Ending Day by Day

Volume 4
Volume 5
Story by Shouji Gatou
Art by Shikidouji

POP
FICTION

A  Prose Novel

TOKYOPOP Inc.
5900 Wilshire Boulevard, Suite 2000
Los Angeles, CA 90036
www.TOKYOPOP.com

Story	Shouji Gatou	Print Production Manager	Lucas Rivera
Illustrations	Shikidouji	Managing Editor	Vy Nguyen
Translation	Duane Johnson	Publisher	Mike Kiley
Cover and Interior Design	James Lee	President and COO	John Parker
Layout	Lucas Rivera	CEO & Chief Creative Officer	Stuart Levy
Editor	Ailen Lujo		

First TOKYOPOP printing: February 2011
10 9 8 7 6 5 4 3 2 1
Printed in the USA

FULLMETAL PANIC ! OWARU DAY BY DAY
© 2000, 2001 Shouji Gatou, Shikidouji
First published in Japan in 2000, 2001 by FUJIMISHOBO CO., LTD., Tokyo.
English translation rights arranged with KADOKAWA SHOTEN PUBLISHING CO., LTD., Tokyo
through TUTTLE–MORI AGENCY, INC., Tokyo.

English text copyright © 2011 TOKYOPOP Inc.

Library of Congress Cataloging-in-Publication Data
Gatou, Shouji.
[Furu metaru panikku. English]
Full metal panic! / by Shouji Gatou ; [illustrations by Shikidouji ;
translation by Duane Johnson].
    p. cm.
  Summary: Sousuke and company face their toughest challenge yet as they are besieged on all sides by enemy
Venoms and a ghost from Sousuke's past.
  ISBN 978-1-4278-0246-0 (v. 4)
  [I. Spies--Fiction. 2. Adventure and adventurers--Fiction. 3. High schools--Fiction. 4. Schools--Fiction. 5.
Science fiction.] I. Johnson, Duane. II. Arntz, Benjamin. III. Title.
PZ7.G22553Fu 2007
  [Fic]--dc22
                              2007020427

FULL METAL PANIC!™

CONTENTS

OFF TO DISTANT ITALY....
FOR SOME REASON, KANAME SENSED
AWKWARDNESS FROM SOUSUKE ON THE
OTHER END OF THE LINE.

BRINGING WITH IT THRILLS
AND EXCITEMENT, THE FIAT
SOUSUKE WAS DRIVING
MADE ITS WAY THROUGH
THE GUNFIRE!

An unexpected order from Mithril.
A series of inorganic words displayed
on the liquid crystal screen.
A wave of violent emotion swept over Sousuke.

EVERY LAST THING WAS GONE.
KANAME STOOD AND STARED AT THE
EMPTY APARTMENT,
WHERE THERE REMAINED NO TRACE OF SOUSUKE.

WHEN HE TURNED AROUND,
THERE STOOD KANAME CHIDORI IN THE FLESH.
SHE THREW HER OVERNIGHT BAG AT HIM,
SHOUTING THE WAY SHE ALWAYS DID.

Prologue

A small red car was parked behind the north school building. It was a four- to five-year-old model, with a cheap-looking design. It had small scratches in several places, and the tires were somewhat worn down. Because of rain the past few days, the hood and roof were very dirty, giving the domestic model an even seedier appearance.

"I don't recognize that car," said Kaname Chidori, looking down on it from a second-story hallway window.

"Really?" asked Kyouko Tokiwa, her classmate standing next to her.

They were on their way back to their classroom, having returned a borrowed library book. It was now lunch break. Students, who could usually be seen behind that building playing ball, were not there today—probably because it was the day before second semester midterms. Most students were confined to their classrooms, grappling with textbooks and notebooks.

"It's also parked in a weird spot. That's not exactly a parking lot," said Kaname.

"Maybe it's some visitor or something?"

"Maybe."

"Never mind that. Let's get back to the classroom. We've got tests tomorrow," said Kyouko.

"Mmm."

Paying it no further mind, Kaname and Kyouko returned to the room. They sat at their desks and opened their textbooks. Just as they began to ask each other practice questions based on tomorrow's exam material, the school broadcast chime sounded.

"Testing, testing.... This is the Student Council Presidential Aide speaking."

It was the voice of Sousuke Sagara, from their class. Looking around carefully, they noted that he was not in the classroom.

"To whoever parked the small red motor vehicle behind the north school building, please contact the student council office immediately. I repeat: Whoever parked the small red motor vehicle behind the north school building, please contact the student council office immediately. The license number is TAMA 50—"

After repeating the plate number three more times to be thorough, the speaker fell silent. It was the type of summons one would hear broadcast in a department store for someone who had parked improperly.

"That's about that car we saw," said Kaname.

"Just what is Sagara up to?" asked Kyouko.

"Who knows?"

She couldn't be sure, but that broadcast should have been audible in the staff room and principal's office. The owner of the vehicle would probably get in touch with Sousuke after hearing that announcement. It was not particularly a problem.

Kaname and Kyouko continued their quizzing of each other for another thirty minutes.

"Here's one. What's the meaning of 'in spite of'?" asked Kaname, proposing a question based on the syntax in her English text. Kyouko gave her a blank look.

"Huh? I don't know that. Where's it from?"

"Page 88."

"Let's see.... That's chapter ten. It's not covered on the exam," said Kyouko.

"Oh, yes, it is."

"No, it's not. Miss Kagurazaka didn't say so in class."

"What? She said it would be on there."

"No, she didn't,"

"She did!" Kaname insisted.

"Did not!"

At the end of their lengthy dispute, they decided to ask their English teacher, Eri Kagurazaka, directly. They left their classroom and headed to the staff room. Upon opening the door marked with the warning PREPARING FOR EXAMS. NO STUDENTS ALLOWED!, they called for Eri from outside the office.

"Excuse me, Miss Kagurazaka?" said Kaname.

"What is it?"

The answer came from behind them. When they turned around, there stood Eri Kagurazaka holding a white vinyl handbag.

"Oh, did you go out?" asked Kaname.

"Yes, for a bit of shopping at the discount store in the shopping district," she said as she took car washing detergent and wax out of the vinyl bag.

"For those?"

"I just got my license the other day, and today I tried driving my car to work for the first time. I thought, while I'm at it, I'd use the water outlet behind the school to wash it later," said Eri, smiling. It seemed she had been outside the school building since lunch break began.

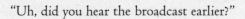
"Uh, did you hear the broadcast earlier?"

"Hmm? What broadcast?" asked Eri.

"Never mind that, ma'am. Please tell Kana! Chapter ten won't be covered on the exam, right?!"

"Right. Chapter ten's not on the exam."

"There, see? I knew it!" Kyouko crowed, triumphantly cocky.

"Ugh. Sorry." Kaname meekly accepted her defeat, and immediately started edging away.

"Kana?"

"Um, something's bugging me. Rubbing it in will have to wait." Leaving Kyouko behind, Kaname walked with long strides from the staff room to the north building. For some reason, she had begun to feel a strange uneasiness. She went to the first floor, left the building through an emergency exit, and headed to the area where the red car was located. She suddenly stopped in her tracks and was stricken speechless.

There was the car, an image of dismantled tragedy.

Four tires lay on the ground, the hood stood leaning against a wall, with the synthetic leather seats aligned precisely next to each other. And then there were the countless bolts, nuts, and engine parts littered about. The doors had been removed as well.

"S ... Sousuke?!" she shouted, and Sousuke Sagara turned around. He held a large detector and had been inspecting a newly-detached seat.

"Don't come any closer, Chidori!" Sousuke shouted in a sharp voice. "I still haven't secured this. We don't need anyone besides me dying."

There was a serious look on his face. With cold sweat beading his forehead, he continued his work.

"Y-you.... Whose car do you think you've taken apart?!"

"Unknown. Hence why I'm investigating it; it's suspicious."

"Wh ... what are you talking about?!"

"It's a car bomb," said Sousuke, deadly serious. "When packed with concealed plastic explosives, such cars become dreadful weapons. In Lebanon in 1983, a Hezbollah truck filled with explosives carried out a kamikaze attack on a U.S. military base. Do you know how many casualties that terrorist act resulted in?"

"How should I know?!"

"Two-hundred and forty-one! Those daring and resolute marines were blown up in an instant. There's no guarantee anywhere that a tragedy of that magnitude won't befall this school!"

"There's plenty of guarantees!"

Kaname ran full speed at Sousuke and knocked him down. His detector and tools flew everywhere as he hit the asphalt.

"Chidori, what are you—"

"This is Miss Kagurazaka's car! A few minutes ago she was all excited about giving it a wash! So how are you gonna deal with this?!"

"But, high powered explosives—"

"There aren't any!" shouted Kaname.

Sousuke attempted to get up, but Kaname knocked him down again.

"Put it back together! Right now! You won't get away with it if she finds out. No, this is *her* we're talking about. She's so timid she might just pass out. And *that* would be a much bigger problem!"

"It's Miss Kagurazaka's? Really?"

"Why would I lie about it?!"

"Hmm."

Sousuke looked over the scattered car parts with grave eyes.

"Not good. I can't reassemble it right away."

"Then don't *dis*assemble it!"

As he was knocked down for a third time, an electronic sound came from Sousuke's chest area. *Bee-bee-beep ... bee-bee-beep.*

"Hmm...." He hurriedly retrieved a cell phone from inside his jacket. He pushed the talk button and answered in subdued English: "This is Urzu-7.... I see, but.... Two and six are? ...Received.... I understand. I'll head there via route 10.... Yes. Over and out."

After focusing on the conversation, he ended the call and started very quickly packing up the nearby tools.

"Hey. What is it?" asked Kaname.

"Something urgent's come up. I'm leaving early."

"Again...? I mean—hey! What about this car?!"

"When it comes to priority—" Sousuke broke off and looked down at the scattered parts in obvious distress. "My only choice is to leave this as it is. Don't tell our teacher."

Sousuke picked up his bag and took off.

"Sousuke?! Hey—come on! Are you nuts?! And, hey ... midterms start tomorrow! Ah, geez.... He's gone again. Damn it."

Kaname watched Sousuke as he ran helter-skelter away from her, then clicked her tongue.

Is it work again?

Why does that place work him relentlessly like this? she thought with a frown. As she took a look around, her glance fell upon the corpse of the car.

I ... I'd better get out of here, too.

Right. In any case, she was under no obligation to put this back together. Not that she would be able to, anyway.

She imagined the explanation that would soon follow—words would most likely fail to describe how difficult it would be to explain—and Kaname took off at a run. She returned to the classroom, and when the fifth-period chime rang, from far away the tearful screams of a female teacher could be heard.

But Kaname only slumped onto her desk and covered her ears.

I'm sorry, ma'am.

It's all his fault.

CHAPTER 1
Code of Silence

Teletha Testarossa and nine ghosts surrounded the round black table.

They were pale, faint images of men. Each of them was hazy, inside a vague veil infused with white noise.

These high officials, scattered around the globe, were all meeting via online conferencing.

What made the resolution of their projected holo-screens low was the application of heavy encryption on satellite communications. Therefore their reproduced actions were by no means smooth—rather, they were nothing more than images which would change completely at intervals of about .2

seconds. The jerky images were closely reminiscent of vintage Claymation.

"So, in effect—" the Intelligence Headquarters staff officer finally said, after an endless thirty minutes of explaining the report summary, "—we feel it was impossible, even for our Intelligence Bureau, to anticipate the actions of John Howard Dunnigan and Nguyen Bien Bo. There are physical limits to follow-up surveys of the histories, characters, and financial situations of individual personnel. Therefore, we believe this calls into question the disposition of the party in authority at the scene. That is all."

Of the nine high officials, four emitted protesting groans. Three were battle-group leaders like Tessa, and one was the Operations head, Admiral Jerome Borda.

The reason for the obvious dissatisfaction of these Operations bureau personnel was clear. Though it was the job of the Intelligence Bureau to do checks on Mithril personnel, they were claiming in a roundabout way that ultimate responsibility lay with the Operations bureau. All Operations could say to that was, "Screw yourself."

This was, in effect, what Admiral Borda had said.

"Thirty minutes to tell one joke. Stop wasting our time." He was usually gentle, but a rare amount of anger threaded his voice. The three battle group leaders agreed with his opinion entirely.

"You said it. Why not let us hear a point of view that's a bit more constructive?"

"A car manufacturer who ships lemons is saying, 'Accidents are your own fault.' Then, what are we supposed to do? Walk instead of drive on a hundred-kilometer trip?"

"It's worse than that. It's like wearing a live grenade on your chest." The Intelligence Bureau staff officer showed some signs of faltering, but his superior officer, Intelligence head General Amit, displayed no hint of agitation.

"The limits of investigation are a grave fact," General Amit said quietly. "Especially in personnel at a level chosen to be SRT members, experience and personal connections abound, as do intelligence and cunning. After all, we're in need of such capable people. If one of them were to feel the urge to concoct some intrigue through convoluted means and accept money from a third party, detecting this could be next to impossible."

"You're saying there's nothing you can do about it!" Admiral Borda sputtered.

"Nothing *can* be done, Admiral," said General Amit, who had remained calm throughout the discussion.

"Would you have personnel in important positions under surveillance 24-7? Or maybe encourage whistle-blowers? Nonsense. It's SRT members themselves who detest such tactics the most."

It was a tough rebuttal. One of the reasons the SRT institution that Operations employed had achieved acceptable results was the combination of their superior independent spirit, pliability, and survival capabilities.

"This is an issue of structure. As Mithril is a mercenary group, loyalty has its limits. However competitively we set our pay rates—if we're to believe this Sergeant Weber's report, five million dollars, it was—if that kind of fortune is waved around, traitors will emerge. The human conscience is a fragile thing."

Silence greeted General Amit's statement.

"Also, we can't forget that it was none other than Operations that was utilizing Lieutenant Commander Bruno."

Lieutenant Commander Bruno, the staffer at Operations Headquarters who had arranged for Dunnigan and Nguyen to be assigned to the *Tuatha de Danaan*. Bruno was a mole of an "enemy organization," so both Intelligence and Operations were agreed that a terrorist had been introduced into the system.

Immediately following the incident on the *Tuatha de Danaan*, Bruno had absconded from Operations HQ. As a result, Mithril had had to change much of their classified information: encryption systems and security protocols, supply routes and safe house locations. The facilities on the Merida Island Base could not possibly be relocated, so it had been limited to enforcing rigid security measures—but the cost of implementing all those necessary measures, though completely necessary, had been astronomical.

"Had the TDD-I been lost as a result of what happened, Bruno probably wouldn't have even been suspected. He might have remained in the organization—excuse me—" The Intelligence head stopped speaking and lit a cigarette. The 3-D online conference image appeared to enjoy the smoke it exhaled. "—remained in the organization, and caused even greater damage."

"That didn't happen, though. All thanks to Captain Testarossa's quick thinking."

"Indeed. This is why her responsibility in losing control was overlooked. Is that not satisfactory?"

The Intelligence head's hazy image glanced at Tessa. She said nothing, but continued to look down at her own hands.

"The TDD-1 was on the verge of sinking; our amphibious assault submarine, suffice to say our single largest asset and military force," said the general. "Because it's a weapon, the possibility of loss always exists. You should have been prepared for that as of a year ago. Since the time we decided to put her to sea, in the hands of a mere fifteen-year-old girl."

Admiral Borda gave a little snort before falling into a dejected silence.

"Is that everything?" Perceiving that no one had anything further to add, Lord Mallory, silent up until that point, spoke up. He was an elderly gentleman in a three-piece suit who wore a monocle. He was quite advanced in age, but his posture was firmly straight. "Very well. Then I shall state my opinion: The structural issue pointed out by Admiral Amit has been anticipated since our inception. Unlike a regular military, we of Mithril, who have no foundation based on race, religion, or national policy, must embrace our policy of preventing international disputes, though opinions of such would differ among individuals. I was under the impression that you all carry on the fight while being aware of that risk.... Was I mistaken?"

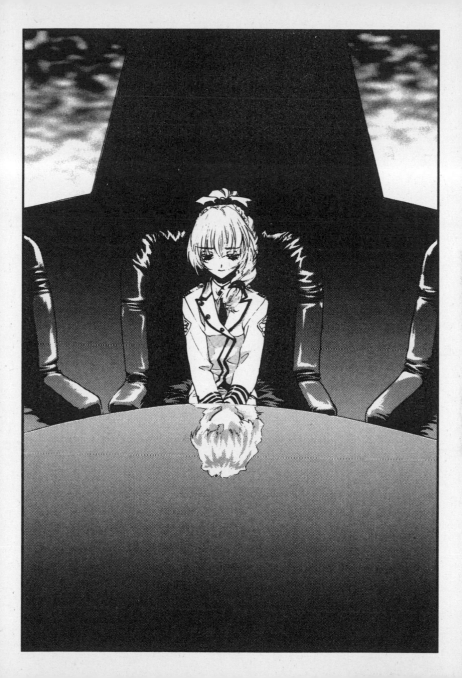

Lord Mallory looked around at everyone. No one contradicted him.

"Good. Then regarding this issue, the exchange of blame ends here. Naturally, pursue countermeasures. It should be possible to reduce a danger of 1% to .5%. Reconsider your current protocols, and each of you propose what countermeasures are realistically executable. Also…," he paused for a moment and adjusted his monocle, "…continue investigating this enemy organization as you have been. That is all. Best of luck, then."

The old man's image disappeared without a sound, and only the words TRANSMISSION ENDED. CIRCUIT DISCONNECTED hung in the empty space. At that signal, the other high officials vanished in sequence from the online conference.

Finally, only Admiral Borda remained.

Borda was a middle-aged man, grey beginning to mix into his abundant black hair. His physique had a dignity becoming of his age, but his face and arms were suntanned and had a tense look about them.

He stared at Tessa and said sympathetically, "I imagine you disagree. You're the only one who lost subordinates in all this, after all."

Mithril was largely divided into three duty stations. Operations, Intelligence, and R&D. Operations was composed of four battle groups (including the *Tuatha de Danaan*), and HQ. Gathering, analyzing, and assessing the information necessary for their operations was undertaken by Intelligence—of which General Amit was in charge. Intelligence also filled the role of offering data and advice to the security agencies of various countries and saw that Operations had to use as little show-of-force as necessary.

The relationship between Operations and Intelligence could not be described as very favorable. It was not so much a matter of hostility, but then they were not exactly bosom buddies, either.

Operations would rant daily, left and right: "The intelligence you provided had errors in it. We almost died thanks to that. What are you going to do about it?!" And Intelligence in like fashion would always shout back: "Do you have any idea how much effort it takes to gather *that* much information?! Stop asking for too much!"

Of course, this was a problem not limited to Mithril, but the sort of problem experienced by any kind of organization.

"Amit does have a point, though. There are always risks involved. And there are many expenses which must be paid."

"I know," Tessa answered feebly.

"I wonder. I really don't feel that your current situation is suited to you. You still have a lot to learn, even if not in the field. Come back to Operations HQ. There's important work to do in R&D, and Mardukas and the others can manage that ship. Don't you think it's about time—"

"As I have said repeatedly, I will not leave this post," she stated clearly.

"I could officially order you to," he pointed out.

"If you do, I will simply leave Mithril."

The 3-D image of Admiral Borda sighed.

"You know, you get that stubbornness from your father. He gave me a hard time, too."

"...I'm sorry, Uncle. But they are all my valued comrades. And—"

"Leonard, perhaps?"

Seen through by Borda, Tessa hung her head.

"...Yes. He has surfaced. And in the worst way. I am sure my powers will be needed to stand against him."

"Even so, are you sure? We still don't know his intentions, but at the least, he doesn't seem to be our ally. Confronting Leonard will probably cause you further pain. You even still blame yourself for what happened to Bani."

Tessa didn't respond.

"Fair enough. That aside, about this traitor, Vincent Bruno."

Tessa flashed a reserved smile.

"Yes. We are currently moving forward on that. Very far away...."

October 13, 22:30 (Central European Time)
Southern Sicily, Mediterranean Sea
The outskirts of Agrigento

A stoutly built *capo* entered the old Baroque-style room. Following him were guards—two young members of the family—but at the man's signal, they bowed and exited the room.

Already getting up from the couch, Bruno greeted the boss with a warm embrace.

"Vincenzo Bruno. Have you gotten used to life here?" the capo asked.

"Thank you, Boss, it is comfort personified," answered Bruno in fluent Italian.

"Call me Papa. I think of you just like my own son. And these days, there aren't many left who call their father 'boss'. It's the same as there being more women who go to university. Utterly lamentable. But amusing as well," said the *capo*, smiling heartily.

In actuality, Bruno and the *capo* were not far enough apart in age to be called father and son. Bruno was an American in his forties, of medium build with brown hair. He certainly did not have a look that stood out, but a spark of boldness and impishness twinkled in his blue eyes. He had graduated from the Naval Academy and had been an elite employee of the Department of Defense, but now he was a free agent. He had money, too. Until just a few weeks ago, Bruno had been a staff member of Mithril's Operations HQ in Sydney. At the same time he had also been spying for Amalgam—and the organization had paid him a lot of money to do it.

Nevertheless, Bruno had not thought of it as betrayal. It would have been one thing if he been serving his native country's military, but he had been with a glorified security firm. He had never sworn his loyalty. Even if he'd sold information to another organization, wasn't that nothing more than a bit of outside work?

Besides, "preventing international disputes"? There was no way most mature people could stay affiliated with such a wannabe-justice-hero empty slogan. World peace! Oh, very nice. But that was something people with sufficiently stuffed bellies wished for. Right now, the majority of the world was starving, and he had only just eaten his fill.

However, the incidents of his engaging in acts of espionage could be counted on one hand. All he had done was illegally divert Mithril encryption software a number of times, and reassign two SRT personnel to the West Pacific battle group.

Thanks to the situation that winning those two over had led to, he'd had to flee from Mithril. That was unfortunate, but maybe he should just be happy he was still alive.

He had not tried to rely on Amalgam. It was easy to imagine how such a shady organization would have dealt with a mole for which they had no further use. Currently, Mithril and Amalgam were both the same kind of threat to him.

Therefore, Bruno decided to attach himself to a distant connection in the Sicilian Mafia. It was the Barbera family, which had seen sudden growth from weapons smuggling from Europe to northern Africa and the Middle East, as well as procuring heroin. Bruno had accommodated their weapons smuggling a number of times. A shrewd individual would value such a connection.

Their level of firepower rivaled that of a small nation. Of course they had various firearms, but also armored vehicles and armed helicopters on top of that—not that there was a use for them, they even possessed second-generation Arm Slaves. Not even Mithril would tread lightly here. Or Amalgam.

"You may rest easy. Everyone here is a friend of mine," assured the *capo di capi*, Don Barbera. "Many policemen and soldiers are my supporters. Should intruders come to this island, word should arrive at once."

"That is most reassuring."

Bruno had already informed Don Barbera what the men who might come to seize him would look like. Mithril's Mediterranean Sea battle group *Partholon*. He was unable to steal facial shots of its SRT personnel, but they were all in his head. If they were to infiltrate Sicily, it was obvious that they would be murdered within the day.

After chatting briefly, Barbera thumped his shoulder. "Anyway, let's enjoy the evening. It's my daughter's birthday, after all."

"I will, then. Let's toast. To the great *capo's* daughter." Bruno raised his wineglass, expressing his heartfelt respect. After the toast, he separated from the Don and proceeded along the vast hall.

Built in the seventeenth century and having undergone periodic expansion and alteration, this extravagant mansion had a solemn interior that somehow also overflowed with vibrancy. The walls and ceiling were painted a subdued golden color, ornamented with complex curves. An elegant tune floated in the air. And in that hall, chatting, drinking, and eating luxurious cuisine were throngs of people. Though it was approaching late night, the party was still in full swing.

There were also many beautifully-dressed women. In this land where many races had contributed their genetics, individuals of various appearances coexisted. Where there were Middle Eastern beauties of swarthy complexion, there were also Northern European ones with blonde hair and blue eyes. When they noticed Bruno, they smiled and waved slightly at him.

"*La bella Sicilia,*" he murmured to no one in particular.

I swear, this is Heaven. Thank God I ran!

He drank as he wandered the party hall, and just as he was becoming good and drunk, a young woman approached him.

She was attractive, probably Asian in descent. Her long, curled black hair and slightly slanted eyes caused an exotic aura to hang about her. Her long black dress seemed like a subdued design at a glance, but upon closer inspection, the open back plunged so deeply that the tops of her hips were nearly visible.

Bruno felt a stab of lust, and his heart began to beat faster.

"Are you having fun, sir?" the woman asked in fluent English.

Surprised, Bruno smiled and said, "Yeah. This is a nice place. Though when I first arrived, I was concerned by how poor the streets looked."

There were only a handful of extravagant places like this mansion in Sicily. Nearly all the population led simple, quiet lives. Had Bruno's words been a joke they would not have been funny, and she gave him a strained smile.

"You're an American. I lived there for two years."

"Did you? I guess it's easy to tell."

"Yes. Somehow. Maybe you're more urbane ... or refined.... Well, something like that. You have a sense that is different from the other gentlemen here."

"That's not good. It'd be best for me not to stand out." As he said this, Bruno could not stop a smile from spilling out. It was a sense of superiority characteristic of urbanites. He did not fail to notice something like secret intent cross the woman's eyes.

"Where did you live?" asked Bruno.

"Baltimore."

"Hah! I used to live near there, too."

"Really? That seems a bit too coincidental." She chuckled.

"It's true. Of course, that was a long time ago."

Aided by nostalgia and alcohol, Bruno enthusiastically made a play at her. Reminiscent talk and mentions of local connections, and of course, he did not forget to compliment her. Seemingly not as annoyed as he anticipated, she followed along with his conversation.

Then, she made a proposition.

"Shall we go somewhere else? It's noisy here."

Without hesitation, Bruno agreed.

"Yes, let's. I'm renting a room here. We can drink more there."

In any case, there was a bed there. And a bathroom. While she was aware of this, she took his arm without an ounce of shyness.

They left the party hall. Standing in the corridor leading to the annex were two large family soldiers. They each had guns hanging from their shoulders and wore sunglasses-style goggles with night vision sensors.

"*Signore*. Who is this lady?" asked a soldier in a courteous but inorganic voice.

Modern Mafia equipment was high-tech. The soldiers had also received specialized training. Their guns were not Thompson submachine guns such as would appear in gangster films, but the latest model Belgium-made submachine guns. They had a compact boxy shape which used many different reinforced plastic parts, and their rounds flew at such high speeds as to easily penetrate regular bulletproof vests.

"Don't ask stupid questions."

Bruno passed in front of the guards with the girl in tow.

I'm glad the guards are strict, but it's annoying at times like this. He smiled bitterly.

"Sorry. It may not seem like it, but this is VIP treatment," he whispered.

The girl gave him a blank look, and then uttered a sound of admiration.

Before long they arrived at his room. Bruno at once put his arms around her slender waist. She was not all that buxom, but as he liked thin women, she was quite to his taste.

"So, what should we do? You know, I haven't even asked you your name...."

"Hmm ... you want to know?" she said with an enigmatic smile. Now getting a closer look, he could easily see how fine her skin texture was. *Young women are the best.* Anticipation and arousal made Bruno's breathing grow rougher.

"I do. Otherwise, I can't call out your name when the time comes."

He pulled her in close. The slits of her dress opened, and the contours of her long legs became visible.

"Just my name? You don't want to know anything else?"

"Of course I do. Plenty of things. All in good time."

"You want to know everything?"

"Sure, tell me. Everything. Everything...."

"Okay. Then I'll tell you."

Bruno was not really sure what happened next.

He was suddenly shoved up against the wall, and just as he noticed a violent pain emanating from his front teeth, there was a huge handgun thrust inside his mouth. A Heckler & Koch .45 caliber. It was a model designed for Special Forces raiding operations. It was too coarse a weapon for this woman to have.

"Gah! Wah?!"

This time Bruno was truly surprised, and the woman holding the gun said to him, "Listen carefully. My name's Melissa Mao. Mithril Operations, *Tuatha de Danaan* land combat group, SRT member. Rank: master sergeant. Call sign: Urzu-2."

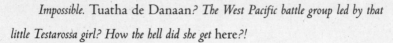
Impossible. Tuatha de Danaan? *The West Pacific battle group led by that little Testarossa girl? How the hell did she get* here?!

"Gack! Ah!"

"While I'm on a roll.... I'm also a lady who not too long ago lost a damn good superior officer in action because of you—and I'm really tempted to pull this trigger."

Those cold eyes of hers brimmed with a fierce hatred and bloodlust.

As his tears flowed and head shook, the gun barrel audaciously in his mouth, Mao felt a profound irritation toward her prey.

Please. Please don't kill me, his eyes pathetically petitioned her. There was not a shred of dignity there. Had he been a braver a man, she would have gladly pulled the trigger. But he was so miserable that it ended up cooling down her hot head.

She pulled her automatic pistol from Bruno's mouth and once again thrust the muzzle to his throat.

"Please don't kill me. Please don't kill me." He whimpered.

"Just shut up."

The nearby hallway was crawling with Mafia soldiers carrying radios. They, the Barbera family, were known for brutality unprecedented in the history of the Mafia. Their boss, Don Barbera, had the outward image of an amiable local man of influence, but his true colors were different. He was the kind of man who would kidnap a judge who turned down his bribe, cut off his head, stick a wad of bills in his mouth, then send a picture of it to the judge's family.

And so, the men patrolling the mansion were nearly all ex-military pros who had been bought out with money. What's more, their equipment was nearly all extravagant high-tech weaponry. Mao could not afford to let her captive have a chance to scream.

"Don't shoot me. I'll do anything. Please."

"So, like I said, shut up."

"I will. I'll shut up. So cut me some slack here. I was an idiot. I didn't mean to get on Mithril's bad side. Yeah, it was just a sudden impulse. I've repented. Please. Oh, please, please."

"You know what.... Damn it."

With her free left hand Mao took a syringe out of her handbag, pressed it into his neck, and pressed the plunger. Ten-odd seconds later, as Bruno inarticulately repeated "please" over and over again, he dozed off and eventually lost consciousness.

"Phew...," she muttered as she took off the stifling wig and false eyelashes she wore, scratching her very short black hair.

"This is Urzu-2. Target is secured. I will now neutralize the alarm system." The ultra-small communicator in her ear picked up the vibrations in her cranium and transmitted her voice to her comrades.

She extracted tools from her handbag and began working on the alarm system's control box. After easily bypassing the circuit, she set the window's alarm switch to OFF. The light, which would ordinarily switch to red, remained green.

That's that. Alarms like this are a cinch if you can get at them from inside.

Mao walked over to the window and unlocked and opened it.

From the small fourth-floor terrace could be seen a stone annex and a high wall, and further beyond, dim in the moonlight, gently rising hill country. The lights of some town stretched out vaguely over the horizon.

"Now, then...."

She leaned against the railing. The refreshing night breeze tickled her cheek. She felt liable to forget this was right in the middle of enemy territory.

"Picture perfect. Like the goddess of night," said a voice from right behind her.

In the shadow of the wide-open window, in a very dim corner of the terrace, stood a man. His arms were folded smugly, and his back leaned against a stone pillar.

"How long have you been there?" asked Mao curtly.

"Since about the time that dick grabbed your ass."

The man advanced out of the darkness. Kurz Weber appeared in the moonlight dressed in a tuxedo; a handsome man with blond hair and blue eyes. Dressed up like this, he looked like a young noble.

"See, what did I tell you? That dress was definitely the way to go."

"True. I had him at 'hello'. But I'd rather never wear this again. I look like some stupid actress at the Oscars."

Kurz approached with graceful steps and whispered near her ear, "No, you don't. I think it looks good on you."

"You have vulgar tastes," said Mao.

"No, no, you look wonderful. From behind, bewitching, isolated.... Did you know? Hecate is also the goddess of revenge. Such an elegant comparison really fits you tonight."

"Are you drunk?"

"*Signorina*, your *charms* have intoxicated me, rendering me a mere poet." Kurz laughed.

"Uh, hey."

From behind, Kurz lightly hugged her shoulders. The cologne he was wearing, a clean citrus scent, wafted in the air. If she wasn't careful, she would surrender herself to the moment. But unfortunately, Mao had a job to do.

She titled her head down and then jerked it back up hard. The back of her head hit the bridge of Kurz's nose, and there was an unpleasant cracking sound.

"Buh!"

"Yes, yes. I understand, now let's get to work."

"*Oww!* What'd you do that for?"

"Get a clue already. How about keeping things where they belong? This place is crawling with scary bad guys."

"What a sad truth."

"Come on, get out the equipment."

"Tch!"

Eyes watering and holding his nose, Kurz reached for the day pack in the corner of the terrace. It was one of the pieces of equipment that yesterday had been smuggled in, mixed with food and decorations for the party.

Making such arrangements and sneaking in as members of the party had been rather difficult. As there was a chance of other moles being somewhere within Mithril, this mission had proceeded completely alone and unaided. Permission had not been sought from Intelligence or the North Atlantic/Mediterranean battle group. It was thanks to their superior officer Lieutenant Commander Kalinin's personal connections, Mao's own computer knowledge, and Kurz's connections from his mercenary days that they were able to infiltrate this unfamiliar land.

They took a very small winch and wire out of the bag, and together carried the unconscious Bruno to the terrace. Kurz continued to grumble complaints.

"This just ain't fair. I had to tear myself away from a sweet young thing to get away from the party hall."

"Sweet young thing?"

"Oh, yeah. A millionaire's widow from Milan. She wore a necklace with this *huge* diamond in it. We had a good mood going, too."

"You lie."

"It's the truth. Her almond eyes got all moist, and she even said, 'I wouldn't mind being married again if it was to you.'"

"Ah-ha."

She attached the winch to the railing. No guards were seen in the courtyard. Kurz had probably put them to sleep with a stun gun before climbing up here. He was about to descend to the shrubbery on the ground when Mao stopped him.

"Wait. I'll go down first."

"Not that it really matters, but why?"

She did not answer. The lech would no doubt love to find out she was panty-less. Not only was this dress thin, but the back was almost completely open, so underwear was not an option. What was more, the slit ran deep, so if a strong wind were to blow while Kurz was down below....

He would see everything.

"Now it's buggin' me. Come on, why?"

"Shut up. It doesn't matter why."

Mao took off her high heels, and barefoot, hurriedly climbed over the terrace railing. There were no real problems, and she swiftly descended to the shrubs at the bottom. After next lowering Bruno down, Kurz was the last to reach the ground.

"Our route to the car?"

"No problem. I put the guards around here to sleep."

"Good. Let's get out of here."

If they could just get to the visitor parking area, all they had to do was put this man in the trunk of the Ferrari they had arrived in, then get past the front gate and leave.

Kurz shouldered Bruno's limp body. With a silenced pistol in one hand, Mao had started walking toward the visitor parking area when a husky feminine voice shouted from the courtyard.

"*Signore!*"

"Ugh...?"

"Signore Carius! Please wait!"

A middle-aged woman wearing gaudy jewels came running from the direction of the annex. She was rather plump and well-rounded. Her fully fleshed stomach and bust swayed every time she moved, making her seem just like a giant beach ball.

"Might that be the sweet young thing of a widow?"

"Huh? N-no ... well...."

"And 'Carius'?"

"It's just an alias. It's the name of this old guy who runs a pharmacy in my old man's hometown. He let me hang out there a lot on summer holiday. For some reason he had a ton of plastic model Japanese tanks—"

"*Carius!*"

The woman screamed crazily, charging toward a flustered Kurz at full speed before latching onto to him. She seemed to give no regard whatsoever to Bruno, who was still slung over his shoulder, or Mao, who was dumbfounded.

"Carius, my darling. I've been looking for you! Where are you going, leaving me behind?"

"Well, um...."

"If I said something to hurt your feelings, I apologize from my heart. You are probably one who is easily hurt, no?! I can see it. The sadness hiding behind those blue eyes! So let us talk some more. Love is like a plant. It puts down roots, and it takes time before it flowers. But I am sure you and I can understand each other. So, so—!"

Mao and Kurz panicked when the woman began speaking loudly.

"Look, ma'am. Please just keep your voice down, okay? Okay? Hey—"

"Please, Carius! Do not depart from before my *eyes! Per favore!* Ahhh! Ah, ah, ah! Ahhhh!"

"Well, as much as I'd love to...."

"Quiet her down! If she keeps shouting like that...."

The frenzied woman's shouting must have gone on for no more than thirty seconds, but it was plenty of time for those nearby to catch an earful.

A man dressed in black and carrying a submachine gun appeared around a corner about twenty meters away.

"What's all the noise?!"

The guard's expression changed as soon as he noticed the large screaming lady, the beautiful woman holding a handgun, and the slender man carrying an unconscious American VIP.

"Intruders! *Intruders!*" he shouted and aimed his submachine gun at the group. Mao pulled her trigger at the same time, hitting the Mafioso in the shoulder and flank. The Mafioso fell forward and pulled his own trigger, his gun discharging at the ground. Muzzle flashes. A soaring cloud of dust.

The submachine-gun fire was far louder than the woman's hysterical voice.

A siren that sounded a lot like that of a patrol car resounded throughout the vast premises.

The private Mafia army suddenly flew in like an avalanche from the main building, annex, guardroom, and lodging house. A succession of gunfire and shouting voices was heard. Trained Dobermans barked ferociously as they ran. Multiple spotlights lit up and tracked down the intruders. The entire old-style estate was suddenly reminiscent of a weekend disco.

"Son of a bitch!" Driven by a downpour of gunfire, Mao cursed loudly.

"I thought it would go smoothly this time! Now it's down to shooting again. Tell me why?!" she shouted, practically in tears as she hid behind a waist-high stone wall.

"Come on—it's an act of God." Kurz protested as he belatedly rushed behind the wall. He was breathing heavily as a result of running around while carrying Bruno.

"I mean, I'm a suave guy. I was polite, I complimented her a bit here and there, and I guess she took it seriously. But now I think I see why her husband died at an early age."

"Is this any time to get all emotional?! We're in really deep here!"

Incidentally, the widow in question jumped in the air at the sudden firefight, and then passed out on the spot. Mao and Kurz left her there and ran across the yard, reaching a corner of a garden where flowers of various sizes were growing all over. They'd hit a dead end.

"There's a three-meter wall behind us, and a hundred Mafia in front. There's nowhere to run! And all we have for weapons are one Socom pistol and a stun gun!"

"But there's one good thing. That gun was expensive but you still hadn't had to chance to use it in combat, right? Weren't you complaining about it being a stupid buy the other day?"

"That's not good at all!"

As they carried on, enemy rounds flew all around them. Bits of stone and black soil sprung up and rained down on their heads.

"Aw, shit!" Mao shouted, sticking the pistol in question out from behind the cover and squeezing out five shots. The two Dobermans who were rushing toward them took hits and went down, writhing on the ground where they fell.

"Oh, man. Poor things," said Kurz.

"Ask me if I care. I'm not about to become their dinner."

"Yeah, that's true, but—"

Kurz used his stun gun on a man who had dashed out from the opposite cover a few meters away. Sharp electric bolts ran through the air, and the man went down.

"Shit, I'd love a rifle. There's a guy who looks like a commander in the window of the main house over there."

With Kurz's skill, he most likely could have taken out the commander. His name meant "short" in German, but with a rifle he could reach any enemy, no matter how far away.

"At this point, taking out their command structure would be meaningless."

"This is bad, though. They're starting to surround us," said Kurz as he exchanged his stun gun's battery cartridge.

"It's your fault. I say we ice this guy before we buy it."

Mao changed her gun's clip and looked down at the heedlessly sleeping Bruno.

"You wanna kill him? We came here to kidnap him."

"I'm kidding. It's just wishful thinking."

Just after that, a new voice came over the communicators in their ears.

"Don't get desperate, Urzu-2."

"Wha—?"

"Looks like I made it. Keep your heads low."

"What? Are you close by? Sou—" A roar and shockwave cut off Mao's words.

The wall behind them was blown out, and violent explosive flame and shrapnel flew about.

Someone had exploded the wall from the outside.

Black smoke billowed up from the explosion, and visibility dropped temporarily to zero. The Mafia soldiers shouted to one another as they haphazardly discharged their weapons.

"Wha—?!"

"Keep to the wall behind you. Move toward 4:00. Run."

Smoke stung their eyes. Ignoring the tears that blurred her vision, Mao pulled on Kurz's shoulder and ran toward 4:00—to the right and behind—as they had been told. A space two meters wide was collapsed in the high wall. It had been blown in from the outside by a bomb or something. When they stepped over rubble and arrived outside the wall, they heard the sound of brakes beyond the smoke.

"This way!"

An old Fiat was visible, parked on the estate's perimeter road—a cream-colored boxy coupe. It was a small car, and would probably be packed tight with four people in it.

Mao and Kurz spotted the driver, and their eyes opened wide.

"Sousuke?!" they shouted in unison.

The person who had come to their rescue was their colleague, Sousuke Sagara—with his usual messy black hair, sullen face, and tight-lipped mouth. He currently wore an olive-colored flight jacket over his black combat uniform.

It was very natural for them to be surprised. Sousuke had not taken part in this mission, and was supposed to be in Japan.

"What's going on? Don't you have midterms today?" asked Kurz, tossing Bruno into the back seat.

"Affirmative. But your escape route's been changed. I'm here on the lieutenant commander's orders to brief you and offer assistance."

"Changed?"

"It's not to Marseilles by sea anymore. The captain of the secured fishing boat is apparently in the hospital for alcoholism. We'll use a different intermediary, and then from a NATO—"

A bullet came whistling through the smoke and shot off the Fiat's rearview mirror.

"Whoa!"

"From a NATO air base, we'll fly to Turkey. Together on an air shuttle, the usual way. Forged U.S. military IDs and orders, along with Marine Corps uniforms, will be at a post office in Catania tomorrow morning—"

"Forget explaining, go!" shouted Mao as she got into the passenger seat.

"Yes, ma'am."

Sousuke stepped on the accelerator.

The engine howled, and the rear wheels kicked up dirt and pebbles. The Fiat accelerated like it had been kicked from behind, and Mao was nearly thrown through her still-open door.

"Whoa, now. Isn't that a little dangerous?!" Mao lectured, her face angry as she restrained the hem of her dress from wildly fluttering.

"So are bullets. Still, though...." Sousuke gave her a sideways glance. "That's a strange swimsuit. Did you plan to swim to Marseilles?"

"No! This isn't a swimsuit, it's an evening dress!"

"I see."

Sousuke cranked the wheel hard. The frame inclined sharply to the left, and Mao hit her head with a thump on the passenger side window. The unevenness of the unpaved road was intense, and it could soon be the death of this loaded-down car's suspension.

"Your driving sucks!"

"No problem."

"Oh, yeah. Hey, girl, what should we do about the Ferrari we left in the parking lot?" Kurz grumbled.

"Leave it be. It was a rental, anyway."

"Yeah, but you know, there's a satellite communicator and whatnot in the trunk."

"Huh?! You *idiot!*"

"I *did* rig it with explosives. If I push this switch, in fifteen minutes it goes boom. So we *could* get rid of it."

They had left a satellite communicator with a code entered into it. Next to a shocked Mao, Sousuke asked moderately: "Well? Do we go back?"

"Of course not! Right now—"

Chewn. A sound ripped through the air, as a bullet flew by just over their heads.

About a hundred meters behind them on the road was a black 4WD. A Cherokee. It was approaching at full speed. A man whose top half rose up from the sunroof fired a submachine gun on full auto. *Grash.* A dry impact sound. A hole opened in the Fiat's rear window, and glass fragments were scattered around the interior.

"Look at the situation we're in! Push the detonator button!

Whatever. Just make it go boom!"

"*Yes*, ma'am. And—"

Kurz pushed the cell-phone sized, remote switch.

"That activated it. Farewell, Ferrari. Hello, Fiat."

"This car has its advantages, too."

As Sousuke tried to control the struggling steering wheel, he sped up even more. But the Fiat's lack of power was impenetrably problematic. What was more, the pursuing 4WD had more than twice their engine displacement.

"They're gaining on us."

The black vehicle was quickly approaching. When Mao perceived there was a large curve coming up, she stood up through the Fiat's sunroof.

"You son of a bitch!"

She fired, both hands squarely aiming the handgun. The enemy gunman took a hit and fell into his vehicle. She fired again. The frame of the Cherokee sparked. It appeared to have been made bulletproof, as her shot did not penetrate it. Even so, she stubbornly continued firing until her clip was empty.

Over ten .45 caliber rounds were focused in front of the driver's seat.

The enemy's bulletproof glass stopped the bullets completely, but countless thin cracks formed, and the surface of the glass became totally white.

The sudden curve approached.

With graceful movements she loaded her last clip and fired again. Three shots each to the left and right, blowing out the headlights.

"I'm turning!"

The Fiat's suspension creaked as it plunged into the corner. The frame inclined considerably, and the right tires floated slightly. Mao, Sousuke, and Kurz simultaneously shifted their weight to the right.

"Wow!"

The frame righted, and the tires touched ground. Its grip back, the Fiat somehow managed to turn the corner. As if tottering unsteadily, the underpowered car again accelerated.

Meanwhile, with the Cherokee's windshield covered in cracks and with its headlights gone, the driver apparently could not see the corner. He hardly slowed down, and his front wheels hit the sudden incline running along the road.

With a shrill howl from the engine, the black vehicle soared into the night sky.

It was a short flight.

It crashed into the ground as it flipped heavily to the left. Two, three rolls, and parts of various sizes scattered. The heavily damaged 4WD, starting to catch fire, quickly grew small in the distance.

"Pity. It could've flown if it had wings, hmm." Mao blew a kiss like a salute.

"Today was like, I don't know, a spy movie," muttered Kurz.

The Fiat swerved from the unpaved road and landed on a paved one.

The area around them was covered by low hills, so the road gently curved left and right. Maybe it was because of the time of night, but there was hardly any oncoming traffic.

One minute, then two. The car drove just fine along the night road.

"Is that it, then?"

"It didn't seem like it was enough," said Mao.

Far behind them, a pair of headlights appeared from beyond a hill. A car was driving erratically, moving fast. Apparently it was a new pursuer.

"Just one again?"

"One's bad enough. I'm out of ammo."

"No. Look closely," said Sousuke.

At first, it was definitely only one set of headlights. But as they moved further along the road and their angle changed, making their view through the hills clearer, another set of headlights showed itself. Then another. And another. There was no interruption in the row of lights, just a straight line.

"Th ... thirteen." Kurz opened his mouth wide.

"Sousuke, can't you go any faster?"

"This is the limit. We're carrying a lot of weight," said Sousuke, unperturbed. This car was definitely small and underpowered, designed for cities. It was not made for a car chase while carrying four adults. And they were unarmed. They had hidden guns and ammo in a rustic church for a worst-case scenario during their escape, but that was in a far-distant deserted village.

Mao gave the man leisurely sleeping in the back seat a hard stare. "Maybe we should kill and ditch him after all?"

"Yeah. I'm liking that idea more and more," answered Kurz. Vincent Bruno did not seem to be aware of the discussion.

"You want to lighten our load?" asked Sousuke.

"Right. Otherwise they'll catch up."

"Then that man alone would be insufficient. There are weapons and ammo under the back seat, so you can eject those. An assault rifle, shotgun, disposable rocket launcher, and high powered hand grenades. I estimate it's about forty kilograms total—"

"Say, what?"

Kurz pushed Bruno aside and, struggling and flailing in the cramped car, managed to lift up the rear seat.

The inside was a small armory. A German-made assault rifle, an Italian-made shotgun, and an American-made rocket launcher. All heavy weaponry which would easily break through protective glass.

"Say something sooner, you moron!" Mao and Kurz yelled simultaneously, their faces red with anger.

"I didn't say anything?"

"No, you didn't! Goddamn it!"

They finished their verbal abuse and grabbed guns, levers clacked as they moved, and loaded ammo was verified. Kurz knocked out the bullet-pocked rear window and chose his rifle's target. Mao again stood up through the sunroof and aimed the slug-loaded shotgun.

"Time to party some more." She was used to the touch of steel. The sensation wound up enthralling her.

"You ready, ladies?!" screamed Mao.

"Anytime."

"Anywhere."

The pursuers bore down on them. Very close now.

Yeah. This is how I like it, in the end, thought Mao.

"Rock 'n' roll!" she screamed.

Just after she shouted over the wind, Mao let loose with the shotgun.

"I have never seen been so disgraced!" shouted Don Barbera, his whole being filled with anger. "This is my daughter's birthday party! And yet a guest of mine was abducted. If that was not bad enough, the thieves continue to elude my soldiers."

"I am most sorry, *Capo di capi*," said the Mafia guard chief more politely than necessary. Where they stood in the estate's parking lot, about half the vehicles that had been parked there were pursuing the thieves.

"However, we will not let them escape. The circling net is contracting. We *will* retrieve Signore Bruno, and massacre these insolent thieves."

"I could care less about Bruno!" the Don shouted, finally airing his true thoughts.

"He is a burden. Kill *all* of them for all I care! By any means necessary! Use Arms Slaves as well! Trample anyone who stands in your way, even women and children!"

"Uh, ASes, too?"

"Yes. I bought those robots for times like these. Now dispatch the mercenaries posthaste! You hear me, kill them! Bring their heads before me!"

"Yes, sir, but if we deploy ASes, surely the state government will—"

"Stop nitpicking! If they escape, I will twist *your* head off, too, *chiaro*?"

"Yes, sir! If you would excuse me!" As was probably a habit during his stint in the military, the guard chief stretched his back straight and ran toward the guard center at full speed.

"Hmph!"

The don watched him leave. Making it seem laborious, he took out a cigar and lit it. He thought it would calm him down a bit, but that was just not the mood he was in. When he thought of the humiliation he had suffered, his head felt like it would explode with anger.

Until now—until rising to this position, he had made a bloodbath of all his enemies. No matter what kind of person it was, he was capable of killing their whole family. Naturally, some of them had been very young. Even then he had shown no mercy. It was to plant fear and indecision in his enemies. He had been sure to make his own son and daughter witness these spectacles with their own eyes.

Yes. I have to comfort my daughter. She is easily hurt, and this must have been a terrible shock.

Shifting his thoughts, Barbera began to leave the parking lot with guards in tow. That was where his guests' luxury cars were lined up: a Jaguar, a Benz, a Lotus, a Porsche, a Rolls-Royce, a Lamborghini. Just as he was striding past a deep red Ferrari F-40, he heard a brief electronic sound emanating from the vehicle.

The tone of the sound quickly became high-pitched. Without stopping to think, Barbera paused to examine the Ferrari.

In the next instant, the five kilograms of plastic explosives that had been rigged to the car detonated.

The shockwave of the explosion blew the car to pieces instantly. The igniting gasoline became a fireball, devastating the area in a tremendously violent storm. The blown-off hood sliced through the air like a Frisbee, stabbing into the wall of the main house fifty meters away.

Barbera himself did not even realize he was dead. Unfortunately, the aggressively lethal order he had given was to be in effect for some time to come.

At the same time
Chofu, Tokyo, Japan
Jindai Municipal High School

Naturally, Kaname Chidori had no way of knowing about the firefight that had occurred half a world away.

She, of the long black hair and school uniform. While she had a lively personality, she possessed the bearing of an adult. She wasn't flashy, but her eyes were both sharp and beautiful, and while her proportions did not reach the level of supermodel, she was undeniably thin.

A peaceful high school in a peaceful Japan, in peaceful, clear Japanese weather.

Probably because the chaotic one was not around, yesterday's exams were practically peace personified.

At the moment, it was just before the first exam of the morning was to begin, so Kaname was getting ready for it. In the seat next to her, a classmate was talking on a cell phone. Her voice was audible to Kaname's ears.

"Uh, hello? It's me.... Yeah, test's about to start.... Yeah, so-so.... Mmm-hmm.... No, it's *true*.... Pfft.... I mean, I'm trying my hardest. You know that, don't you, Hiro? ...Yeah.... Yeah."

She was probably talking to her boyfriend. He was likely a college student.

"Yeah.... What are you doing now? ...You've been up all night? ...Ah ha ha, sorry. Oh, you had a report.... Yeah.... Yeah. That's true. Gotta do your best."

Her classmate was absorbed in the phone call, in direct odds with how she usually was.

Hmm, well isn't that special, Kaname thought judgmentally. *Getting all excited in class first thing in the morning; lost in a world of her own with just her boyfriend, who comes from who-knows-where. Damn it. I don't think I've ever seen such a stupid-looking face!*

Despite her uncharitable thoughts, it would be a lie to say she wasn't jealous. To have someone's voice she specifically wanted to hear right before an exam was to begin—what did it feel like to have someone like that? Someone of the opposite sex? What kind of things was she talking about, and with what kind of guy?

If I were in a relationship like that with someone, and if we lived in different places— would I have that kind of expression on my face, too? All because of one phone call?

What if, hypothetically, it was with him*?*

That's a little hard to imagine....

Kaname was lost in thought when her classmate Kyouko Tokiwa spoke up.

"Hey, hey, Kana."

"Eh?"

"How will you do on math today? I'll probably suck."

"Huh...? My condolences. I might do okay." Kaname evaded the question with the tried and true answer of one who had crammed for exams.

She would probably get a nearly perfect English score. Classics, she might be able aim for something around that level. Chemistry, definitely a hundred. Math II, most likely a hundred.

Once again, for these tests she was confident she would ace the math and science, subjects she was supposed to be weak at.

Tessa's prediction had come true. Her awakening as a Whispered involved a suddenly-heightened degree of knowledge. As for whether or not this was disturbing, it really wasn't. All it really meant was that she had the ability to think a little harder.

Strangely, Kaname hardly felt any sense that she had actually gotten smarter. At this point, she could explain at length the chemical formula and manufacturing method of the conductive shape memory polymer used in AS drive systems. Not only could she speak about the principle of a single electron in a quantum sense, she could also propose a unique way of applying it that no one else had realized yet.

It felt no different to her than discussing how to cook mackerel in miso. What was more, the people of the world did not know that when shredded ginger was added to boiled miso it added that much more of a spicy taste.

That was the nature of it.

She would watch stupid comedy shows on TV and cackle at them, and her conversations with her friends were the same as always. Worrying about this would only discourage her, so she had decided not to think too deeply about the issue. The troubling thing was that there seemed to be people who wanted to know about these delicious uses of miso at any cost—

"Uh, I doubt that," said Kyouko, sensing Kaname's momentary self-confidence.

"Kana, didn't you score the highest on last semester's math exam?"

"Yeah, well.... I got lucky."

"How do you study? Or do you actually cheat? I don't care which, just tell me." Her big eyes glittered under her huge glasses.

"It's a secret. You have no 'need-to-know' clearance. Y'know?" Kaname laughed.

"Hmph." Probably reminded of him by Kaname's mimicry, Kyouko changed the subject to Sousuke. "Oh, that reminds me, looks like Sagara's not coming today either."

Even though they were in the middle of important midterms, Sousuke was absent from school. There had been times before now when he suddenly did not show up for two or three days, but this was the first time it had happened during exams.

"Yeah. That idiot—is he cool with failing, I wonder? All he ever does is get in trouble, anyway."

Her tone was light, but Kaname was actually worried. He did not take being a student seriously enough. If things kept going like this, teachers would not keep quiet about it, regardless of how laid-back this school was.

"So annoying. Ugh."

"Have you tried calling his cell? If you threatened him, he might still come," said Kyouko as she excitedly took out her new cell phone. She had just bought it and wanted an excuse to use it.

"Forget it. You can never get a hold of him at times like this. I'm sure he's fishing or something, out in the sticks or deep in some mountains."

"You never know. He might surprise you and answer."

"No, no way. Just forget it." Kaname tried halfheartedly to stop her, but Kyouko still punched some buttons and put the cell phone to her ear. She said nothing for a bit, quietly waiting for an answer.

"See? No use, right?"

"Hmm...."

"It's always like this. It doesn't even go to voicemail. Y'know, when it comes to this guy—"

"I got through."

"Huh?"

"Here." Kyouko held out the cell phone.

Nearby, the classmate from before was still murmuring words of love to her boyfriend. For some reason Kaname saw that image overlaid on herself. Feeling an unfounded embarrassment, she timidly took the cell phone and, half in doubt, spoke into it.

"Hello?"

"Chidori?! What is it?!" It was a distant shout. A terrible noise was mixed in, but it was unmistakably Sousuke on the other end.

"Uh.... Sousuke. Where are you?"

"By Canicatti!"

"Buy manicotti.... What?"

It made no sense. What was it supposed to mean? It also bothered her that the timing of his responses seemed random.

"Hey, look, we've had exams since yesterday. Did you forget?"

"I remembered, but something urgent came up! I couldn't help it!"

"I don't want to hear 'I couldn't help it.' I spent a whole three hours helping you with classics, which you're always terrible at. The test's about to start."

"—ry about that!" The static got worse for a moment.

"Saying you're sorry doesn't make up for it! Urgh! And you know what? I had to make up a cover story for how you demolished our teacher's car!"

This was how Kaname explained it to Eri Kagurazaka:

Sousuke had tried to perform auto maintenance on her vehicle out of kindness. But he started feeling poorly in the middle of it, so he left early and ended up going to the hospital he usually went to. He said that once his condition improved, he promised to come back and put it back together, so he needed Eri to bear with him for a few days.

It was quite a painful explanation, but kindhearted Eri had said with teary eyes: "Oh, all right. This is the first I've heard of this chronic disease, but if that's how it is, I'll wait and not make a big deal of it."

The disassembled car was still behind the school building, covered with a vinyl sheet.

"Do you know much stress I'm under?!"

There was no answer for a short while. Five, six, seven seconds. Just as she was starting to get irritated, a short response came back. "I know!"

"No, you don't! You're insincere! What the hell do you think someone's good will is, anyway?! You know what?! Why do you always have to cause so, so many problems for people—hey, are you listening?!"

"Yeah! I'm lis—"

He was interrupted by a roaring, thunderous sound, followed by high-pitched static. A beat later, Sousuke said, "I'm listening!" And then, strangely, "We're on a straightaway!"

Kaname was taken aback.

"Wh-what?"

"Never mind—something on my end! I'm driving!"

On the other end of the line Kaname could hear a sound like a big rocket firework soaring.

At the same time
Southern Sicily
The outskirts of Canicatti

The Mafia Benz was hit on the lower right side by the rocket round and flames erupted. The flaming vehicle inverted, and when it skidded sideways on the stone-paved road, the pursuer hit it and spun hard. The vehicles entangled and plunged into an empty market. Sousuke paid them no notice.

The Fiat raced at a wild speed and without hesitation along the road in the dead of night. They fled past old streets with stone buildings pressed tightly together.

"That makes ten! Three more!" Mao shouted, hurling the disposable rocket launcher away. Her dress was covered in soot and some spots were ripped—she was practically half-naked.

"Was that the last rocket?!" shouted Kurz as he changed the magazine on his rifle. He had already thrown off his tuxedo jacket, and his blond hair was a disorderly mess.

"Affirmative. All that's left are grenades!"

"Son of a bitch."

"Focus your fire on the grills! I'll keep the shooters' heads down!" Mao shouted.

The pursuers fired even more. Kurz and Mao returned fire. Then, right in the middle of a horrendous noise, on the other end of the satellite connection Kaname asked, "Hello? Driving, as in a car?"

"Affirmative!" Sousuke shouted into his communication headset as he roughly handled the steering wheel.

"Well, that's dangerous. Using a cell phone while you drive is a traffic violation. And you're a high-school student, you know. Pull over somewhere so we can talk."

"Can't do that! If I stop, I won't be able to take the make-up test!"

"Huh?"

Sousuke's Fiat was full of bullet holes, and covered miserably in abrasions. It was practically a scrapheap on wheels. That neither the engine nor the occupants had any conspicuous damage was nothing short of a miracle.

"Well, guess you've got no choice but to do make-ups. But you're really in danger of failing a class, all right? You always skip school like this."

"It's my missions! I can't help it!"

The Fiat crashed with gusto through a pile of vegetable crates piled on the side of the road. Making the rear wheels slide, he drove onto the sidewalk and into a narrow alley. The enemy followed persistently. Mowing down trash cans, a bicycle, a cart, and a case of wine bottles, the BMW quickly bore down on them.

"I don't suppose you can explain that situation to our teacher, though. If you fail a class, you won't go up a grade. You won't become a senior."

"That's true, now that you mention it!"

Bang, bang, bang.

The walls of the meandering alley flew by with violent speed. The pursuer's front bumper rammed the Fiat's rear with a *klunk*.

The steering wheel rebelled. The frame grated.

"What if you repeat a year? The rest of us will end up graduating before you."

"That would be a problem!"

The pursuer's engine spouted smoke. Apparently Kurz's rifle had been effective. After staggering, it slipped and spun. It hit the stone wall, and then was still.

"That leaves two!"

When the Fiat rushed out of the alley, one enemy vehicle that had gone on ahead cut across the road and was hot on their heels.

"...It would be a problem for me, too."

"Say, what?!"

Mao and Kurz were shouting something to each other, as their shotgun and rifle blasted.

"Hmm.... Nothing."

"I couldn't hear you! Say it one—"

They concentrated gunfire at the enemy's front wheels. The wheel cap was blown off and bounced off the road surface. A T-intersection approached. Sousuke nimbly cranked the wheel.

Unable to make the turn with a busted front wheel, the pursuer drove onto the sidewalk and plunged into an empty restaurant, kicking up flying glass fragments and dust. The shrill scream of a car horn echoed.

"One more!" shouted Mao.

"What's going on? Is someone there with you?"

"Don't worry about it! So, what would be a problem?!"

Tires squealed and the final vehicle charged from behind. It was a gigantic pickup truck. It approached with just enough speed to overtake, came alongside, and violently ram into them.

"Just forget it. You probably just weren't paying attention."

"No, things are noisy he—"

A powerful impact shook the small car intensely and caused it to scrape the wall.

The truck again rammed into the Fiat. The rear bumper hung off and scraped the road, generating enough sparks to hurt one's eyes.

"Sousuke?"

"Things are noisy here! It'll be over soon!"

"Uh-huh. Sometimes I get the feeling you aren't seriously listening to anything I say."

"I'm always serious! Even now—"

"Sousuke, brake!" shouted Kurtz as he pulled a hand grenade's pin and threw it into the bed of the nearby truck.

Sousuke reacted immediately. The brake rotors screamed. The enemy pickup flew past the Fiat, which pitched forward roughly.

"Get down!"

"Hello?"

Just then, the grenade Kurz had deposited in the truck's bed exploded.

Shrapnel flew toward the Fiat as well, punching holes in the exterior like it was paper.

The rear half of the pursuit vehicle was destroyed, and it suddenly lost its balance. Billowing black smoke, it slid sideways as it plunged into the town plaza, crashing into the edge of the central fountain. Even then its momentum was not spent, as the frame sprung up, spun over laterally, and fell right in the middle of the fountain.

The crunching scream of tearing metal rang out.

From the Fiat, which had stopped suddenly at the side of the plaza, Sousuke and crew looked at the fountain as the black pickup was skewered upside down on the spire-like sculpture.

The spinning wheels pointed at the sky, and smoke smoldered.

"Yeah, that's art. Like, the fusion of the medieval and modern." Kurz put the fingers of both his hands together and made a rectangular picture frame.

"And that makes zero. But, huh, what a thing to say." Mao groaned as she fixed the top of her dress, which had begun to slide off.

The Mafia private soldiers squirmed out of the open doors and kicked up fountain water as they raced to get away.

That took care of all pursuit for the present.

Sousuke readjusted the transmitter headset and hurriedly called out to his counterpart. "Chidori, it's taken care of now. So ... what were we talking about?"

A sullen silence greeted him. After a short while, Kaname whispered, "I don't know anymore."

"Huh?"

"Look, just get to school as soon as possible."

"Yeah. Oka—"

"Jerk."

The connection cut out. The circuit via satellite from his cell phone, which he left behind in Japan, closed. Sousuke flipped the communicator switch and sighed deeply.

The pursuing cars had been dealt with, but they still could not relax. The local police would soon arrive. As they had no replacement vehicle, Sousuke and the others decided to drive away from the town in the busted-up little car. Although it had become quite rickety, somehow the Fiat was still running.

"Let's head east, anyway," said Mao.

"We'll ditch the car near a town called Delia. We'll change cars and get clothes there."

"Method of procurement?" asked Sousuke.

"I guess stealing would be best. If we bypass the main road and drive all night, we should be at Catania by midday."

"Ah, man. All night. Damn it."

Next to the grumbling Kurz, the sleeping Vincent Bruno let out a muffled sound. He mumbled some unfamiliar woman's name, and smiled slackly.

"He sure is easygoing. Is this guy really a spy?" asked Kurz.

"Both the lieutenant commander and Tessa said so. As did he himself," Mao answered and peered into the cracked rearview mirror. She vigorously wiped the soot from her face and adjusted her crazed hair.

"I could cry," said Mao.

Kurz groaned, tore off the bowtie caught on his neck, and threw it out the window.

The frame rattled and the tires kicked up pebbles as their car drove right through the middle of the gently sloping hill country. Were it daylight, a rich green rural landscape would probably be seen. But the farm road their single headlight shone upon was dark, and the only other light was cast by the moon and stars in the night sky.

I'm not sure if I can be back in Japan by the day after tomorrow, Sousuke muttered silently to himself.

A slightly agitated feeling lurked in his mind. He had missed exams. He was not confident about make-up exams. If his homeroom teacher Miss Kagurazaka found out why he had been absent, how would he ever be able to deceive her again? He also worried about the disassembled car. Not reaching the next grade would be a problem. Without knowing why, he felt very troubled.

How many minutes had he spent in such thoughts? As the car crested a small hill, he heard a sound. At first he thought he had imagined it. But, no.

He thought maybe it was sounds coming from the troubled engine. It was not that either.

He definitely heard it. From far away.

Krrrrn. The sound of turbine blades spinning. A low, muffled sound. Intermittent heavy footsteps. They came together in complete harmony and gradually approached.

"Hey," he called to Mao and Kurz. But he need not have bothered, as they were already alert, looking around the area. Pitch dark shrubbery grew thick on both sides of the country road the Fiat traversed, so visibility was poor.

"Five o'clock," said Kurz. On the other side of a distant thicket to the right rear of the Fiat, the leaves of a tree rustled. Some huge thing was pushing its way through the trees as it ran.

The sounds grew louder. Now they were clearly discernible. A bipedal object loaded with a gas turbine engine. In other words....

"An AS. Not good," said Mao.

"The Mafia?"

"It's one of their commodities. They buy up second-hand mechs from Eastern Europe and Russia, then sell them off to African dictators and guerrillas. Regulations are strict on western models, but lately Soviet ones are—"

"Incoming!"

The shrubs behind them were mowed down, and a giant humanoid shape appeared.

It was a Soviet Arm Slave, an RK-92 Savage. In the midst of the flying foliage stood an eight-meter-tall giant with a short, stout, egg-shaped torso and a large head reminiscent of a frog. Its right hand was equipped with a small machine cannon.

Two red eyes glowed dimly as they gazed at the Fiat. The next instant, it kicked up earth with explosive acceleration power as it broke into a run. "Damn! If it's not one thing it's another. They're *really* persistent. I hope this is the end," said Kurz.

"It's the end for us, at this rate! Can't this go any faster?!" shouted Mao.

"As I said before, this is top speed."

Four people in the small car, on a rough unpaved road—no matter how hard they pushed, 100kph was the best they could do. Conversely, the pursuing Savage could run at 130kph even on terrain such as this. And those figures were nothing more than safe operating levels in a catalog. Depending on the mech's tune-up, it could possibly run faster.

There was more than one pursuer. Two, no, three. One after another they broke through the shrubbery and pounded up the road as they closed in.

"We can't outrun them," muttered Sousuke. Forget guidance counseling and make-up exams. If things went badly, he might never make it back to school at all.

"I guess they won't let us surrender."

"Well, not after all the trouble we caused."

As they were having this conversation, the first Savage approached the Fiat. It bent forward and ran at high speed. The dark green mech held up its thick left arm. It meant to hit them rather than shoot them.

"Get down!" Sousuke stepped on the brake. The Savage's arm came in sideways and swiped at the top of the car. The Fiat's roof was torn off, and the frame inclined heavily to the right.

Another blow. Sousuke yanked the wheel, making the car take refuge at the Savage's feet. It left them in danger of being stepped on, but it allowed them to dodge the enemy's strikes.

The Fiat, however, was practically at its limit. The front wheels emitted a peculiar screech, and white smoke spouted from the engine block. The revs were not increasing. The car was only decelerating.

The Savage reduced its running speed a little and adjusted its posture. It was going to shoot rather then hit. The machine cannon in its right hand aimed at them.

"This is it—"

It was just as they were resigning themselves to the end that something long and thin collided with the Savage's front armor, sparking a simultaneous explosion. An ear-splitting roar rang out through the area.

"Wha—?!"

It was only visible for an instant, but that was an anti-tank dagger, deduced Sousuke instantly. An AS throwing explosives had flown in from somewhere and hit the enemy mech squarely in the chest. The Savage staggered, was suddenly engulfed in flames, and toppled down.

Confused by what had happened, the other two mechs spread out with sharp movements.

"Who? Where?" Mao looked around the vicinity.

A dim shadow rose up directly ahead of them on the gloomy farm road. The air shimmered, pale lightning welled up, and—as if oozing through an invisible membrane—a single AS appeared. It had invisibility mode ECS.

"An M9?" A silhouette with which they were well familiar. This new AS which had shown itself was an M9 Gernsback, a third generation AS which Sousuke and crew used regularly.

However, some details looked subtly different from the M9s they used. Besides there being more bulk on the thighs and upper arms, the shape of the head was quite different. It looked more like the Arbalest. Its coating was not grey, but matte black. It was black from the top of its head down to its feet. Only the sensor bits on its head gave off a slight orange light.

"Who does that belong to?"

"I don't know."

The black M9 sprinted.

The two Savages postponed dealing with the car and entered combat with the mech of unknown affiliation. They broke left and right, moving at high speed, attacking so as to outflank the M9.

Just before the enemy mechs fired, the black M9 jumped.

It cleared the machine-cannon fire and cleverly used obstacles as it weaved its way through the terrain with sharp movements and approached one of the two mechs. The distance was closed in the blink of an eye, and the M9 drew the monofilament cutter beneath its armpit and pierced the Savage's chest as it ran past.

The armor gave off a terrible screech.

It was a precise attack on the cockpit. The operator probably died instantly. It was a certain, but ruthless methodology.

The remaining mech apparently did not even have margin to flinch. Firing its machine cannon wildly, it charged at the black mech. The M9 used the enemy it had just slaughtered as a shield, easily staving off the bombardment.

They approached each other. The M9 ditched its shield and moved nimbly.

In the next moment, the final Savage was exploding. The M9 drove an anti-tank dagger into it at point-blank range, and instantly retreated from the blast radius. An amateur watching probably would not even have deduced what had happened.

The fuel tank of the mech the M9 had used as a shield eventually caught fire and blazed up.

Now, around the Fiat which could do nothing more than hobble, three Savages were on fire and emitted black smoke.

Hardly thirty seconds had passed from when the Savages had first attacked. Kurz gave a short laugh. He was amazed. To take down three mechs without firearms, just using standard issue knives.... Even if an M9's agility exceeded a Savage's by several levels, that mech's operator had considerable skill.

The black mech ran along beside the Fiat. It showed no sign of stopping. The M9's head was equipped with a dual sensor like the Arbalest's.

After looking down at them with sharp, raptor-like eyes, the M9 growled deeply. It was the sound of cooling equipment venting. It was nothing more than a transitory heat disposal right after combat, but it sounded a lot like a lion or tiger growling.

Without saying a word, the M9 pointed east once, and then it changed its own course to the south. It quickly distanced itself from them. In absolute silence.

"Hey...."

Parts of the mech's armor slid, and a red lens-shaped part was exposed. ECS activated. A laser screen scorched the air, and a veil of light enveloped the mech. As if suddenly melting into the darkness, the back of the M9 disappeared.

All that was left were traces of a light purple band.

Stillness returned to the scene.

"What's going on here? Who's piloting that?"

"I don't know."

"But it was one of ours, right?"

"It *should* be."

"Then who was that?"

As if entranced, all they could do was look after the vanished unidentified mech.

In the end, they still did not know the identity of the M9's pilot.

Currently, Mithril was supposedly the only organization in the world making use of the cutting-edge M9s. Even in the American military, Engineering and Manufacturing Development prototypes were still in the testing stages. And the only ones who knew about their mission in Sicily were Tessa, Mardukas, and Kalinin.

That Kalinin had sent in even more reinforcements from somewhere was the most natural explanation, but why had it said nothing to them, much less reveal its affiliation, before it vanished like that? It didn't make sense. In the end, Mao called Kalinin with Sousuke's satellite communicator and requested an explanation.

"You three have no-need-to-know." Kalinin gave the standard businesslike reply.

"Not even myself, the highest ranking officer here?"

"You'll know at some point. Right now, focus on escaping," said Kalinin.

"Roger, sir. Over and out."

After ending the transmission, Mao began complaining immediately. "Ugh, that pisses me off! Why does he always—always!—have to be like that? Damn it!"

"Yeah, I'll say. And yet, I hear women at the base talking about him behind his back. I'm younger than him, more handsome, and nicer while I'm at it," Kurz grumbled, and Sousuke looked surprised.

"The lieutenant commander?"

"Oh, yeah. You didn't know? Try listening around in the mess hall. I hear girls from Supplies and Communications carry on about how awesome he is all the time. They even say that lately he's been having all these secret meetings with Nora the engineer."

"With Ensign Lemming? What kind of meetings?"

"Secret meetings are secret. The lieutenant commander's a man, too. I guess one way or another, they're getting along well." Kurz laughed.

"Hmm." Sousuke had no idea what Kurz was getting at. But judging by the way he smiled, it must have been rather un-Kalinin-like behavior.

When it came to Kalinin's relationships with women, Sousuke knew only of his wife who had died in an accident during his time in

Russia. She, Irina, a well-known violinist, had been a fleeting beauty of slim features. Come to think of it, the aforementioned Ensign Nora Lemming seemed to vaguely resemble Irina somehow.

"Rumor mongering is nice and all, but let's just hurry and get off this island."

"Yeah, let's."

The discussion over, they decided to stick to their plan and hurry to Catania.

The rest of their escape went anticlimactically smoothly. They switched cars in a nearby town and drove through the night, acquired the forged IDs and U.S. military uniforms in Catania, and went to a nearby NATO air base. Mao was a former U.S. Marine, and security was lax at the rural base, so slipping in was exceedingly easy.

There were also no problems boarding a transport headed for Aviano Air Base in northern Italy.

The kidnapped Vincent Bruno had been kept asleep the entire time. Dressed in a retired officer's uniform and riding in a wheelchair, it was explained that he had been seriously wounded in a top-secret mission in the Middle East, which also explained his comatose state. Sicily held a lot of memories for him when he was whole, so it was his family's earnest request that he be brought there. One of his family members was a famous senator, so this trip was a secret one. But sadly, even coming into contact with the scents of this land did not allow him to regain consciousness. That was the story.

"Comatose? Him?"

Seeing Bruno, well-padded for someone in a coma, the transport's steward seemed quite in doubt.

"Correct. But his internal organs couldn't be healthier. What are you looking at?" said Mao—who was wearing a first lieutenant rank insignia—imperiously to the sergeant.

"Well, I just...."

"You do not look at him that way, soldier. He became this way fighting for his country. Do you even remotely realize the hell he's seen? I will not allow you to pity or disdain him!"

"I-I beg your pardon, ma'am. I beg you to forgive such rudeness—"

"No, there's something incorrigible about your attitude. State your name, rank, serial number, and unit!"

The sergeant looked like he wanted to cry. He stated his post and serial number, apologized again and again, and left Bruno quite alone afterward. Things would, of course, not have gone this way in a civilian airport.

"What an actress," said Kurz

"Admirable." Sousuke agreed. Kurz and Sousuke marveled at her after the sergeant left, and Mao flashed them a weary face.

"Ahhh, it's seriously draining, talking like a refined officer. I came *this* close to dropping the F-bomb."

With almost no further problem, their transport took off ten minutes behind schedule.

That was one less worry.

Next, Mao and Kurz planned to head to Mithril's operations headquarters in Australia to deliver Bruno. Sousuke would part with them en route, and return to Japan alone. He would probably arrive in Tokyo tomorrow.

The roar of the turboprop engine permeated through the cabin. It was a terrible sound, but it was tolerable once one got used to it.

The seats were nearly empty, with only five or six occupied by soldiers.

The autumn Sicilian sunlight shone through the windows. Its brightness made sleep seem unlikely. They had not slept since last night, but it would probably take a little more time for their high-strung nerves to calm.

A post-combat, weary feeling lay heavily among them.

"You know, though...," said Kurz, sinking down into his rough seat. In the ten minutes since takeoff, it was the first thing anyone had said to break the languid silence that had descended. "Are you sure you're okay?"

"In what way?" Sousuke asked sullenly, as he looked through his world history vocabulary notebook.

"That way. Tests. Didn't you miss some?"

"Yeah."

Missing midterms really did hurt, thought Sousuke.

His multiple unexcused absences due to being called suddenly overseas for missions had resulted in poor grades in a number of subjects. At this rate, there was the chance of him repeating a year like Kaname said.

"My job is important, too, though. What would've happened if I hadn't shown up last night?" Sousuke pointed out the time when Mao and Kurz had been surrounded at the Mafia mansion.

"We'd have managed. Right, girl?"

"Hmm. Probably," answered Mao, reclining in the seat ahead of them.

"To be honest, I'd thought a few steps ahead."

"Oh," Sousuke murmured, feeling slightly alienated. He felt like he had somehow been told, *You don't need to get involved. Just be a good boy and go to school.*

"Well, it's true that you saved us," added Mao, perhaps picking up on things.

"But, you know, I'm a little worried, too. Like, I don't know...." Mao trailed off.

"My advancement?"

"No. Your whole situation right now. You guard Kaname at school, you go on missions like this, and you've had that Arbalest pushed on you. Isn't that overwhelming?"

Sousuke remained silent.

"At first I was like, well, as long as it's temporary, and you were getting your job done no problem. But lately—"

"I haven't made any mistakes."

"That's not what I'm getting at. It's purely a physical and temporal problem. Just like how things are getting worse at school right now."

"That's true, but...."

"No matter how shorthanded we are, there's a limit. If I were in your shoes, I'd definitely throw it back in the lieutenant commander's face."

"Yeah, but—"

Kurz cut in. "When you think about it, well, so what? So long as he does go to school. I mean, he got in with forged papers, anyway, and there's no reason he has to force himself to graduate."

The reason Sousuke had started attending Jindai High School was to facilitate guarding Kaname. His principal occupation was still as a Mithril mercenary, and being a high-school student was nothing more than provisional. Therein lay the fundamental difference between Kaname and the other students. As Kurz said, there was no reason to force himself to graduate.

"Well, yeah, true," Mao said flatly and glanced back at Sousuke. "This may sound personal, but what do you think?"

"About what?"

"About your plans for the future."

"I'll follow orders. That's it." He answered plainly, gazing at the window through which dazzling light shone.

Mao would usually smile at such an artless response from Sousuke, but this time she groaned as if annoyed.

"It's always like that with you. I'm talking about your life plans. You're only seventeen, right? What will you do from here? Don't you give it any thought? Aren't you just using duty and orders as a means of escape?"

"Escape? Me?"

"Yes, you. I guess it's a lot easier to live when all you do is what other people say."

Sousuke made no response.

"Whoa, pick a fight, why don't you?" said Kurz.

"Not really. I've been thinking about this," Mao said and then fell silent.

Far in the distance through the window, Mount Etna was visible. It was Europe's largest active volcano. Maybe the air was turbid today, as it looked ashen and hazy.

Plans for the future....

Despite everything Mao had said, Sousuke was not angry. Rather, it made him think. Kaname had also said something similar last night.

Life plans.

He had a rough idea what that meant, but when he thought carefully, it felt like he had never heard the words before. To put it another way, it probably meant a protracted war strategy. What would he be doing in five, ten years—to foresee that and decide on lifestyle guidelines? That was what it was.

Until now he had never thought of himself five years hence. He had not even been conscious of that existence. The majority of Sousuke Sagara's past was spent in a storm of conflict and survival. Would a wild animal that does not even know about tomorrow's food worry about things five years in the future? No word had sounded more false to his ears than *future*.

Future? Whatever. Securing ammunition was the priority.

That had always been his main concern—at least it had been until half a year ago.

He had vaguely sensed change coming to that desolate mental state. Going to Jindai High School and spending time with Kaname and the others had begun to have unseen effects on Sousuke's mind. Like a sheet of ice melting, and the land, abundant with life, faintly showing itself.

A future. Is that something I have, too?

He would sometimes ask himself that in a corner of his consciousness. He did not know the answer. But at least he had reached the point of asking it. That was change.

As time went by, everyone would change.

Every type of lifestyle had an end, and the wave washed away even him.

The ending days brought about the next future—an obscure truth that made Sousuke feel restless.

"Kurz?"

"What?"

"What will you be doing in five years?"

Kurz looked at Sousuke blankly. "Who knows? Well, I hope living the good life with a good woman."

"Do you think that could be?"

"Who knows?" Kurz repeated and pulled the shabby field uniform hat down over his eyes. Then he folded his arms, and after a large yawn, added, "I dunno, but there's no loss in thinking it. Sweet dreams."

Kurz fell silent. When Sousuke looked at the row in front of them, he saw that Mao had leaned her head against the window and was gently breathing in her sleep.

Mount Etna grew distant.

Their transport was moving away from Sicily.

CHAPTER 2
Underwater Scene II

October 16, 08:53 (Japan Standard Time)
Chofu, Tokyo
Jindai High School

The first subject of the fourth day of midterms was world history.

Twenty-three minutes had passed since the test started. The rustling sound of question sheets turning and mechanical pencils clicking. It was so quiet that when a car rode down the street in front of the school, the engine noise was disruptive.

Kaname's eyes ran over the problem sheet.

The height of the Roman Empire; The Five Good Emperors; Augustus; Cicero; the Sicilian revolt, and numerous other minutiae. Many terms she remembered but did not understand. Once the exam was over, she would likely completely forget the words. Fixed-term tests were such a meaningless and unproductive ritual.

She glanced over toward the window.

Sousuke's seat was empty.

There had been no word whatsoever from him since the pre-test phone call the day before yesterday. She had thought he would come today, but he was absent. Ultimately, he had been out since the first day of tests.

I swear....

For some reason, a sigh escaped her. The school was blessedly quiet without Sousuke there, and she should have been able to relax. But what was this uneasiness, this sense of something missing?

Stop it; I'm in the middle of a test. I've got to focus.

She regrouped and faced the questions again.

The fall of the Han Dynasty; the Hun invasion; the Yellow Turban Rebellion; Emperor Ling; Cao Cao; the Battle of Red Cliffs, and even more minutiae. Because she had read about things related to *Romance of the Three Kingdoms* in manga, she knew a lot about this part. She just could not recall the kanji. How did one write the "Kong" in Kongming, again?

Where's he gone, anyway? she thought while stumped on an answer.

Wonder what kind of work it is. Maybe he's in danger again. I wonder if he's okay. Or maybe he's with her *again. He did sound odd during that phone call the other day, come to think of it.*

She came back to herself with a start.

No, I did it again. I wound up ignoring the test and thinking about him.

Enough, already.

It's his fault. He's taking unexcused absences and missing exams. That's why it bothers me. I'm class rep, and it's not like he's a complete stranger. That's the only reason, but I still can't get it out of my mind. What a pain. If he weren't absent, I could concentrate on this test!

The classroom door suddenly opened.

"Sorry I'm late."

Breathing heavily and speaking between gasps as he entered was none other than Sousuke Sagara. He seemed to have arrived in quite a hurry. His sullen face was bathed in perspiration. And for some reason, he wore not his school uniform, but deep green camouflage. The design was subtly different from the field uniform he sometimes wore. On the chest was printed U.S. MARINE.

"Sagara. Fine time to finally join us. And what's with those clothes?" said the proctoring teacher with a frown.

"I apologize. There was no time to change."

"All right. Fine. Hurry and take your seat."

"Yes, sir!"

Sousuke headed quickly for his chair. Just before he reached his destination, his classmate Shinji Kazama whispered to him, "Sagara, why are you dressed like that?"

"I had my reasons," he answered shortly and sat down. He took the test sheet from the teacher, took out his pencil box, and hurriedly began going over the test.

Kaname was absent-mindedly watching him from a distance. A feeling of relief, like a weight being lifted from her chest, washed over her.

Their eyes met for an instant. In place of a greeting, Sousuke lifted his mechanical pencil just a little. Kaname, flustered, averted her gaze and focused on the exam.

October 17, 16:09 (Australian Eastern Standard Time)
Sydney, Australia
Mithril Operations Headquarters

This is the second time I've come to an interrogation room with Lieutenant Commander Kalinin this way, thought Tessa. The previous detainee was a fifteen- or sixteen-year-old boy, but this time it was a middle-aged man.

Vincent Bruno, who Mao and the others had abducted, reclined with an impudent attitude, a faint smile on his face.

It was probably just a bluff. This was no police station. It was Mithril Operations Headquarters. There was no lawyer to protect him, and there would be no trial. Bruno should have known that, on the other side of the magic mirror.

Tessa wore only a light coat over her usual uniform. She had ridden in a Mithril jet to the airport, then in a limousine from there, so no civilian eyes had seen her. Kalinin likewise wore his olive-colored field uniform.

They had both received the successful report on the Bruno kidnapping mission, then had flown to Sydney from the West Pacific Merida Island Base.

This man had introduced the conspirators who had driven her ship into a desperate situation. There was no mistaking this, but it still did not feel real to Tessa. She was supposed to loathe him as an enemy. But now all that lurked in her chest was a chilled sense of contempt.

"It's unbelievable," she muttered.

"That— That seemingly worthless person nearly sank my ship."

"It could be said that it is because he appears worthless that he was able to do such a thing. It was probably not too difficult for an enemy to win him over to their side," said Kalinin.

There were two men besides Bruno in the interrogation room on the other side of the magic mirror, a lieutenant junior grade, based out of Ops Headquarters, and likewise a petty officer third class. According to Kalinin, the lieutenant was once a Peruvian intelligence agent, and thus knew much about this form of questioning.

"Let's start with a simple question, Mister Bruno." The lieutenant began. "You were the secretary of the chief of personnel, and in late June of this year, you maneuvered for John Howard Dunnigan and Nguyen Bien Bo to be assigned to the SRT of Mithril's West Pacific battle group, *Tuatha de Danaan*. You downplayed, or perhaps deleted, data on four other higher priority NCOs, as well as recommendation data from training camps in Belize and other places. You then maintained to the understaffed *Tuatha de Danaan* that there were no other options. Do you dispute this?"

"I don't know what you're talking about," Bruno said, not looking at them. The lieutenant smiled gently, then turned to the waiting petty officer and said, "Do it."

"Yes, sir," the petty officer said and then hit Bruno with an eye-opening punch to the face.

"Guh!"

The petty officer grabbed the nape of Bruno's neck when it looked like he would tumble out of his chair, and resettled him. He then pressed Bruno's wrist down on the desk, grasped his little finger, and wrenched it hard in a direction it was not meant to bend.

"St-sto—!"

There was an unpleasant snapping sound. A bone in his little finger had broken. An earsplitting scream rang out in the interrogation room.

"No need to worry. This will be the end," Kalinin announced from behind Tessa, as she drew back and made to avert her eyes from the sight. Sure enough, he was right. Bruno's shoulders shook, he sobbed, and when his ring finger was grabbed, he shrieked, "Stop ... it! Okay, I'll tell you everything! So ... so, forgive me!"

"Answer me. You were the one who sent Dunnigan and Nguyen onto the TDD-I, weren't you?" The lieutenant coldly repeated his question.

"Yes! It was me!"

"By whose request?"

"I don't know."

"Don't lie."

"Hold on! I—I really don't know his name! He said he was a messenger for Amalgam!"

"Amalgam? What's Amalgam?"

"I don't know. I really don't. I thought it was probably an intelligence agency for the Soviets or something. They never denied it. At first ... it seemed simple enough! They paid me $200,000 up front.... Can you believe that? Two-hundred K! Of course I had no reason to refuse! Right away I said, sure—"

"What do you think?" Tessa asked Kalinin, who watched silently.

"He does not seem to be lying. Nor can I think of a reason for him to hide it. Of course, he does not seem to know very much," said Kalinin, gazing at the nearby LCD.

The computer was analyzing Bruno's words as he spoke them. By minutely checking the stress in his voice, the system was quite accurately able to know the authenticity of a suspect's testimony. It was an expansion of the lie detector. The first violent attack was also to stimulate the suspect's excitement and make the analysis even simpler.

"Amalgam.... That may be some kind of insinuation," said Tessa.

Mithril was the name of a fictional type of silver. In the face of that, the enemy called itself Amalgam, a mercury alloy. It was like a bad joke.

"I don't know who they really are! Honest!" Bruno screamed on the other side of the mirror. His face was pale and bathed in cold sweat, as he glared at the adjoining dark room.

"Are you satisfied now?! You're listening, aren't you?! How 'bout you show yourselves instead of spying from in there?! Treating me like this— Mithril, so what?! The 'silver of justice'?! Hypocrites who act like heroes!"

"Calm down, Mister Bruno."

"What is it I'm supposed to have done?! The devil take every last one of you! You're murderers and you deserve to die! Pieces of shit, all of you!"

Tessa endeavored to ignore it all. But she was unable to keep a phrase—a phrase that spewed out as if stifled to death—from emerging: "How dare he?"

The faces of the men she'd lost during that incident came to mind, and she felt like all the blood in her body had come to a boil. She wanted to immediately turn on the lights in the room, appear before him, and hurl bitter words at him.

You're *the murderer. Give me back my men.* You're *the one who's damned. You don't know anything. You're a worthless man, in there spouting poison. You're a vile imbecile who doesn't know his place, and you push your views on* me? *Enough with your conceit! I wouldn't mind ordering that petty officer to break the rest of your fingers!*

Muddled, intense emotions welled up inside her. It wasn't simple anger that tried to stir her, but something more violent.

"Captain—"

The sound of Kalinin's voice made her come back to herself. Her palms were clammy with sweat and she felt a little dizzy.

She felt a terrible self-hatred. She could not deny it if she wanted to. She had just been enjoying watching the man suffer.

"Captain, let us leave the rest to the lieutenant. Admiral Borda is apparently waiting."

"Yes," Tessa answered feebly, and turned her back on the ranting Bruno.

"This is an unpleasant way to do things."

On both sides of the glass, she thought.

"I do not deny that, but it is effective. His life is not in danger. Besides, fingers heal quickly."

"That's true." Tessa glanced at Kalinin's expressionless profile, and faltered.

Doesn't he feel anything? Did that scene play out before his eyes, and his feelings not even tremble? It's also true for Kalinin that he lost men because of him.

Just after she thought this, the Russian added in a cool voice, "I'd be cutting his fingers *off.*"

Tessa and Kalinin left the interrogation room and headed for the office of the Operations chief.

The Mithril Operations Headquarters that they were currently occupying was in a section of midtown Sydney. Most people involved with Mithril found it hard to believe that such a world-wide organization would have an important base here in Australia. Even in light of transportation facilities and correspondence with other agencies, everyone in the "business" believed that it would be advantageous to establish such a base in Europe.

Be that as it may, such common sense stopped applying twenty years ago. Satellite communication and the Internet had developed, and today when the flood of information had covered the world, a headquarters' physical location was not too important. Moreover, Paris, London, Brussels, and Geneva had long since been ridden with excellent intelligence agencies—establishing a high-functioning base amongst them was problematic.

To put it simply, it was an issue of turf.

Mithril was a young organization. Ten years ago when its prototype was inaugurated, there were plans to build Operations Headquarters in Europe, but small problems kept emerging, and it was eventually abandoned. The majority of currently-active Mithril bases in Europe belonged to Intelligence, but they were of a very limited scope.

Operations Headquarters in Sydney was a little short to be called a skyscraper. The owner of the building was ostensibly Argyros Security. Argyros was one of the enterprises Mithril used as a front, but it really did manage security firms all over the world, which managed to bring in a tidy profit. Most of Mithril's members publically worked for this firm. It was quite common for discharged soldiers to find employment with security firms, so this front was rather convenient.

Mithril maintained this enterprise and a number of others.

M9 power reactor manufacturer Ross & Hambleton; marine shipping mainstay Umantak; long-established aerospace firm Martin Marietta—the branches extended in many directions. From fast-growing up-and-coming enterprises to those with financial difficulties saved from bankruptcy. There were also supporting financial institutions and firms posing as paper companies.

Fronts, financial investments, equipment supply, talent discovery—Mithril put these enterprises to all sorts of necessary uses in order to manage the organization. Most of the people who worked for them did not even know Mithril existed.

The Argyros building that housed Operations Headquarters was at a glance old, but its actual security system was extremely advanced. Every part of the building was bugged, and countless surveillance devices and plainclothes guards were watching for intruders.

Tessa and Kalinin came to the Operations chief's office, and the male secretary came out to receive them.

"It's been a long time, Captain."

"Yes, Mr. Jackson. You seem well. But please, do not call me Captain," she said and the secretary, not quite forty, smiled cheerfully.

"Yes, but calling you 'Little Miss' like before would not be appropriate. From what I've heard, you've done quite well for yourself since leaving here. Showing you respect is a matter of course."

"Then, thank you. Well, I suppose I manage one way or another."

For a period before she assumed command of the *Tuatha de Danaan* battle group, Tessa worked as staff here at Operations HQ. While assisting Admiral Borda, she had studied amphibious, specialized, and underwater warfare. During that time when she met this secretary, Lieutenant Jackson, he had called her things like "Little Miss" and "Little Tessa." It was when she became the *Tuatha de Danaan* battle group commander that she received the rank of captain.

"So, the admiral?"

"He is on the phone, but he doesn't seem to mind you going in. By the way, he will probably try to detain you again. Be sure to keep your guard up."

"Yes, I will. Thank you." After thanking him, Tessa was admitted into Admiral Borda's office along with Kalinin.

The office opened up like a small café, but the walls were nearly completely covered with tall bookshelves. Most of the furniture was made of wood and well-used, giving off a darkened luster. The indirect lighting of incandescent lamps and sunlight lent the atmosphere of an old library to the room.

Admiral Borda was seated in his office chair, talking on the phone.

"Yes.... Mmm-hmm. I know.... Yes.... Took the words right out of my mouth. We'll take care of our own mismanagement. Of course we'll forward the interrogation record. Have a little faith.... His person? I'm not sure what you mean." As he spoke to whoever it was on the other end of the line, Admiral Borda returned Tessa's and Kalinin's salutes, indicated reception chairs, and mouthed the words "Have a seat."

"If you say so. Do what you want.... That's right. We should discuss that again another day.... Mmm-hmm. It's something to think about.... No, I have to go. I have visitors," he announced and then pressed the switch on his phone. He threw the receiver onto the desk like it was some filthy thing and then slowly stood up.

"Glad you're here. Care for a drink?" the admiral asked, walking to the minibar in a corner of the room.

"Thank you. Water will do."

"Lieutenant Commander?"

"I will have the same."

"Hmm, not much of a drink order." Admiral Borda shrugged and retrieved a Perrier bottle from the refrigerator.

"How are the M9s handling, Lieutenant Commander?"

"Sir, there is room for improvement, but they are generally satisfactory. However, the issue regarding maintenance still remains. Part compatibility is so low, our inventory status will likely become problematic." Kalinin answered the opening question crisply.

"I see you're true to form. But bear this in mind," the admiral said and smiled.

If one were to concisely describe Jerome Borda, Mithril's Operations head, one might say he was a good-natured man one might find anywhere. He had a moderate bearing on which a hotdog-stand apron might look more fitting than a military uniform.

His age was supposed to be around sixty, but he had a full head of grey-streaked black hair, which made him look ten years younger. Even Tessa, who was young enough to be his granddaughter, found his features to be somehow charming. It was not polite to say, but his droopy eyes and mouth suggested the sweetness of a small puppy.

That was not to say he had no dignity. An ordinary person could guess after one encounter that this was a man of resolute intelligence and experience, and also leadership qualities and fortitude. In actuality he had been in the U.S. Navy for over thirty years, working his way up from seaman to admiral. Sadness toward the world was hidden in his eyes—that part of him was no different whatsoever from a man like Kalinin.

"That phone call was from the Intelligence head," said Admiral Borda, pouring water into glasses.

"They appear to be in a bad mood over us abducting Bruno without permission. They, too, had ascertained that he was in Sicily. They were even keeping a close eye on *Partholon*'s activities to make sure we didn't beat them to it."

Partholon was one of the four battle groups which were part of Operations. They were originally supposed to be the group carrying out the Sicily abduction. The movements of *Tuatha de Danaan*, the Western Pacific battle group under Tessa's command, meant that both Bruno and Intelligence had been outwitted.

Of course, only a small number of people in the group had done the moving.

"Intelligence wants us to hand over Bruno?" asked Tessa.

"Yes. I refused, of course. By the way, you watched his interrogation?"

"Yes, sir."

"There's something you need to learn from seeing that, if you intend to remain a battle-group commander. The path you travel is one of violence. The long, grim corridor of the warrior." Borda's tone became enigmatic.

Tessa understood then that it was probably none other than Admiral Borda himself who had maneuvered it so that she would be the one to witness the interrogation. As soon as she had arrived, the NCO who met them had said, "The admiral is currently busy with something that cannot wait. Would you care to oversee Bruno's interrogation until he's free?"

Why did he want me to see something like that? What was I to learn from it?

Clean and dirty don't exist in combat. He did not seem likely to give her such a commonplace sermon. Of course, compared to the admiral, Kalinin and many other adults, she had not yet seen anything truly dirty. She was aware of that.

But it was a more abstract concept that this older gentleman was conveying. It was simple in its complexity. Was there not something symbolized by that scene which language and logic could not express?

An ominous suggestion. A gloomy personification. A fragment of the future.

Was he not suggesting that she would eventually be confronted by the severe dilemma of that spectacle? No matter how much a genius she was at sixteen, seventeen years of age, there were rules at work on the underside of events, rules which she had no way of understanding—that perhaps those rules had appeared before her by way of the admiral?

"Don't think too much about it," the admiral said, presenting a glass to Tessa. "You'll understand in time. Sooner or later."

"What will happen to Bruno now?"

"The maximum penalty, or so I'd like to call it. But we're not a regular military. A lynching. Regulations allow for death by shooting, but to date that's never been carried out. Confining him for quite a long period of time is the usual punishment. Until all the information he knows about Mithril's equipment, organization, and personnel become outdated."

Tessa knew of that regulation. Five years or so would probably not be sufficient for his confinement. Ten years, or maybe fifteen. *But will this organization still exist that far into the future?* She was suddenly seized by that baseless thought.

"We're not some chummy club. Penal regulations must be applied. Well, his actual punishment will probably be decided by the council once all the interrogations are over."

Borda sat on the opposite sofa and changed the subject. "Now, the reason I summoned you both was to discuss something besides that. I thought our structure could use some adjustment."

"Meaning what, exactly, sir?"

"I've looked over all the reports of the incident at the Perio archipelago. The roles played by those two Japanese, the Kaname Chidori girl and Sergeant Sagara, are immeasurable. You stressed it in your report as well, but it seems the TDD-1 was saved by those two."

"Yes, sir. That is the case."

"It's now becoming hard to deny their significance. The Whispered matter, the ARX-7 matter. Meaning, we're already no longer at a stage of treating them as a 'pending item.' Intelligence is even making random claims about them. Then there's the issue of Wraith."

Tessa and Kalinin remained silent.

"It's time we reevaluated their situation. Don't you think so, Lieutenant Commander?"

At Borda's question, Kalinin looked down slightly and answered in a reserved voice, "You are quite right. However—"

Borda raised his hand, interrupting him. "I don't need a bureaucratic answer. However you temporize, it doesn't change the fact that our current methodology is inefficient."

"Yes, sir."

"Your opinion, Teletha?"

"What you say is correct. But—"

Borda made an exaggeratedly surly expression and pointed directly at her.

"But? But what?"

"Nothing, sir.

"Good. Then let's get down to brass tacks."

October 19, 14:59 (Japan Standard Time)
Chofu, Tokyo
Jindai High School

The week after exams the school underwent guidance counseling.

Of course, as important as "guidance counseling" sounded, it pretty much meant a bunch of long-winded lectures from teachers.

Sayeth the principal:

"You might all be thinking, 'But I'm still just a junior.' It is during your second year, though, that you must think seriously of your direction after graduation. In these especially hard times, you will be asked at business interviews not about your academic background, but about what you're trying to learn, what kind of abilities you have. So you need to focus your thoughts on those areas, making a plan for your future—"

And so on.

That's easier said than done, thought Kaname and the others.

Sayeth their class president:

"Get this. Stop thinking you won't have a job or be in college the year after you graduate. That easy way out just creates worse problems. Sumo who work to become *yokozuna,* even though most of them are inexperienced *sekitori*, if one of them thinks, 'I just need to make it to juryo,' will he really even get that far? I don't think so. That's how rigid society can be. In other words—"

And so on.

But we're not sumo wrestlers, thought Kaname and the others.

The three-hundred-plus juniors gathered in the gym had little in the way of aspirations.

Just as Kaname's head was beginning to nod from the boredom, the final lecture ended.

"Bear all that in mind and think carefully. All kinds of materials are available in front of the guidance office, so whoever needs them, take them."

Dismissal. Starting with Class I, the students left the gymnasium in turn.

The assembly was during sixth period, so school was going to end soon.

Sitting on the clattering train on the way home from school, Kaname let out a big yawn.

"Kana, you were totally asleep," said Kyouko, who was sitting next to her.

Standing in front of them was Sousuke with his sullen face. Apparently in need of sleep, there were dark circles under his eyes. It was probably because he had been putting Miss Kagurazaka's car back together without rest or sleep since Sunday.

"Well, duh. I can't take guidance stuff like that seriously," said Kaname, stifling another yawn.

Rather than such idealism, she wanted them to talk about practical things like an attorney's average annual income, how difficult it was to get into a particular famous company, or that it was best to give up on becoming an animator.

"They said some pretty good things, though. It made me think a little."

"Ugh. Kyouko, you were listening?"

"Yeah. I mean, it's about us. I'd planned to get a job once I graduated, but now I don't know."

"Hmm," Kaname murmured ambiguously. Kyouko's profile always looked childish, but for some reason it looked a lot older than her own just then. Maybe she noticed Kaname's quiet gaze, as she smiled a little awkwardly.

"Well, it's not all that serious. But you know what?" Kyouko suddenly looked closely at Sousuke, standing before them.

129

"Sagara, I've been thinking about this. Isn't your hair getting a little long?"

"Hmm?" Sousuke looked puzzled.

Kaname imitated her and stared rudely at Sousuke.

His hairstyle was the same as always, messy but adequate. But upon closer inspection, it was overall longer than before. The thickness of his bangs, long enough to reach his eyes, seemed to be increasing—at certain angles his eyes were hidden from view.

It was not at the point of being unsightly. It helped that his face was dauntless, and it had not grown extremely long. It was just growing in a way that was somewhat bothersome.

"Yeah, now that you mention it...," said Kaname as Sousuke lifted his bangs with one hand.

"Does it look odd?"

"No, it's not that bad. Hey, do you usually go to a salon or something?"

"What's a salon?"

"A barber."

"Ah. No, I've never used one. I cut it myself."

"With scissors?"

"With this," Sousuke said, and took a rough combat knife out from his uniform.

"Ah-ha. Now it all makes sense." She finally understood why his hair was always uneven and unkempt.

Then, as if Kyouko'd had an epiphany, she raised both her finger and her voice.

"Hey, hey! I just thought of something. Why don't we take Sagara to a hair place? We'll give him a whole new image."

"Huh? That sounds ... pretty interesting," said Kaname.

"Doesn't it? I think a pompadour would work."

"No, more like a simple crew cut."

"How about a mushroom cut? And maybe have him wear some colorful glasses."

"Pfft!" Kaname laughed and said, "A punch perm would be funny, too."

"Could you picture him using slang like some street punk?"

"Maybe we should add some dog ears, too."

"That's not what a barber does."

They went off on a tangent with their crazy ideas.

The suggestion was a joke from the start, but Sousuke suddenly spoke up with an idea of making it a reality. "I wouldn't really mind."

"Huh?"

"A barber. Isn't that where typical high-school students get their hair cut?"

Kaname and Kyouko took him to a chic barbershop a short walk from Chofu Station's south exit.

This looks a lot different than barber shops in Afghanistan, thought Sousuke, looking at the exterior. There were barbers in the conflict zones in which he grew up. It was just that he was totally indifferent toward such establishments until now. It was a desire to improve himself that had motivated him to come here.

He had to adapt more to this town, this lifestyle.

That motive was equivocally at work. He may not have thought such a thing if not for what Mao had said the other day.

Of course, he was also simply curious.

"This place okay?"

"Sure. I leave it to you."

Thus did the three of them enter the barbershop.

"We'd like to get his hair cut, please," said Kaname to the stylist who greeted them. The stylist seemed to take in the situation just from that, because he grinned and said to Sousuke, "This way, please."

"Hmm."

With awkward movements, he sat in the chair. The stylist put a towel around his neck and covered him with a vinyl sheet.

"Now, what kind of effect are we going for?" the stylist asked Kaname and Kyouko, who stood nearby.

"What do we do, Kana?"

"Hmm. I guess we should give up on gags like mohawks, etcetera."

"Oh, nice, a mohawk. I've always wanted to try one of those." The stylist joked. As the girls laughed, he made several suggestions. After chatting for about three minutes, they ended up settling on something safe.

"Okay, at least make it short enough to see his eyebrows. And he has a lot of hair, so please comb it out really well. Sound good, Sousuke?"

"Sure."

"That'll do it, then. Thanks so much. We'll wait over there." The girls waved and went over to the waiting area. For some reason Sousuke felt helpless.

No, it's not just that.

He had a bad feeling. Even though nothing should have been irregular, something inside him was stirring. His long-cultivated intuition and sense of danger were trying to warn him of some peril.

Is it just my imagination?

He did not know. And his intuition was often off in this peaceful town. It was practically unreliable. How many blunders had he made thus far, relying on that intuition?

"Okay. I'll give you a shampoo now, sir." The stylist made to apply some bottled shampoo to Sousuke's head.

"Wai...."

His voice stopped as soon as it started.

"Yes?"

"No ... continue."

Looking a little doubtful, the stylist put shampoo on the top of his head, rubbing it into his hair, and bubbles quickly appeared. The unknown fingers of a complete stranger moved vigorously over his scalp.

"Does it itch anywhere?"

Sousuke paused and then said, "No." In truth, his whole body was itching, but he had decided to make his answer brief.

I can't relax. I really can't relax.

What if the contents of the bottle were a deadly dermal toxin? What if this stylist had a poison needle in his hand? What if there was a small automatic handgun concealed under this white robe?

He would have absolutely no way to resist.

Don't worry about it. This is just soap. He just works here, Sousuke told himself. The idea that this stylist was an assassin was nonsense. It was Kaname who had picked this place, and what had brought him here was his own momentary whim from a few minutes ago. There was no way an enemy who was after the two of them could already be lying in wait to ambush them here.

"Okay. Right over here, please," the stylist called to Sousuke while running hot water in the washbasin in front of him.

"Huh?"

"We need to rinse out that shampoo."

"Ah." The hairstylist seemed to be telling him to stick his head in the washbasin.

But if he did that, his field of vision would drop to zero. It would also mean exposing his defenseless neck to the guy. There was probably no way the stylist would bring a weapon down on his spinal cord or inject him with a syringe. Perhaps it was more likely that someone outside the building had him in his sights.

"Is something wrong?"

"Well ... is it absolutely necessary that I do that?"

At first stylist looked at him blankly, but then he smiled uncertainly.

"Well, of course. I can't cut it the way it is. Come on, over here."

In a state of terrible mental agony, Sousuke slowly and wordlessly began to move. He then put his head in the washbasin. He drew his automatic pistol from its holster under the sheet. That at least was one consolation.

As he rinsed Sousuke's head, the stylist asked, "How is the water temperature?"

"It's fine." He felt suspense even as he answered. He did not know the temperature of the water.

If he showed even the slightest opening, wouldn't this man attempt to end his life? Wasn't it strange that most of the stylist's commands would result in completely rendering him defenseless?

Could someone have outwitted him with some unfathomable trick, somehow anticipating this visit to the barbershop, and impersonated a stylist? Or maybe there was another enemy, waiting to strike the instant he was totally defenseless?

Yes. There was no reason for him to feel secure. Even now, someone was after Kaname. If he died here, who would protect her?

"And there we go. See, that wasn't so bad."

Wrapping a towel around his head, the barber slowly returned him to the chair. It was nearly torture, having his head rubbed vigorously, his view obstructed by the towel.

"Time for your cut."

The barber worked his scissors and casually grasped his hair. A man whose identity he did not know stood behind him, grasping a sharp tool.

Somewhere in his head, an alarm bell went off furiously.

This is bad. Enough already. At this rate—

He reached his limit.

His body moved on its own volition. Before the scissors could get close to his head, Sousuke grabbed and lifted his opponent's arm, and standing up from the chair, slammed the stylist into the mirror in front of them.

"Wh-what are you—"

"Don't move!" Sousuke shouted sharply, running his eyes over the other astonished stylists and customers. He waved his gun around in all directions.

Everyone was speechless with shock.

However, no apparent enemies were to be seen. The hairstylist, who was still pressed against the mirror, emitted a feeble voice as he struggled against the hold.

There was no threat. Inside the shop, or outside.

He had went off again. It was always like this.

"Sousuke?!"

Kaname charged over from the waiting area. At full speed, with a rolled-up fashion magazine. She was unmistakably angry.

Correction. There is one *threat.*

Sousuke bravely awaited the downward swing of the improvised cudgel at his head.

138

"For God's sake!" Kaname remained angry for a while on the walk back to her apartment.

"I only took you there because you *told* me to. Why did you go nuts like that?!"

"I'm ashamed."

After the situation, though Kaname joined him in bowing her head in apology, the stylist had treated them as if they were yakuza, driving them out with: "I'm sorry, but could you go someplace else? And of course you don't owe us any money."

Afterward, Kyouko had smiled and said, "Oh, well, can't help that," and then left them to walk home alone.

"But it's too dangerous to leave yourself that defenseless with a complete stranger holding an edged weapon," explained Sousuke.

"Oh, right. Then don't suggest going to a barbershop! Are you saying that you didn't know from the start that's how haircuts work?! One wrong move and an innocent man might have been seriously wounded! You need to get away from images of assassins and enemies for a change!"

"I won't do that." That part alone he said in a resolute tone. "Enemies exist. That's a fact. It would be no surprise if one attacked you."

"Well...." Kaname was at a loss for words.

Unless it was so bluntly pointed out, she was liable to forget. She was definitely a target because she was a Whispered, whatever the heck that was.

"My highest priority task here is to protect you from enemies."

Hearing it said so plainly, Kaname lost the urge to chastise him any further. Instead, she mumbled a little grumpily, "Yeah, but ... nothing like that's happened once since then."

"That's true. But it doesn't mean we can lose focus."

"Ugh."

Since the class trip incident, no so-called enemies had taken any action directly against her as a target. At least, not as far as Kaname had noticed. She had seen her share of danger since then, but none of situations was anything more than her getting involved in things she perhaps shouldn't.

Life here in Tokyo was by and large peaceful. Although perhaps Sousuke-ish slapstick made the days noisier than typical high school life.

Do these enemies really exist? Aren't he and Mithril just making a bigger deal out of it than necessary?

It was natural for Kaname to have such doubts.

Unconsciously, their pace slackened.

There were many signs of life this evening in the residential area. Autumn was deepening, and the air was growing chillier. The sun was also setting earlier.

"It's been half a year already."

It had been spring when Sousuke first appeared before Kaname. Almost exactly six months ago.

"Seems like such a short time."

"That it does."

"But, Sousuke, you haven't made any progress."

"No?"

"No."

When she giggled, Sousuke inclined his head. In the end his hair had not been cut, but it was wet and unkempt. His appearance, somewhat lacking in spirit, suggested a worn-out stray dog.

It was quite slovenly, to the extent that it seemed irresponsible to leave him this way.

"Hey, you know...," she started to say, after thinking for a bit.

"What?"

"Want to come over to my place? I might as well finish cutting your hair."

The proposal was apparently quite unexpected. Sousuke's eyes went round and blinked with surprise, a rarity.

"You'd rather not?"

"No. I mean...."

"Worried that even I might attack you?" she asked. He shook his head slightly back and forth.

"It's nothing like that. I'm not worried. You're an exception."

It felt awfully pleasant to Kaname that he denied it so seriously.

Even in a three-bedroom apartment in which a family could comfortably live, the bathroom was cramped. As she carried a chair into hers, Kaname said, "Okay, sir. Please have a seat."

Sousuke sat. Kaname cheerfully wreathed a towel and vinyl sheet around his neck. She had already changed her clothes, and was now wearing a thin T-shirt and jeans.

"Not too tight?"

"No. No problem."

"Okay, then, here I go. Hmm-hmm-hmm."

Picking up the scissors, Kaname smiled boldly. Sousuke became anxious for a reason entirely other than assassins or enemies, and asked, "Chidori, do you ... well, have any haircutting experience?"

"Nope," Kaname answered readily. "But I've messed around with Kyouko's hair before. Guess this is my first time cutting it, though."

"It's all right. It'll at least be better than you cutting it yourself," she said after a brief silence.

"Don't cut off my ears."

"Sure. I'll do my best."

After she laughed, Kaname grasped part of Sousuke's hair and snipped it. Then once more. At first her hands worked cautiously, but gradually her rhythm improved and the speed of her cutting increased.

"So, hey...," Kaname said without pausing in her task. "You had to miss exams for work."

"Yeah."

"Were you in combat again?"

"Yeah. What about it?"

"Nothing, really. You weren't injured?"

"Just scratches. No problem."

"Okay." Kaname went on cutting silently for a while.

She looked from his head back to the mirror, sometimes hummed, "Hmm," and worked the scissors with a face tense with concentration. The shorn hair fell bit by bit, and slipped off the sheet.

"You know, I...," Kaname said slowly, after a while. "I heard from Tessa. That there's someone besides you protecting me."

This was the first time she had ever touched on this topic. Maybe she had been thinking about it ever since their earlier conversation when they were on the way home.

"I see."

"But there's no sign of that whatsoever ... is there? So, sometimes it doesn't seem real. It's like everything until now, everything about Mithril, is a lie."

Sousuke's duty in Tokyo was basically as Kaname's guard. In reality, though, he was not alone in watching her. An agent had also been dispatched by Mithril's Intelligence branch, and was always somewhere near her. It was because that agent was there that Sousuke could part from Kaname and go overseas.

Sousuke's and Kalinin's Operations branch called the agent Wraith.

"Sousuke, have you met him?"

"No. We've never spoken."

"Do you know who it is?"

"No. It's probably someone you don't know."

"I wonder if he's reliable."

Sousuke made no response.

"For that matter.... Well, Mithril and everything." Her words hung thickly in the air with the scent of doubt.

No matter how cheerful she usually seemed, she was frightened. It was then that Sousuke realized that obvious fact. When one seriously considered that someone was out to get Kaname, Mithril was the only thing upon which she could rely. The police would be no help.

"Of course. Have faith in him." Even as he answered, Sousuke had absolutely no faith in his own words.

Wraith was always far away.

Outside the school during class. Several blocks away from this apartment building after school. Maintaining a reasonable distance, watching her from somewhere. This was why Sousuke was not at her side twenty-four hours a day.

The agent would never respond to a call from her end. No matter what happened.

Wraith had not taken action even when danger loomed for Kaname. To this point, she had gotten involved with local delinquents, been taken away to some unidentified person's villa, and even abducted by A21 terrorists, but Wraith had not moved. In the end, Kaname had been saved in all of those cases, but Sousuke had always felt a severe irritation afterward.

Why won't he move?

Why didn't he protect her in my place?

In the reports submitted to the higher-ups, Sousuke had repeatedly written: *I harbor strong doubts regarding the capabilities of the agent from Intelligence—code name: Wraith.* But the response was always: *Under consideration. Continue your mission as is.*

Neither Kalinin nor Tessa attempted to explain that decision. "Never mind, just continue," they said. Thus it persisted. So when it came time for Sousuke to put distance between himself and Kaname, he always felt a strong anxiety. *Just leave it to Wraith.* Despite those orders, Wraith did not seem to be fulfilling his duty.

Was Wraith very patiently waiting for a true enemy to appear? Did he intend to not lift the fishing rod at all, no matter how much the float moved, until something big struck at the bait called Kaname? If so, it was understandable why he had never shown himself.

No, that's strange.

If Kaname died before that, it would all mean nothing. It was repulsive to think of, but she had already been in situations multiple times where one wrong move could have meant death. So what was the reason for continuing to not lend a helping hand?

I don't know.

Some cold, unknown logic must have been at work somewhere. Wasn't Intelligence confident about something, and hiding it from him?

"Sousuke?"

He had been lost in thoughts when Kaname addressed him.

"Hmm...?"

"What's wrong? You look like you're brooding."

"No."

"Don't worry about what I said. I mean.... No matter what I say...."

Kaname's hand stopped cutting his hair and hesitated a little. Then she said, as if she had made up her mind, but while averting her eyes from the mirror: "I have plenty of faith in you."

He was silent as a strange sensation assailed him.

This unknown warm, soft thing tightened around his heart. His face was hot. It felt like something was welling up from inside him.

I wonder why. It's like I've missed this.

What's the name they have for feelings like this?

I can't remember.

"...That helps," he barely managed to answer.

"You're welcome," she said in a normal tone, then resumed the haircut. "Okay. Could you turn a little more to the right?"

"Huh? Sure."

"Not that way, the other way."

Kaname's slender fingers gently pushed his cheek. Her slightly cold fingertips felt nice. It was like a refreshing, momentary breeze rustling a tropical jungle.

In a corner of his field of vision, Kaname's white T-shirt and black hair swayed. The shirt seemed to be cheap, as the thin cloth became see-through where the light hit it. When she went around in front of him to cut his bangs, the contours of her body from her armpit down to her hips became dimly visible: smooth, slender curves. Sousuke averted his eyes as if he had looked at something blinding.

"Hmm. I think I'm slowly getting the hang of this."

Kaname's handling was careful and gentle from start to finish. Grooming shears shortened his hair, a razor evened up the details with diligent combing. As this was happening, he began feeling sleepy.

What's going on here? he thought.

A person's this close to me with edged weapons, and I'm sleepy.

Me, of all people.

So unbelievable.

But what's this indescribable peace?

Chidori.... Could I possibly be—

"Okay, time to rinse you off."

His head was pushed into the washbasin and suddenly drenched by a lot of cold water, and his drowsiness quickly came to an end.

"Yeah, that should do."

Kaname switched off the dryer and nodded eagerly.

"It doesn't feel like it's all that different," commented Sousuke, staring into the mirror with a muted expression.

It technically was shorter than before the haircut, but the overall effect did not seem to have changed that much. It was simply back to the way it was about a month ago. His hair was as messy and unkempt as always. And he had the impression that the left and right sides were of asymmetrical lengths.

"What are you talking about? You just don't see it."

"I don't?"

"Nope. It's a lot better. Try asking everyone in school tomorrow."

"Hmm." After gazing closely at himself in the mirror once more, Sousuke stood up.

"Thank you, in any case. If it's convenient, I'll cut your hair next time."

"Not a chance," Kaname said with a grimace.

After helping clean up the bathroom and sharing a simple meal, Sousuke said good-bye.

Kaname seemed somewhat reluctant to let him go.

When he exited the apartment, it was completely dark outside. It must have been after 8 o'clock. There were still many people on the sidewalk: a salaryman on his way home; an elementary school student on the way home from a cram school; a housewife taking her dog for a walk. He traversed the flow of such people and headed for his apartment building, across the street from Kaname's.

For some reason his gait was light and his feelings were uplifted.

Maybe the best expression would be to say that his morale was high. Wraith, his duty, what Mao had said about his future—just a few hours prior his head had been filled with such things, and there should have been no room for buoyancy.

Things were different now. He felt like it was all worth giving it a shot.

Guarding Kaname. Adapting to this society. Training on Merida Island. And combat. He would try to do well in all of them.

She found him reliable. What would happen if he did not have self-confidence?

That's true.

Worrying could wait until next week.

He had a ton of things to do: first was to return home and send today's report to Merida Island; then equipment and firearm maintenance; checks on the sensors deployed around the neighborhood; followed by studying for makeup exams.

He returned to his own apartment with quick steps, started up the laptop directly connected to the satellite communicator, and spent five minutes writing a concise report. He applied a strong encryption and sent it immediately. Before long, a message confirming receipt came from Merida Island's communications center, along with another, separate encrypted file.

It was a tasking message from headquarters.

Top priority order: 98J005-3128 191121Z

Sender: West Pacific Battle Group Headquarters (Merida Island Base)

Recipient: Urzu-7/Sergeant Sousuke Sagara

A: It was determined by Integrated Operations Headquarters, as well as Battle Group Headquarters, that as of today at 15:00 (GMT), existing priority order 98E001-3128 (operation name: Guardian Angel) is rescinded.

B: Urzu-7 is to withdraw from the current safe house, and return quickly via route 3b to the Merida Island Base.

C: Notification of withdrawal from the currently infiltrated Jindai Municipal High School is to be tendered by postal mail. Rationale for withdrawal is left to the discretion of Urzu-7.

D: Guarding of Kaname Chidori will henceforth be taken over in full by code name: Wraith.

E: Following 15:00 (GMT) today, contact with Kaname Chidori is forbidden.

—End

Sousuke rubbed his eyes and read the order again.

There was no change in content. However many times he read it, however much he tried to distort the interpretation, it came down to one thing.

You are permanently released from guard duty of Kaname Chidori. That was what it said.

An Operations HQ determination meant that someone higher ranking than Tessa or Kalinin was involved. No matter how Sousuke protested, it would probably never be accepted.

He looked down at the LCD screen and did not stir an inch for several minutes. It might have lasted for even longer than that.

His molars made a grinding sound.

Guarding of Kaname Chidori will henceforth be taken over in full by—

Before he knew it, he had brought his fist down on the laptop. The alloy frame was crushed, and keys broken off the board scattered through the air. A rage close to madness spurred him for an instant.

He left the destroyed laptop behind and headed straight for the balcony. He opened the glass door, grabbed the railing with both hands, and looked around the area.

"Where are you?" he muttered, his shoulders shaking.

There was nothing to see but a nighttime residential area. Nothing out of the ordinary, a quiet night....

"Get out here, Wraith! Talk to me!" he shouted as loud as he could.

Getting angry was meaningless. Even if he complained to someone, the order would not be reversed. He was aware of that, but he could not remain quiet.

"I know you're close by! How about you answer me?!"

His voice rang out through the whole vicinity. Those walking on the street beneath him looked up, wondering what was going on.

There was no response. Sousuke knew full well that this was not nearly enough to make his counterpart appear. Therefore he continued to shout.

"I'm Sergeant Sousuke Sagara! I work for Mithril Operations, Western Pacific battle group *Tuatha de Danaan*! I was dispatched here to Tokyo on April 20th with orders to guard a certain person! That she's being targeted by someone is conceivable for the following reasons: One! She's a special type of person known as a Whispered! Two! Whispereds are said to possess as yet unknown knowledge, apparently chiefly in the field of military appli—"

A phone began to ring from inside the apartment.

Sousuke closed his mouth at once and went back inside. He picked up the receiver of the phone on the table, and pressed the switch.

The person on the other end immediately shouted, "Are you insane?!"

The voice had a deep, throaty, synthetic quality. It was being electronically altered. It sounded like a monster's voice, but it was still obvious that the person had called here in a hurry.

This was Wraith, the other agent, dispatched by Intelligence.

"What kind of agent divulges classified information to the entire neighborhood? This is clearly an obstruction of the operation!"

"It's because you ignored me," Sousuke said coldly.

"There's no way you're unaware of the danger of us talking this way. Urzu-7, what you're doing is—"

"Answer me. Is your mission to guard Kaname Chidori? Or is it simply to observe?"

"I'm under no obligation to answer."

"I could stand on the balcony all night and continue shouting everything I know. I've been relieved of this post, anyway."

"Are you threatening me, Urzu-7? I'll lodge a formal protest of this with Operations."

"Be my guest. But, you *will* answer the question."

There was a sound like a tongue clicking. After a short hesitation, Wraith said resignedly, "Of course it's to guard her."

"I can't believe that."

"That's your prerogative. But the task given to me is not to let code name: Angel fall into the hands of another organization. Nothing more, nothing less."

"Then why don't you save her? She's been in danger multiple times."

"And each time it was the acts of worthless punks. There's no reason for me to emerge over trouble caused by the town's delinquents."

"Of course. But how do you explain the A21 incident? You didn't even try to help her then."

After he said that, Sousuke thought suddenly that maybe it was not "you," but "you people."

Wraith didn't respond.

"Well? Answer me."

"While it was my intention to leave the enemy at large, the situation grew to be beyond my control. During the combat at Fushimidai Academy, I was nervous, but ultimately I was correct not to get involved. Those terrorists didn't seem to realize how important she was, did they? In other words, they were essentially the same as the street punks."

"That's a sophism. It doesn't seem to me like you're serious about protecting her."

"I don't expect you to be pleased. Worry about it to your heart's content." The synthetic voice ridiculed him.

"This operation was originally supposed to be under Intelligence's jurisdiction following the Sunan incident. Then Operations butted in, and arranged for you to remain. Operations' excuse was that you'd be an effective decoy, but to me you've been nothing but a nuisance. Oh, the number of times I've thought of taking you out and making it look like an accident."

"It's still not too late. Try it."

"I'm joking. If you and I went at it, I don't think I'd come away unscathed. Of course, you *have* made for good recreation."

"What?"

"All I had to do was point a rifle at you from afar, or move the bolt on a submachine gun while in hiding, and you'd become extremely nervous. Your soldier's sense of danger is superb, but you've made a lot of mistakes because of it. I had fun with today's scene in the barber shop."

"You bastard."

"Don't get so angry. It's in the past now."

There was a thread of triumph in Wraith's voice.

"In any case, that fun ends today. You go back to your base and return to your original duty. I'll continue my work. We're both pros. Let's end this trivial dispute."

"I don't think so. What about Chidori's safety?"

"That's no longer your concern. Don't you have official orders to withdraw? Surely you don't intend to disobey orders?"

"Well...." Sousuke was at a loss for words.

"Don't forget that your life here was furnished by Mithril. You were no high-school student originally. You're just a mercenary, a hit man. Both your origins and school records were completely fabricated.

"You criticize me, but did you seriously believe in the first place that a person like you could protect her? You've been entirely inept at adapting to Japanese society these past six months. It's *your* presence that's exposing her needlessly to danger."

A minor shock wave erupted. The air around him seemed to grow heavy and stiff all at once.

Wraith's point was not necessarily in error.

"Sorry, but you're worse than third-rate as a guard. In the end, you'll only cause her harm. For that matter, you might even involve the people around you.

"You're done playing house, Urzu-7. Obey your orders and return to base."

When he did not say anything in response, the phone call ended.

He set the receiver down shakily.

After a short time, a sense of helplessness set in.

CHAPTER 3
Black and White

October 20, 08:10 (Japan Standard Time)
Chofu
Jindai High School

"'Morning, Kyouko!"

Kaname thumped Kyouko on the back after meeting up at Sengawa Station.

"Good morning. You seem kinda cheerful, Kana," mumbled Kyouko, looking a little tired.

"Do I?"

"Yeah. Did something good happen?"

"No, not really. Maybe something did? But I guess it's not that big a deal. Hmm."

"*Ooo-kay.*"

Kaname and Kyouko walked on to the road bustling with students on their way to school.

It was unfortunately rainy today, so the air was unpleasantly chilly. Her umbrella up next to Kyouko's, Kaname was a little nervous. Her friend was a lot shorter than she, so the edge of her umbrella was right at eye level.

"Yesterday was a mess, as Sagara was his usual self," said Kyouko after walking for a while. Kaname nodded and said, "For real. He doesn't make any progress. No matter how much you say, he goes nuts. It makes me want to hook up a remote-controlled electric shocker to his head or something. Every time he does something stupid, I'd zap him. It might be unexpectedly effective."

Kyouko laughed. "He's not a dog, you know. Oh, right, what happened afterward?"

"Hmm? I-I went home. What about it?" She feigned ignorance. Somehow, saying she brought him to her apartment and cut his hair seemed awkward.

Upon closer examination, had she made a rather bold move? Would she normally have been that kind to one of her friends? If everyone in class knew about yesterday, would it be weird, and would they make fun of her again?

Oh, well.

When I see Sousuke later, I'll tell him as soon as I can that the story is that he gave himself the haircut. That'll settle it. No problem.

"Somebody's mood sure seems good, though."

"Whose?"

"Yours."

"Huh? Y-you're imagining things. " Kaname laughed nervously.

"Uh-uh. Somehow I doubt it."

And that was the end of that topic. They passed through the school's main gate as they got worked up talking about that year's Japan Series, changed into indoor shoes, and headed for their classroom.

She put her bag on her desk and looked around the room.

There was no sign of Sousuke.

He's still not here.

She glanced up at the clock. It was 8:27. Almost time for school to start.

What's he up to?

She wanted to see everyone's reactions when they saw his hair.

As she chatted with her other classmates, the chime sounded. Students shuffled to their seats.

Sousuke's remained vacant.

Is he late again? What an idiot. He's got make-ups to take soon.

Kaname opened her textbook, feeling a little disappointed.

Sousuke failed to show that period, or the next.

He failed to show at all.

October 20, 17:19 (Western Pacific Standard Time)
Merida Island Base

Tessa was perusing documents at her base office when the intercom on her desk beeped. It was her secretary in the adjoining room. Tessa picked up the receiver.

"Yes?"

"Captain. Sergeant Sagara is here."

His immediate superior, Lieutenant Commander Kalinin, was not at the base, so he had probably come here to report his return. The lieutenant commander was still at the Sydney Operations HQ. There were still consultations regarding equipment to be had with the Ross & Hambleton engineers.

"Show him in."

"Yes, ma'am."

Tessa put down the receiver and temporarily cleared the document being projected on her desk's holoscreen. The testing and planning files on the new type of submarine communication system—the VMEbus receiver—were still treated as confidential documents. Sousuke Sagara had not been given the clearance to read it.

She felt heavy-hearted.

It was none other than she who had issued the order for him to return. It was, of course, unavoidable, and it was under the admiral's and Operations' orders, but now it was as if she had torn apart Sagara's and Kaname's lives. The fact that she was jealous of their relationship made her feel all the more guilty.

If only Kalinin were here. She was discouraged at her own weakness for thinking it. The very idea of giving orders on her own, then wanting to hide behind her subordinate. That was enough to disqualify her as a commander.

But how should she go about facing him?

She had been thinking of this ever since coming back from Operations HQ in Sydney, but she never reached a conclusion.

"Begging your pardon." Sousuke entered. He walked directly to the front of her desk and saluted smartly. She returned the salute, and he immediately lowered his right hand and stood to attention.

"Thank you. At ease."

"Yes, ma'am." Sousuke quickly shifted to standing at ease.

Sousuke's attitude toward superior officers was like this at any time with anyone, but today it felt more overly polite than necessary. Was she thinking too deeply into it? Or was he really displaying the kind of attitude normally shown in front of a newly-met officer?

They remained silent for a time, a silence that seem to last a long, long time.

He was not looking at Tessa. He gazed straight ahead, back straight, at a large map behind her.

It was if they were not even acquainted. And they were the same age.

This act of courtesy seemed as much a silent protest, for him.

"Did you say farewell to Kaname?" said Tessa, no longer able to stand the silence.

"Ah," answered Sousuke vaguely. "May I ask for an explanation, ma'am?" he said, still looking at the map.

Tessa clenched her fists hard, and launched into the extremely painful explanation.

"This decision was mine and that of the higher-ups. Now that Intelligence has completed its preparations in Tokyo, it's become practically meaningless for you to be attached to Kaname."

"It does not seem that way to me. Intelligence alone is insufficient in guarding her."

"No. You seem to underestimate the gravity of your own situation. Were I to assign you on any further missions of dubious efficacy, it would mean the abandonment of my responsibilities as battalion commander. There is other work that is more demanding of your focus."

"What work would that be?"

If there's work more important than guarding Kaname, then go on, tell me what it is, he seemed to want to say.

"The Arbalest," said Tessa, and the skin around Sousuke's mouth tightened a little. "You will devote yourself to the operation of that mech. The Arbalest will accept no operator other than you."

Sousuke remained silent.

"During the Sunan incident, your brainwave pattern was registered in the Lambda Driver. No, it would be more accurate to say that it was imprinted. The blank slates of each system arranged themselves in accordance with you during its first combat. The moment the systems were run, the pseudo-nerve network composing the mech's system frame copied your nervous system via TAROS. That structure cannot be altered afterward."

"I do not understand very well."

"What I mean is, since that time you piloted the Arbalest, it became an offshoot of you," Tessa said and leaned into the back of her chair.

"Mithril currently lacks the power to construct new ASes equipped with the Lambda Driver. In other words, the only ones who can oppose enemy mechs like Venom and Behemoth are you and the Arbalest. Intelligence will take over guarding Kaname. Therefore, I want you to concentrate on mastering the Arbalest."

After the very patient explanation, Sousuke hung his head and sighed a little.

"Then I have no say in the matter?"

"No," Tessa answered weakly.

"Please understand, Mr. Sagara."

"Would that be an order?"

Hearing those words filled with bitterness, Tessa felt like her head had been struck by a hammer.

He's saying it on purpose. He's talking to me like this on purpose because he blames me. Here I am trying my hardest to get him to understand, and he asks if it's an order. He might as well be openly rejecting me as a friend.

And the reason he's angry—it's because of her.

"Yes, it is." Unconsciously, her tone grew stronger. "If that ... will make you consent, then I will order it. After all, it's matter of course that I do. I will show absolutely no favoritism. Even if it means keeping you from Kaname, if it is a necessary measure, I will do so."

"Colonel?" Sousuke's demeanor displayed a bit of consternation, but that did not stop Tessa's discourse. The image of Sousuke became hazy. Words poured out of her like a dam had burst. Her voice grew shrill, beyond her control.

"You do not understand the dynamics at work in the upper echelons. There's nothing I alone can do. As you can see, I'm a young girl. But you don't know anything about organizations, politics, or diplomacy, do you?! How nice and convenient. You distract yourself by aiming your bitterness at me. But I'm different. I have to think about not only her safety, but the safety of my crew! Listen. Think about it a little. If you've fought Venom and Behemoth, shouldn't you comprehend that danger?! Not even an M9 can stand up to an AS equipped with the Lambda Driver! If that enemy shows up again, someone else might die! One of my subordinates! Next time it might be Melissa. Or Mr. Weber. There's even the danger that the entire land combat team will be destroyed in an instant. But I can never afford to let such a thing happen!"

Oh, this is pathetic. I'm crying. Whoever heard of such a commander? This is the worst.

No matter how much she thought so, she could not stop her feelings from bursting out.

"Th—"

"What are you looking at? Is she the only thing in your head? Did you stop to give any thought to *my* feelings?"

"I-I apologize, Colonel. I—"

"Stop it, please!" she said, her eyes swollen and red. "You're horrible. You act obedient and kind, but you're really a terrible egotist. And you're misrepresenting yourself. Why not just come out and say it? 'I want to be with her. Don't interfere!'"

Now *Sousuke* made a face like he had been hit with a hammer. He looked stupefied. He blinked, shook his head a few times, and not knowing what to say, opened and closed his mouth.

"Besides ... it would be so much easier ... if you did...."

170

The rest found no verbalization. Realizing that at some point she had stood up, Tessa's strength left her and she plopped back into her chair.

"I'm sorry ... Colonel. I must reconsider my conduct. I ... that is ... the situation.... At any rate ... I guess I failed to realize ... um...."

Sousuke's whole body was stiff, and as he wrung the words out a few at a time, the intercom on the desk sounded again.

She slowly picked up the receiver as she wiped her tears away with her cuff.

"What is it?"

"Captain, First Lieutenant Clouseau has arrived," announced the secretary, Ensign Vilan.

"Please ... have him wait a minute. I will call for him soon."

"Yes, ma'am."

After replacing the receiver, Tessa took a tissue out of her pocket and blew her nose. Sniffling, she again wiped her eyes with her cuff, and bitterness made itself clear.

"Mr. Sagara, I hate you."

"...I'm sorry."

"I also hate how quick you are to apologize."

"...I am ashamed."

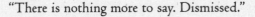

"There is nothing more to say. Dismissed."

"Yes, ma'am." Dejected, Sousuke left the office.

When the door closed, a terrible sense of self-hatred tortured her.

Throwing it back in his face and crying just because a subordinate snarled at her. It was beyond indecent. It was deplorable. This was the first time she had ever behaved so disgracefully. It could only be termed lucky that no one else witnessed it.

In any case, I held nothing back and bluntly said all that. He might totally hate me now.

Tessa needed three minutes to calm herself down and regain her composure. After she checked her appearance in the mirror, she called her secretary to let the visitor in.

A tall black man came through the door Sousuke had gone through, and saluted.

"Belfangan Clouseau, reporting."

"Welcome to the West Pacific battle group, Lieutenant. I am its commander, Teletha Testarossa," Tessa responded, not showing the slightest evidence of her tearful encounter with Sousuke.

"Your achievements precede you, Colonel. I am extremely delighted to meet you."

"Likewise. Have you seen your new post yet?"

"No, ma'am. By the way, might that sergeant have been Sousuke Sagara?"

He must have encountered him while waiting in the next room. "Yes. You should have introduced yourself."

"It was not necessary. I have already met *them*, you see," he said without smiling.

"So, in short, this time you made *Tessa* cry?" Sitting at the bar counter in the base's only pub, Kurz's eyes went wide.

"Affirmative," said Sousuke from the seat next to him. His shoulders slumped and head down, he gazed dimly at the glass on the counter containing his grapefruit juice.

"Hey, man, you sure you don't got talent as a gigolo?"

"What's a gigolo?"

"Don't worry about it. But you know.... Hmm. Damn, dude."

Sousuke glanced sideways at Kurz, who for some reason folded his arms and looked deeply impressed.

"You sure seem cheerful."

Before, when Sousuke had made Kaname cry, Kurz had punched him. Occasionally, he did not understand his partner's behavioral principles.

"Not terribly. You probably think it's your fault?"

"Well ... yes, I do."

"Then don't take it so seriously. Tessa's not a bad girl. She'll forgive you eventually," Kurz said lightly, then took a gulp of his scotch.

The room was crowded with PRT (Primary Response Team) members and maintenance team members who had finished with training and work for the day. Someone was foolishly bragging and telling a funny story of a woman he'd ensnared while he was off duty in Guam. Rough laughs and stories of various homelands flew about and cigarette smoke hung thickly in the air.

"I'm no match for the colonel," said Sousuke after a short time had passed.

"It looks like I didn't know anything about her heavy responsibilities. For her to react that way ... she must have been very offended by my attitude."

"I doubt that alone would make her cry," Kurz said drily, curling his lip.

"What do you mean?"

"Oh, you— It's *so* annoying, I just *have* to tell you, don't I."

Sousuke only looked at him, uncomprehending.

"You really don't get it. Man, no wonder she got mad," Kurz said in amazement, and Sousuke's shoulders slumped further.

"I guess I really was a fool. Her assertion is correct. There's definitely no reason for me to make myself Kaname's guard. When you think of it as a situation in which the right person is in the right place, the measures we've taken until now have been unorthodox, I guess."

Kurz listened to Sousuke's monologue, frowned for a while, and before long shrugged and muttered to himself, "This is hopeless."

"Like I said, what do you mean?"

"Nothing. Forget about it," was all Kurz said about it, before shifting the topic to Sousuke. "Well, SRT or not, expecting someone to test a prototype AS and guard a girl at the same time is nuts."

"You're right. But...."

"But?" Kurz urged him on.

But Sousuke only gripped his glass tightly. "No. Never mind," he forced himself to mutter before shutting his mouth.

Talking to Kurz about it would not help him with the dilemma with which he was confronted. Order. Obligation. This thing with

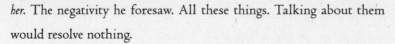

her. The negativity he foresaw. All these things. Talking about them would resolve nothing.

But in reality, he wanted to confess everything to his colleague.

Kaname had trusted him. She had relied not on the Intelligence guys, but him. Despite that, he'd had to betray that trust. He knew the Arbalest was necessary. As the colonel had said, only it and he could stand against Venom, Behemoth, or the like. He should just leave guarding Kaname to the Intelligence specialist. But, then, in that case....

He could not agree. Not just with the reasoning. Not just with rationality.

No matter how many times he solved this simple equation, the same solution was all that emerged. That solution was correct, tactically. But why did the right answer irritate him so much?

"What is it? I'll listen if you've got a complaint. Say it."

"No, it's all right."

"You really are awkward. Well, that's the part I—" Kurz said, cutting himself off abruptly.

"What?"

"Nothin'." He laughed carelessly, then finished off his scotch.

"So, how'd you say goodbye to Kaname?"

"Uh...."

"Made her cry, did you? Well, I didn't think you'd part with a smile."

"I don't want to talk about it."

Actually, he had not said anything to Kaname. Not a word—no announcement of his departure. What kind of explanation could he have given, right after the exchange during the haircut? He was not brave enough to face her. He had sent his notice of withdrawal to the school, but most of the things in the apartment had simply been moved elsewhere in the city.

He had hesitated and neglected everything.

What am I supposed to do from here?

I never had to worry about this on the battlefield before.

"Oh, okay."

Kurz surprisingly halted that line of questioning. He told the bartender he wanted another scotch, exchanged some meaningless insults, and laughed a spiritless laugh.

Suddenly the loud din of the bar became muted.

The sounds of rough jeering, tableware scraping together, and singing ceased, and an air of vigilance floated across the room. It was different from the hostility commonly seen in rundown bars in

Westerns. This was an ordinary bar where ordinary people hung out. It was more a casual reaction to a small irregularity.

The reason was soon apparent. A commissioned officer—an unrecognized CO, had entered the bar.

The officer was a black man in field uniform. He had a badge on his shoulder with FLT embroidered on it, signaling that he was a first lieutenant. He was solid around the shoulders, had a build like an inverted triangle, and long straight legs. Even at a distance he was quite tall, taller even than Kurz, who was 180cm.

"That's a new face. Where'd this lieutenant come from?" murmured Kurz. Sousuke had the feeling he had seen the man somewhere before. Had he been the one waiting outside of Colonel Testarossa's office?

He traversed the length of the bar, passed behind Sousuke and Kurz, and sat next to Kurz.

"Water."

He put a five dollar bill on the bar and ordered. The bartender made an obviously disagreeable face. "Idiot. This is a bar. Order something with alcohol in it."

"Alcohol goes against Allah's teachings. Water."

"Then don't come to a bar, moron." Even as he said that, the middle-aged bartender poured Volvic into a glass, and shoved it forward on the counter. As the lieutenant took the glass, he shifted in his seat to shoot a direct glance at Sousuke and Kurz. He seemed to immediately lose interest in them because he turned forward and drank some water.

For some reason, a philosophical air hung about him. Brown skin, intellectual but guarded eyes. His lips were thin and tightened. Perhaps he had some Caucasian or Arab blood in him.

"Uh, excuse me, Lieutenant," said Kurz. "I don't know who you are, and I really don't want to sound stingy, but could you sit somewhere else?"

"Why?"

"These three seats at the bar, starting from this corner, are kind of reserved for us in the SRT and you're sitting in one of them."

"Is that a battle group regulation?" he asked the bartender. The bartender frowned and shook his head.

"Those guys just decided it on their own. Of course, other groups have likewise claimed possession of all the seats at that first table and the opposite side of the counter. That's how they divide up where they sit when they come here."

"So it's custom."

"You could put it that way. But the seat you're sitting in, yeah, I guess you could say it *is* reserved."

"I don't get your meaning."

"That's the seat our late superior officer used to sit in a lot," said Kurz. "Sorry, but I don't want some stranger parking his ass there."

"Ah-ha." The man nodded, looking downward.

"What was your dead superior officer's call sign and name?"

"Urzu-I. Captain Gail McAllen."

"Then there's no need for me to switch seats. He was a coward," the man said and smiled coldly.

"What'd you say?"

Kurz leaned forward. Sousuke, who until then had been carefully watching the exchange from the side, did not fail to notice the tension enter his partner's hand as it gripped a shot glass.

"Coward? Did you just say coward?"

"That's right. He was an incompetent, little man."

"Wow. Ha ha. Talk about severe. Hey, d'you hear that, Sousuke? An incompetent, little man. But hey, when it came to that guy—"

Kurz suddenly threw liquor in the man's face and simultaneously attacked with his right fist. It was too quick for even Sousuke to stop it. But that fist did not sink into the man's right cheek. The lieutenant dodged the attack, literally by a hair's breadth.

The man stuck fast to him, and firmly shoved at Kurz's chin.

That was all he had appeared to do—but in the next moment, Kurz's body was thrown back forcefully. As if to draw Sousuke into the mess, he hit a table chair several meters behind him back-first.

Tableware and glasses fell to the floor, making an especially clamorous noise. The bartender frowned, shook his head, and the soldiers in the bar suddenly focused their attention on that spot.

"You lack patience, Sergeant," said the Lieutenant, wiping the booze off his face with a paper napkin. "And here I heard you were a sniper. Is this some kind of joke?"

"You son of a bitch. You want a piece of me?" Kurz put his hand on the overturned table and tried to push himself up, but his knees buckled when he was halfway there. It was like some unseen hand had hit him on the back of the head. He landed on his butt, fell face forward, and muttered, "Shit!" He stopped moving.

"Kurz!"

"Leave him be. It's only a slight concussion," said the lieutenant from behind Sousuke, who had run over to check on Kurz. "Though I'm surprised he managed to stand after that blow. This should be good medicine for a fool who'd get drunk and try to hit a superior officer. Judging by that sergeant and the dead captain, it looks like the SRT here is a real ship of fools. What a disappointment."

Sousuke turned his accusing eyes on the lieutenant, who was not even trying to hide his disdain.

"What's that look for?"

"I don't know who you are. I apologize for my colleague's rudeness. But I want you to take back your contemptuous comments about Captain McAllen."

Usually Sousuke would not react to disparagement, but even he could not keep quiet here.

"That's an amusing jest, Sergeant. Are you ordering me? What would you do if I said no? Would you swing at your superior officer? I doubt you could. At a glance, you look like a steady man. Well, you might just be a coward."

Feeling like his internal conflict had been seen through, Sousuke clicked his tongue. He would be bound for the lockup if he hit this

man. But that in itself was irrelevant. Kurz had probably been aware of that, too.

The reason Sousuke hesitated now was not because of discipline. It was that he felt a more fundamental resistance to the idea itself of breaking the rules.

Hitting a superior officer? Disobeying orders? Each time such an act was committed, the order of the world surrounding him would fall to pieces—that sense of danger put the brakes on his mind. Always.

Despite all that's been done to me, why can't I act? he asked himself.

"I see you can't do anything without orders. So, Sergeant. Shall I call you out for a little game?"

"Game?"

"You want to protect this Captain McAllen's honor, don't you? I could use a little diversion. Come with me."

After leaving a hundred dollar bill on the counter, the lieutenant started walking.

"Where—"

"The AS hangars. You're qualified to pilot one, aren't you?"

185

I walked right into that challenge, thought Sousuke.

He was now in the ARX-7 Arbalest's cockpit, riding the elevator up to the surface of Merida Island.

It was a simple, huge elevator with an open, rust-coated steel frame.

The majority of this base's facilities were built underground. Living quarters, all kinds of communications facilities, weapons and ammo storage, the *Tuatha de Danaan*'s maintenance dock—nearly everything. Most of the surface was still untouched jungle, a clever camouflage for hiding runways and communication antennas. The island's area was about the same as that within JR's Yamanote Line in Tokyo—usually put to ample practical use as practice grounds by the land combat forces.

His Arbalest had again been restored to its white color. By the time that ship combat in late August had ended, the dark grey paint had been completely peeled off. The engineering officer who saw it said it was proof that the Lambda Driver had functioned. Apparently somehow connected to that mysterious force field, regular paint would not stay affixed to the Arbalest's armor.

He checked over his mech. It was nearly the same procedure as with an M9.

Generator: normal.

Control systems: normal.

Vetronics: normal.

Sensors, drive system, shock absorption system, cooling system, FCS (fire-control system), various warning systems: all normal.

His sole weapon was on the left armpit, a training knife stored on a weapons rack.

The elevator reached the surface.

He walked his mech onto the wet ground, out of the twelve-meters-high cage covered by the same leaves and ivy as the jungle. *Zushoon, zushoon,* went the footsteps, flinging mud all over.

A deep red sky. A sub tropic twilight.

Surprised by the emergence of the eight-meters-tall giant, the wild birds in the area all took off into the sky at once.

Depressing the vocal command switch on his stick, Sousuke said, "Al."

"Yes, Sergeant?" replied the mech's AI, Al.

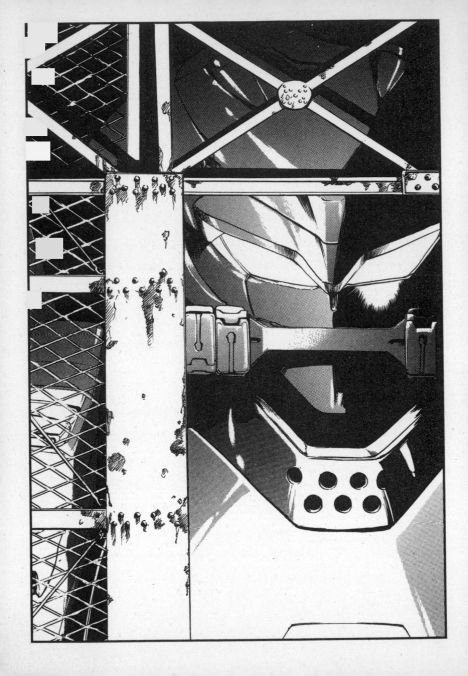

"I want to know this area's temperature and humidity."

"Temperature, 26° Celsius. Humidity, 83%."

"What's the muscle package's mean EOF value?"

"Check ... 99. The highest level."

An unemotional, deep male voice. The voice of this vocal confirmation system could be freely altered, but Sousuke used it at its default setting. Incidentally, Kurz had gone to the trouble of sampling a Japanese idol singer for his own AI's voice.

Kurz....

He had ended up leaving Kurz in the bartender's care. Was he really okay? That technique the lieutenant had used on him was a palm strike or something. But for someone of Kurz's caliber to be knocked out by such a seemingly casual action was unexpected. It must have been more than just a physical blow, more profound, maybe some Asian martial art.

The elevator, which had descended once, again began to climb. The lieutenant must have brought an M9 from a hangar other than the Arbalest's.

Yes, that lieutenant was an AS pilot. And he had proposed a mock battle with Sousuke using an AS, on condition that if he lost, he would take back what he said in the bar.

"If you're afraid to use your mech without permission, I can always make it an order." After being told that, not even Sousuke hesitated.

Fine. I don't know who you are or what you're after, but I'll show you what I can do. If you think I'm the same as those rookies, you're gravely mistaken. I've been piloting ASes since I was ten. During my Afghanistan guerrilla days, Hamidra and I remodeled an RK-89 we stole from the Soviets so that even a child's arms and legs could move it. Despite that handicap, I crushed ten-odd RK-92s—cutting edge at the time.

It's been seven years since then. I've fought my way through many battles, piloting every possible mech. This weapon called the AS is the same as a second skin for me.

I'll make you regret this, Sousuke muttered in his heart.

He was extremely vexed by all the things that had happened lately.

He waited a short while. The elevator reached the top.

"Sorry to keep you," came the lieutenant's voice through the external speaker. Sousuke saw the AS step out of the cage into the dusk, and his eyes went wide.

The mech was a jet black M9.

He noted the additional armor on the thighs and upper arms. It had two glowing eye sensors in its head. Aside from the lack of a "scroll" in its mouth, it was exactly like the Arbalest.

A black M9.

There was no doubt. It was the mech they encountered while on assignment in Sicily.

"I've yet to introduce myself. I'm First Lieutenant Belfangan Clouseau, transferred from *Partholon* in the Mediterranean. As of today, I'm part of *Tuatha de Danaan*'s SRT. By the way, my call sign is Urzu-I."

Urzu-I. It meant he was Captain McAllen's successor, a post which had remained vacant since that incident.

"Sergeant Sousuke Sagara, according to Lieutenant Commander Kalinin, there's no one better than you at AS grappling. Why don't you show me what you can do?"

The black M9 released the weapons rack on its left flank and drew its training knife.

October 20, 18:43 (Japan Standard Time)
Chofu, Tokyo
Sengawa shopping district

Sousuke never did come to school that day.

The school seemed awfully quiet without him there, as it had been during exams. It wasn't as if he constantly waved guns around and went berserk twenty-four hours a day. Just once every day or two he would, for some unforeseen reason, act without any common sense, generating confusion and chaos around him.

Even so, school without him was quiet.

Whatever other students thought, Kaname thought so. Though she chatted normally with classmates, and was loud and rowdy as she always was, she still felt a sense of something slightly lacking.

"Maybe I've caught his disease, too," murmured Kaname on the way home from school, the sun having completely set. Kyouko laughed.

"What?"

"Come on. It sounds like a pretty weird disease when you say it like that."

"Huh?" Truly not understanding her meaning, Kaname looked at her blankly.

"It's okay if you don't get it. You know what, Kana? When I stop and think about it, you're an odd type."

"I am?"

"Yeah. How to say it.... It's like I'm not sure if you're mature or childish. At a glance you look like a college student, but, it's like, you've got a grade schooler thing going on, too."

"Hmm."

Because the person who said it was someone with whom she was close, Kaname actually considered it. But it felt like Kyouko, too, was so different from her. Though at a glance she looked like an elementary school student, she would occasionally say grown-up things like some college girl.

Of course, that was probably why Kaname liked her.

Kyouko Tokiwa was very short compared to Kaname. It was not that their interests coincided that much. Kaname had a strong personality and hers was reserved. Kaname's reflexes were excellent, while hers were not so sharp. All they had to do was walk together and their contrasts became blatantly apparent.

However, Kaname had often looked at Kyouko and thought, *I don't match up to her.* It held true in regard to their conversation yesterday, and other things felt that way, too. At times she had even thought, *Why do you suppose Kyouko smiles and goes along with an idiot like me?*

Ever since hearing from Tessa about the other Intelligence guard who had been assigned to her besides Sousuke, Kaname had several times thought that maybe it was Kyouko. But no amount of thought made it seem possible. Kaname had been over to her house to hang out many times, and had frequently seen her mother and siblings.

"Kana?"

"Hmm?"

"Ah. Are you thinking about Sagara again?"

"...Of course I'm not. Enough of that already."

Just then when Kaname laughed, something sparkled out of the corner of her eye.

They were walking through the shopping district in front of Sengawa Station, on a road that was so narrow that a car could just barely pass. There was lots of pedestrian traffic, and the shouts of the nearby greengrocer echoed around noisily. A sharp light glinted from the roof of a stationery shop along the way.

Was that the reflection of a lens?

It was evening, so that rooftop was dark and also far away.

But Kaname saw it. On that roof, dim, vague, and melting into the dusk, a black shadow had suddenly moved.

It was probably one person. The face had been visible for a second. It felt like their gazes had met for a moment. It was a thin, short-haired man with narrow slits for eyes and inorganic facial features. He was reminiscent of that knife-wielding guy she had encountered on the ship over summer vacation.

It seemed to Kaname that the man had been smiling.

He was no longer visible.

She stopped and fixed her gaze upon that spot, but there was no further movement.

"What's wrong, Kana?"

"Hmm? Uh, nothing," answered Kaname, still looking toward the building's roof. "It's nothing. Let's go."

Kyouko looked at her curiously, but Kaname had started walking again.

What was that?

She felt uneasy. She was unsure of how to express it, but something was off. It was not a tangible physical threat that she sensed. But what was this feeling of discomfort she felt regarding what she had just seen?

Yeah. A sense of discomfort.

A sense of discomfort that something she had secretly feared these past six months had finally arrived. Indescribable footsteps of death that she had long felt would eventually come.

That simple glint of white light on top of that building reminded Kaname of it all.

Of Aomi Wharf at the end of June; in the submarine at the end of August—the sense of foreboding she felt then was recalled to her mind.

Weird. Bad. When it's like this, it's horribly bad.

No, that's not right. It's scary.

"Kana...?"

Ignoring Kyouko's query, Kaname took her cell phone out of her bag and called a frequently dialed number.

SOUSUKE SAGARA. His name was displayed on the cell phone's LCD screen.

It's okay. I got through the other day. Using Kyouko's phone, no less. I'm sure he'll pick up. He'll answer, and come right away. Then—then he'll say, "No problem."

Sousuke....

What's going on here? Why am I so panicky? Why am I irked that it's taking so long for it to start ringing?

Sousuke?!

Click, went the sound of something switching over.

"Hello? Sou...."

"*The number you have dialed is currently not in use. Please check the number and dial again. The number you have dialed is currently not in use. Please check the number and dial again. The number you have dialed—*"

How cold and cruel the voice sounded.

[To be continued in Part 2]

Afterword, or rather, Midword

Sorry for the wait. This ultimately wound up being a two-part story, but here you have Part I of *Ending Day By Day*. I know that for students who get by on a small allowance, separated volumes have quite the negative impact on cost performance. Having said that, due to various circumstances and my lack of efficiency, there were reasons beyond my control. Please be lenient with me. I apologize.

The focus of this book is, one way or another, on interval-esque episodes. At its core are the aftermath of ITB, Mithril internal affairs, school life sans slapstick, and drama which is usually not covered. The title has the word *ending* in it, but in truth this series does not *yet* seem near its end. Unlike in the short stories, Sousuke and company are changing here and there in the long stories, though the upheaval is still a bit in the future.

However, looking back over just Part I, strangely, everyone's moods are taking a turn for the worse. Every single character who shows up is in a foul mood, irritated, or lashing out in response to anger. This does not, however, indicate that I, the author, am in a foul mood.

By the way, Admiral Jerome Borda, who appears in this book, is modeled after a real military man who passed away several years ago of a rather suspicious suicide, but those in the know, please think of him as someone else. He was, after, all just a model, and Borda is simply the result of the author's imprudent delusion: *What if he lived in the FMP universe?* His personality and manner of speaking are simply what I imagined after talking to people who knew him.

I would like to get Part 2 out to you as soon as possible, but it appears it will happen around early next year. Slow? I really am sorry. I thank you for your patience, and ask that you please continue with them on their journey.

The story still is not over, so I will leave it at this for now.

A Sousuke who cannot live up to his potential. The true hand of evil bearing down on Kaname. The starring entrance of truly formidable enemies. And will our two leads manage to meet up again?

Putting aside readers of the short stories who would say, "But in 'Cursed'...." Just wait for Part 2. And forget what you already read. Okay?

I'll wait until Part 2 to offer my usual thanks.

See you again. Come follow Sousuke through hell again next time.

Shoji Gatoh
October 2000

CHAPTER 3
Black and White (continued)

October 20, 19:05 (Western Pacific Standard Time)
Northern Merida Island Base
Practice grounds

The cockpit screens were in battle mode, and they whirled with surging waves of information. A digital image of the landscape, picked up by the optical sensors, flowed by dizzyingly.

The jungle was beginning to sink into twilight, dying the entire sky red and purple. Flora swayed violently from the squalls produced by the mechs.

All of this appeared and disappeared on-screen, accompanied by afterimages.

There were many types of gauges, including a G-meter moving haltingly up and down. Also present were a freely rotating attitudinal grid and a variable reticle in grappling mode. The target box and motion indicator lines went all over the place, the power gauge expanded and contracted, and the AI thrummed buzzers in rapid succession.

"Warning: Incoming!"

First Lieutenant Clouseau's M9 sprinted through the jungle and closed in on the Arbalest from the left and rear at eight o'clock.

The jet-black mech's two orange eyes glowed like fires as it advanced.

"Urgh!"

Sousuke's Arbalest narrowly dodged the contact. The black M9's training knife grazed its armor.

There was an even sharper flash, then stab, slash, roundhouse kick, all in rapid succession.

It was a strangely calm and yet provocative dance. And while it was kinetic, it evoked the tranquil depth of a lake.

What are these movements?

They were human—exceedingly human movements. His opponent seemed very much unlike an Arm Slave. It was like he could even sense the throb of muscles, the scent of sweat, the beat of a heart, and the creak of bones.

Yet there was still another word that better described this M9.

He's powerful!

He was indeed powerful. On par with Sousuke himself—no—beyond him. Even at this point in his experience, he could still count on one hand the number of operators he had met who were this skilled in hand-to-hand combat.

Just who the hell is this First Lieutenant Belfangan Clouseau?

Sousuke jumped backward as he launched a containment attack.

The jumping power of third generation ASes like the Arbalest and the M9 drastically exceeded that of earlier models. On a human-sized scale, they had enough power to easily leap over a two-story building. The explosively accelerative energy produced by the legs, which borrowed from the joint structure of a grasshopper, surpassed that of any land vehicle or aircraft.

But Clouseau's attacks were endlessly persistent. The black M9 leaped a beat later, hot on the airborne Arbalest's heels. Headed for a midair collision, it roughly seized the Arbalest's ankle.

By the time Sousuke realized it, the sky and ground had switched places.

Clouseau used his own mech's momentum to throw off the Arbalest's posture. Now it was face up and beginning to fall, and the black M9 coiled itself around it.

He meant to slam him into the ground while riding on top.

Sousuke skillfully manipulated his mech, combining a knee and elbow strike and bounding away from his opponent. The ground drew near. He wasn't going to make it in time. He twisted his mech into a shoulder-first landing. A muddy splash flew up, and the Arbalest tumbled onto the ground. An impact that even the most cutting-edge shock absorption system could not fully negate attacked Sousuke's entire body.

ASes were frequently referred to as "cocktail shakers" amongst smart-mouthed soldiers. This term had originated because of the terrible shocks pilots were frequently subjected to in battle. Right now Sousuke certainly felt like the ice inside a shaker in a bartender's hands.

Ignoring the pain, he regained control of his mech and sprang it back up. He quickly checked the on-screen damage report, and turned toward the enemy mech. Clouseau's M9 swayed as it stood up.

"That's what I thought. Sergeant Sagara, you're a second-rate operator," said Clouseau's voice from over the radio.

"What?"

"You have a skillful fighting style, but it doesn't have any art. Do you understand?"

Sousuke didn't respond.

"You don't, which is why I called you second-rate. A second-rate predecessor and now-second-rate subordinates. This is *some* team I've been made part of."

By predecessor he meant Captain McAllen. It seemed he was going to keep taking potshots at the dead.

As Sousuke watched, Clouseau's mech slowly turned, and threw away its training knife. The edge of the knife was urethane-foam coated in water-based paint. In other words, it worked like a felt-tip pen. Unlike combat monofilament cutters, all a training knife left on its cut was a paint mark, so there was no danger of injuring your training partner with one.

"Get rid of that toy. Let's have ourselves a real fight."

The black M9 drew a large knife from the hard point at its waist. Actually, it might have been more appropriate to call it a dagger. It was more than twice as long and thick as a typical knife and had a sinister edge.

The Israeli Military Industries (IMI) Crimson Edge monofilament cutter was an oversized model of the Dark Edge series, widely used for their reliability. The Israeli army's ASes had made a meal of many RK-92s, Mistrals, and similar ASes belonging to Islamic nations. It had an unaffected and sincere form, tempered through combat, and had many times been employed for various uses. The Crimson Edge posed a problem for heavily armored opponents and was designed to be able to kill with one blow.

That cutter could probably sever one of the Arbalest's limbs in one slice, and even split the cockpit block in two.

"Aren't you going to draw? You should have a GRAW-2 on you."

GRAW-2 referred to the monofilament cutter with which the Arbalest was equipped.

Is he serious?

As Clouseau pointed out, the Arbalest currently had a GRAW-2 stowed on its weapons rack. But this had already gone beyond just some fight that originated as a barroom brawl. Having a fistfight in these pricey ASes was no admirable deed, but fighting with combat knives was on another level altogether.

Was there really an officer out there who would take a fight this far just to kill time? Who the hell was this?

"Here I come."

The black M9 kicked up a column of mud as it dashed forward. He approached at high speed, and the dark grey knife moved in a sharp arc as it came toward Sousuke.

The moment he quickly drew back his upper half, there was the ear-splitting sound of rending metal. The practice knife the Arbalest had been holding had been bisected right through the middle. Had Sousuke not been moving his mech, there was no doubt that his cockpit might easily have been cut in half.

Clouseau stepped in mercilessly. He slashed up from below with his knife, slashed sideways, and brought it down diagonally. Dazzling sparks jumped away as the Arbalest's armor suffered shallow cuts.

That effortless action conveyed an icy killing intent.

He's serious.

Sousuke hesitated no further, and extracted the monofilament cutter from his own mech's weapons rack. He made no attempt to hesitate or to question why. If his opponent was of such a mind, he had no obligation to go easy on him.

"That's right. No need to hold back."

Mud splashed as both of them jumped back.

"Al! Set GPL to max. Change the motion manager to DI, and release all practice limiters!"

"Roger. GPL, max. Running Delta-I. Releasing all PLDs," recited the AI. Generator output began to rise, and the motion control software toggled fully to combat mode.

"Warning. Recommend setting motion manager to Charlie-I."

"What?"

"Charlie-I is speculated to be appropriate for Lambda Driver operation. Six principle bases—One: statistical data from five previous combats. Two: Chief developer Bani Morauta's original setting was CI. Three: Settings for bilateral angle under Delta-I are—"

"Save it for later!"

"Roger."

Clouseau's M9 bore down. The Arbalest stood ready.

The two mechs clashed furiously as the practice grounds sank into dim darkness.

Data on the two dueling mechs was projected from various angles on the large screen in the base command center. The two mechanical silhouettes charging through a jungle as it descended into darkness was a dance of giants. Many trees were trampled and pulverized by limbs of steel as the two came together and moved apart.

Tessa held her breath as she watched the fierce combat.

"I cannot say I think highly of this methodology," said Commander Richard Mardukas, who stood beside her. "Even if it has a goal, it denotes our acquiescence to personal combat between soldiers. This will not promote discipline. We need to be consistent with regulations."

He pushed up his glasses and aimed a suspicious look at the screen. Tessa glanced at his profile and sighed lightly.

"It's unavoidable. The Arbalest's power can probably never be drawn out unless we do things this way."

"I don't really understand, Captain. We regularly perform maneuvers that simulate combat. So, why should we employ a farce of this nature? We've now condoned a bar fight, the unauthorized use of the organization's equipment, and even the use of dangerous combat gear."

Yes, this fight had been contrived from the start.

Clouseau had proposed it and Tessa had agreed to it. The plan was to pressure Sousuke through provocation, contempt, and personal struggle. By doing so, they would determine whether he could activate the Arbalest's Lambda Driver—or at least, whether data could be collected from a failed attempt.

"I have no intention of holding back. You should be prepared for the worst case scenario—his death," Clouseau had said to Tessa. When she had tried to tell him that it would mean losing everything, the new first lieutenant had callously added, "If I can kill him, the man isn't worth much—and neither is his machine. I doubt Ops Headquarters will put any further stock in that mech."

Tessa had no way to refute his cold but logical words. Had she said no, it would have meant she had no faith in Sousuke.

Mardukas continued speaking as he gazed at the command center screen. "This is a bit excessive from a security standpoint, too. We are a group who makes its living through combat, but we are not a street gang. Acts of violence should be carried out in a gentlemanly fashion via planning and regulation. A savage duel like this is—"

"There are no such things as savagery or gentlemanliness in war, are there?"

Mardukas showed a bit of surprise at Tessa's uncharacteristic words.

"Do you feel I was impertinent to ask such a question?" Tessa asked.

"No, Captain. You were correct," he answered, and a hint of sadness and compassion showed in his eyes for an instant.

The relay device installed in the Arbalest transmitted a multitude of data: The operator's pulse rate, brain waves, neural magnetic fields, measured value of near-infrared rays, the mech's frame temperature, strain, the AI Al's status, and many other things. Everything was being recorded, and the engineering officer, Ensign Lemming, looked over them in detail.

What would he think if he knew we were using him as a guinea pig this way?

What does he think about being forced to become one?

He'd probably react with contempt.

Even just today's events make me feel like he's growing ever more distant. Much more so than the distance between Tokyo and Merida Island.

Bani....

The face of the deceased boy crossed her mind.

Would you condemn me, now that I lost you, lost myself, and developed feelings for him? How many times has that mech you left behind saved us? I can't thank you enough. But at the same time, its sheer presence—it's creating a gap between me and him. A gap that's apparently impossible to fill.

Why was he the one who got into the Arbalest back at the Sunan incident? Why—why couldn't it have been someone else?

She had spent several seconds lost in thought. Snapping out of her reverie, she noticed Mardukas now looked even more displeased.

She said, "The Lambda Driver will not operate under the stress of ordinary maneuvers. A soldier's mental state is decisively different in training than it is in combat. I assume you're well aware of this, Mr. Mardukas?"

"Naturally. I learned that at the Falklands."

Tessa remembered that at the time of the Falklands Conflict in the early eighties, Mardukas had served as executive officer on a nuclear attack submarine in the British Navy.

"Captain.... What I'm saying I don't understand is why we have to go to such lengths regarding the effectiveness of that mech. A weapon that is not guaranteed to function when the trigger is pulled is no weapon at all. Perhaps rather than relying on that thing, we could develop some other strategy? A weapons system's absolute requirement is not a sense of innovation or destructive power. It needs genuine reliability."

"Are you trying to say that the Arbalest is defective?"

"Aye, ma'am. It really has not grown on me at all."

She sensed some melancholy humor in those words. Tessa was vaguely aware that Mardukas did not think too kindly of Sousuke. It occurred to her that both he and Sousuke held the exact same opinion of the mech.

"I suppose Sergeant Sagara feels the same way.... And therein lies the problem."

It was a battle with constantly alternating offense and defense. The black and white silhouettes ran through the jungle as if intertwined, surging up flashing bolts and thunderous roars. Sudden gusts were kicked up, giving rise to turbulence that violently scattered ivy and leaves.

"Ugly. That's what your fighting style is—ugly," said Clouseau.

"Ugly?"

"Like a tin plate doll. Clumsy—"

He attacked the Arbalest with a roundhouse kick to its blind spot. Sousuke stepped his mech in close and forcefully softened the blow, as if trying to ram his opponent.

"—coercive—"

Submitting to its lost balance, the M9 tail spun in the air. It put its rotational speed into a knife strike and with a quick slash cut off the Arbalest's left shoulder. One of the two wing-shaped radiator units was lost, and a shock-absorbent tank had been ruptured.

"—and inflexible."

He did a one-handed handstand and let out a brilliant whirlwind kick. Right leg, then left. The Arbalest staggered, having been struck on the side of its neck.

While spinning like a top from the inertia, the M9 stepped firmly onto the ground and reassumed an upright posture. The Arbalest backed off, white smoke rising from its shoulder.

"See that? If you pilot a mech from the M9 family, I want you to at *least* be able to mimic what I did."

"Are you bragging about your acrobatics?"

"Pardon?"

"If I were you, I'd have focused on finishing me off."

"Looks like you're still lively enough for small talk. Fine, we'll do this your way."

Just then, they clashed together. The two explosive powers made the air tremble, stirring the surrounding jungle. Taking light steps, the Arbalest lunged like an arrow. Clouseau leaned in to avoid it, at the same time trying to chop at Sousuke's frame. Sousuke twisted his waist at the last second, jumping sideways to avoid the attack.

Despite his previous banter, Sousuke was honestly struggling.

Clouseau was strong, and there was more to it than that. His every movement gave the impression of flowing spring water, possessed of a certain harmony. He resisted every lure—saw through every feint. If Sousuke showed the slightest carelessness, Clouseau would no doubt become a raging torrent and break through his defenses.

Not letting up on attack or defense, Clouseau said, "Enough already, how about you fight for real? Europe's littered with pilots at your skill level. If this was an SAS mechanized assault team, you'd fall below the median."

"So, you were SAS?"

That was England's Special Forces unit that was proud of its world-class strength and achievements. Judging by the name Clouseau, Sousuke had thought he might be a Frenchman of African descent.

"That's not important."

An especially vehement roar and vibration assaulted Sousuke. Clouseau's dagger stabbed deeply into the Arbalest's abdomen.

"Worry about your life first. That coward McAllen's waiting for you."

The AI reported damage details in rapid succession:

"Warning! Generator damaged. Extent unknown. Main power cable severed. Number two cooling apparatus non-functional. Rectus abdominis muscle actuator damaged—"

It was not in the AI's report, but the air conditioning system seemed to be damaged, too. The smell of burned metal invaded the normally airtight cockpit.

"What's wrong?"

Another merciless blow.

"What are you looking at?"

Yet another ruthless slash.

"Are you even *trying*?"

A follow-up knee kick sank into the flank of the staggering Arbalest. The eight-ton machine went flying, landing with its back on the ground.

There were AI warnings, shrill alarms, and the shriek of frame, muscles, and armor grating.

At this rate, I'm....

Sousuke was totally at a loss regarding how to deflect the severe chain of attacks, or how to land an effective hit on his opponent.

"I thought I told you to get serious!"

The M9 jumped high in the air, raised its knife in a backhand grip, and dove at the Arbalest. It was coming at a ferocious angle, swooping down at its prey on the ground.

Sousuke rolled to the right and avoided the point by a hair's breadth. Clouseau's knife plunged deeply into where the Arbalest's cockpit block had been. Sousuke bisected the dagger with a sideswipe of his own knife. The Crimson Edge broke into two pieces.

From a face-up position, the Arbalest sprang up in the air just from the explosive power of its back muscles. It was a maneuver called the jackknife. This action, closely resembling the bounce of the click beetle, allowed an AS to return to a vertical stance far faster than by using its arms and legs to get up.

With a nimbleness impossible for humans, the Arbalest suddenly regained its posture while simultaneously brandishing its own knife.

But before he realized it, the M9 had quickly stooped down and snuck in close. It squatted deeply and turned sharply. The moment he was aware of this unnatural movement—

His mech was pulled forward.

It felt like, just for that instant, the direction of gravity became horizontal. Immediately after a heavy impact assaulted him, some overwhelming power went into effect, and the Arbalest was blown backward.

The eight-ton mech traversed the jungle, mowing down several trees. A splash of mud misted up, hanging thickly over the area. The Arbalest sank back-first into the ground, gave off white steam—and sprawled powerlessly on its side.

"No...."

No way. What was that impact?

He felt dizzy and his whole body was numb. It was due to the impact. It had not simply been a physical strike. It was something beyond that.

Does that mech have a...?

The black M9's two glowing eyes were clearly scowling at him.

"...It can't be."

Sousuke's throat constricted.

That AS couldn't possibly have been equipped with a Lambda Driver. The only AS in Mithril that had one was the Arbalest. That was why he was in this unfortunate mess. He had been saddled with a weapon of unreliable utility, and with a duty he was reluctant to perform.

"Stand up, Sergeant," said Clouseau. "Try to draw out that mech's full power. *Full* power, understand? Otherwise, next time you're dead."

The Arbalest stood up. Its knees shook and its shoulders moved up and down noticeably. These movements were reflecting the trauma to Sousuke's body.

I guess I have to use it!

He had to use the Lambda Driver, the enigmatic ability of this mech that had him at wit's end. What a time for him to have to rely on it again.

Will it work, though? Won't this machine just betray me again? Whoever heard of a fight this absurd? Wouldn't it be a better plan to abandon this combat and run away?

"Get ready."

Sousuke took a deep breath, planted both feet, adopted a defensive stance, and confronted Clouseau.

The M9 kicked at the ground. The black mech bore down in a flash.

The Arbalest brought its right fist back as if drawing a bow.

He envisioned an image of power, and focused on pouring all the destructive power into one point....

Do it!

He unleashed his fist. Clouseau moved.

The next instant, the Arbalest arched backward and was blown forward. A violent impact hit the cockpit, and this time he started to

221

lose consciousness. The world haphazardly ran riot, and the jungle landscape revolved chaotically. The moment he slammed to the ground, his vision went dark and he saw stars.

The AI barked out damages and a raucous alarm resounded, but Sousuke hardly heard them.

"Weak and fragile," said Clouseau's voice. "I see you're nothing but a pet dog, after all."

I couldn't do it.

Sousuke's consciousness sank into deep darkness as that thought ran through his head.

"It seems to be over," Mardukas said, taking off his navy blue hat. He also removed his black-rimmed glasses and rubbed his tired eyes with the backs of his hands. It felt warm in the room. "And sure enough, nothing happened. It's useless at this rate," said Mardukas.

"It is too soon to conclude whether anything happened or not. How are the figures, Miss Lemming?" Following her curt response, Tessa addressed the engineering officer, Ensign Nora Lemming. Lemming opened a laptop at a nearby seat and inspected data from the M9 and Arbalest. She answered while keeping her eyes on the screen.

"It wasn't even on par with the combat at Berildaobu Island. TAROS is detecting the usual brain waves—gamma waves, but at an unusually low level. The spectral distribution of the core module's phase interference wave quantum device has shifted. From the N pole of the columnar thalamic axis to ... pretty much around E layer, field fifteen. Also a bit apart, around P layer, field forty-two, at ninety degrees."

"The blue area."

"Aye, ma'am. Please look at this. These two locations are connected. That is a promising result, but it is a far cry from a successful activation."

"In the case of the defensive response, it was N layer, zero degrees, plus or minus forty. Perhaps it's related to Miller's Hypothesis."

"I cannot draw any conclusions. The one thing that worries me is—"

Mardukas only gazed with melancholy eyes at Tessa and Lemming as they debated in front of the colorful 3-D images and graphs. He could make neither heads nor tails of their conversation. He presumed it had to do with neuroscience and physics, but beyond that it was all gibberish to him. Though he possessed a number of academic degrees, he knew he could not hope to keep up with a debate so far outside his areas of expertise.

Lemming was a talented MIT graduate. She had no prior military service record, but Tessa had scouted her when the Arbalest had lost its developer. Her unusual abilities were below the level of Tessa's, but she most likely still deserved to be classified as a genius. Thus far, the overwhelming majority of other engineers Mardukas had met who were knowledgeable about things like ASes and ECS were of the younger generation.

Mardukas had for some time felt uneasy about the numerous new weapons these young people had produced. It wasn't limited to that unreliable Lambda Driver. It also included Arm Slaves, ECS, palladium nuclear fusion batteries, the *Tuatha de Danaan's* super AI, TAROS, SCD, EMFC ... all of it.

A mere twenty years ago, when Mardukas was still considered a young man, nobody had ever even imagined the introduction of such equipment. It was an age during which missiles and jet fighters were finally being furnished with computers that one would think

of as true computers. Had he even said the words "giant robots" or "invisibility device," it would have called into question his standing as a career soldier. *Space Invaders* was a big hit with the public, and people were thrilled enough just to see those shabby pixels move across a screen.

The nuclear-powered attack submarine Mardukas once commanded was still one of the most high-powered boats in the world. But in the face of the *Tuatha de Daanan*, it might as well have been a diesel sub from World War II.

Teletha Testarossa is a good girl. But what the hell's this vague sense of apprehension over the things she and her kind have brought about? I work for her, and yes, she and that ship—this force—have saved many lives. But what is it that makes me want to question its origins?

The debate between Tessa and Lemming continued for five minutes.

"What about observation data from unit E-005?" asked Tessa.

"Nothing."

"So no other conceivable electromagnetic waves were emitted."

"Observational environments have inherent limits, so we cannot be certain. The equipment is also makeshift. We will probably need time for an analysis, as far as details are concerned...."

"Fine. Let's reconsider the hypothesis, and first reconstruct a simple model. Maybe we can also improve in some way the issue of leaving it up to the operator. I still have high hopes, Miss Lemming."

"Y-yes, ma'am."

Mardukas did not miss the way Lemming's face briefly showed a lack of confidence. Perhaps it was beyond even her genius to shed light upon that entire system. Maybe she felt something like an inferiority complex when a girl significantly younger than her could so easily tell her such a thing.

But Tessa seemed not to notice it, and she turned back to Mardukas.

"I will be resting for a bit. Should anything happen, please call for me at the medical center."

"The medical center, ma'am?"

"It's just the right place for a nap. I'm all out of compresses, too," she said and began walking toward the command center exit. She seemed to be taking long strides, and her sense of haste was a bit odd, considering she was on her way to take a break.

So she is worried.... Hmm. That's what it comes down to, is it? Maybe she can't help being concerned about the sergeant's well-being.

Tessa's back disappeared beyond the automatic door.

"Excuse me.... Commander, sir," said Ensign Lemming from behind him.

"What is it?"

"Is Lieutenant Commander Kalinin returning to base today?"

"He's supposed to. What about it?"

"Nothing, sir. I just need to discuss the Arbalest's equipment with him. I was just a bit unsure whether to message him ... or speak to him directly."

"That's up to you, but don't trouble the Lieutenant Commander more than is necessary. Strange rumors affect morale."

"N-naturally, sir. In fact, those rumors are misunderstandings. I'd like to say this for the sake of his reputation. He and I would never—"

"All right, all right. Enough." Mardukas waved his hand wearily and walked back toward his own office. As he did, the petty officer in charge of communications called him to a halt.

"Just a moment, please, sir."

"What is it now?"

"Well, sir, we've received a message from Operations HQ in Sydney."

"Hey, wake up, good-for-nothing Sergeant Moody."

When he opened his eyes, a sour-looking Kurz Weber was looking down at him.

Sousuke was lying on a bed in the medical center, with its white ceiling and inorganic fluorescent lighting. He dimly recalled being dragged out of the mech by a maintenance tech, but he wasn't sure what happened after that.

"He took you down like it was *nothing*? What the hell, man? That's pathetic," said Kurz, conveniently forgetting what happened at the bar. At a glance he looked quite sound, but at the same time he was blatantly displeased.

"Where's Lieutenant Clouseau?" Sousuke asked as he sat up. Kurz turned up his nose. Just then, Clouseau emerged from behind the curtain partitioning off the medical examination area on the opposite side of the spacious room and thanked the medic. He was dressed in a T-shirt, with his uniform shirt rolled up under his arm. A brand new bandage was carefully wrapped around his burly left arm.

"That fight was an experiment. That asshole, engineering, and command all got together and set it up. They set *me* up to take a fall too. Shit!"

Sousuke had guessed it was something like that. They had spent all that time fighting with combat weapons, and not a single interruption or warning had come from the command center. It was no stretch even for him to imagine his superiors tolerating, or perhaps *promoting* that fight.

In other words, that AS and I are Mithril's guinea pigs.

It was a doozy of a new duty. All they really needed to do was give the command to fight instead of being so underhanded.

What must Teletha Testarossa have thought about him being treated this way? If nothing else, she probably did not enjoy it. He could surmise that much.

A bitter sense of defeat swirled in his heart.

That lieutenant hadn't played any tricks on him during the fight. Sousuke had simply lost due to their power gap. Had it been a real battle, he would most likely be dead now. The same could be said for his pricey, yet worthless experimental mech.

He wished the AS had been hit with an attack that seriously damaged it—one that would render it impossible to use again. In any case, responsibility would have fallen on Clouseau. Then, Sousuke could once again—

No. That's absurd. Even if the Arbalest was destroyed, I'd probably never be reinstated to the Tokyo mission. The higher ups would never reverse their stance. But still, isn't that AS the main cause of it all?

Chidori....

I'm sorry, but I don't have the power to do anything. And not just about you. I couldn't protect the honor of the fallen, either. Or my pride. I couldn't protect anything.

Had he ever felt this powerless in his life?

"Incoming." Kurz's whisper brought Sousuke back to himself. Belfangan Clouseau approached.

"I see you're finally awake, Sergeant," he said, showing no sign of appreciation.

"Go to the hangar and sign some papers for the maintenance team. Write your report on that little *exercise*, then submit it to me, Ensign Lemming, Lieutenant Commander Kalinin, and Colonel Testarossa by 2400 hours. If there's a single inaccuracy or mistake in form, I'll make you do it over from scratch as many times as it takes. Practice drills start tomorrow morning at 0600. Be in front of hangar one by then. You too, Weber. I'm retraining everyone in our unit who's qualified to pilot an AS. Looks like McAllen went easy on you, but I'm different. You see, I don't want to be called incompetent by *my* successor after I die in a ditch. So be ready."

Sousuke and Kurz said nothing. They really had lost the fight. They had no choice but to endure the lieutenant's contempt.

"If there are no questions, you're dismissed."

"I have a question," said Sousuke in a stifled voice.

"Ask it."

"What was that attack that beat me? Is there a Lambda Driver in that black mech?" he asked, causing Clouseau to snort.

"It was easy enough to crush you and the Arbalest without one of those. This should prove to you the potential that even normal use of a third-generation AS like the M9 can yield."

"Then what was that shock wave?"

"That was a technique compositing what they call in the Orient *tohshi* and *sunkei*. First you send a violent impact throughout the enemy mech and operator, then you follow up by blowing them away. You don't need a blasted Lambda Driver to pull it off."

Sousuke recalled the bar brawl. Clouseau has used the same move there.

From Sousuke's position at the time, it had looked like nothing more than Kurz's chin being pushed, but it was probably not that simple.

"An M9 is more than capable of such a feat. You synch yourself up with the enemy, then guide the flow of energy into the form you choose. Like water. Like flame. You get it?"

"But the human body is different from an AS," said Sousuke.

"That idea is outdated. The parts count in an M9-type AS's frame is more than double that of an average second generation AS's. With that complexity and elasticity, it's on par with the most detailed mechanism God ever created—namely, the human body.

"Earlier, I said your fighting was ugly. That was because you don't put any faith in the Arbalest's inherent power, and just control it like it's nothing more than a car or a helicopter."

"How is that a problem?"

An AS was not a living being. It was just a machine that moved its joints and obeyed programming. "Your second body" was, in the end, nothing more than a metaphor. Even if Arm Slaves were shaped like people, they were just mechanical medleys of titanium alloy, high polymer materials, and so on.

"I guess I'll have to spell it out for you." Clouseau put his hands on his hips and sighed as if amazed. Then he looked straight at Sousuke and said, "You hate the Arbalest."

Sousuke looked shocked.

"I can tell, now that we've fought. The carriage of the legs, the handling of the arms, the flow of the fists, fine points of the swordsmanship ... all of these harbored doubts. I saw distrust, impatience, and indecision. At a reasonable glance, your movements seemed like a pro's—but your will didn't match up. Your mind was absent. Who *cares* about the Lambda Driver? This problem's bigger than that."

Every one of Clouseau's words stabbed Sousuke in the chest.

You're right, I hate that mech. It hasn't shown any real sign of being broken beyond the Lambda Driver, but I still can't trust it. I only put my life in its hands and fight because I have to, not because I want to.

Are those feelings weakening my skills?

Sousuke was struck to the core by this man who had briefly been his enemy, and it made his heart tremble. Even if he wanted to lash back, he couldn't. What this lieutenant was saying was probably correct.

"Listen well, Sergeant." Clouseau leaned forward and peered into

Sousuke eyes. It was close enough for him to feel the breath coming from his nose. He gazed at Sousuke with a serious face, and stressed every single word as he said "These weapons called Arm Slaves aren't just vehicles. They're an extension of your body as a soldier. The operator's mind expresses itself through the mech. In a high-level battle, a slight margin in that regard will decide victory. Be aware that our enemies from this point on can't be defeated by a man who doesn't believe in his own body and his own power. That is all."

Without waiting for a reaction, Clouseau turned on his heel and left the medical center.

"Oh, man. Now we're workin' for a real creep," Kurz said quietly, fully aware that he might still be overheard.

"He does have a point, however. Clouseau's definitely strong." Sousuke stated his honest impression.

"Well ... in hand-to-hand. We don't know about anything else."

"His other skills are probably top-notch, too. He's apparently from the SAS."

"Wow. Maybe the Canadian SAS, then."

When it came to the SAS, the widely known one was the 22nd SAS Regiment of the British Army. However, the armies of members of the Commonwealth of Nations—such as Canada, New Zealand, and Australia—each had an SAS which boasted of the same level of training. Personnel interchange was common, and the units of different countries shared the same insignia, so it would be difficult to distinguish from an outsider's perspective.

"Come to think of it, McAllen's old man was in the Australian SAS."

"Yeah. I'm pretty sure...," was all Sousuke said before trailing off.

In the medical center entrance opposite the one through which Clouseau had left stood Tessa. Her right hand was on the edge of the doorway, and her left hand held her braid. She looked in their direction with eyes that seemed to want to say something. Maybe it was just imagination, but her footing seemed shaky.

She stayed silent for so long, Sousuke and Kurz spoke up first.

"Colonel?"

"Tessa?"

"...Uh, uh—" When Tessa falteringly opened her mouth, the medic, Lieutenant Goldberry, spoke up from the rear of the medical center.

"Oh, there you are, Tessa!"

"Y-yes?"

"Message from Dick! He says to come back to the command center immediately!"

"Uh.... I understand. I will be right there."

After hesitating a little, Tessa hurriedly disappeared from the doorway. She ended up not saying a word to Sousuke.

"Well, well. Maybe she came down because she was worried."

"Worried? About what?" When Sousuke asked that question out of genuine ignorance, Kurz stared at him with a frown, exaggeratedly shaking his head from side to side.

"Holy hell. If I was a scriptwriter for a romantic drama, I don't think I'd *ever* make a guy like you the main character. I mean, the story wouldn't *go* anywhere. Ratings would *plummet*."

"Huh?"

Scowling at a map of the underground base, Belfangan Clouseau wandered around the officer residence sector and finally found the private room assigned to him. The door wasn't locked, and when he entered, there was the pile of his personal effects he had asked a soldier to carry in.

The officers' rooms were about as wide as a double room at a standard hotel. There was almost no affectation, but the illumination was bright and warm. There were only a few pieces of furniture.

Not touching his possessions, he took a look through the empty locker and cabinets. He failed to find anything left behind by the person who had used this room until two months prior.

He walked up to the wooden desk and looked inside the drawers. There was a faint scent of paper and cigars. In the bottom drawer was a well-worn Bible.

Clouseau picked up the small leather-bound Bible and flipped through the pages. He hoped there might be some kind of photo inside, but he made no such discovery.

He opened it to a passage in Ecclesiastes. It was the only page where the right margin was a bit dirty from a finger mark.

A living dog is better than a dead lion.

He said that from time to time during training. No matter how much I insisted I'm Muslim, he just wouldn't listen. And chances are—forgive me, Allah—I liked these words, too.

Gail, old buddy, he murmured in his heart, then closed the Bible.

Just as he was about to take his personal effects to the rear of the room, he turned back toward the entrance. In the open doorway stood an Asian woman. It was Master Sergeant Melissa Mao.

"That must have been you," said Mao.

"That's right."

"What's it been, a year and a half?"

"Six days, to be precise."

"True. Don't bother looking for his stuff. They finished cleaning up in here a long time ago."

"I know."

He turned his back on Mao and lifted up a large olive-colored bag. As he carried his belongings to the back of the room, Clouseau forced himself to ask bluntly, "Did he ... suffer?"

"No one knows. There was no one to tend to him."

"Okay."

He stopped walking for several seconds, then nodded as if convincing himself.

Pacing back and forth, he straightened up his things that lay near the entryway. Making no move to assist him, Mao asked, "That M9's a prototype of the D Series? I remember there being, besides the

E Series mechs I was involved with, a plan on the drawing board for an AS of similar shape."

"That's right. It's one of just two prototyped at Geotron's Dortmund factory, a Falke model. Aside from a little elbow room in the payload, it's no different than the regular issue E Series."

"Does it carry the same device as the Arbalest?"

Clouseau saw that this was what she came to ask.

"Would that bother you?"

"I've almost been killed twice by enemies who had it."

"That true. I read the reports. But the answer is ... it doesn't have one. It was in the plans, but the developer committed suicide before implementation."

"So the only one in Mithril really is the Arbalest?"

"Correct. That's why I'm going to train you all and that sergeant. Thoroughly."

They needed to be thinking about countermeasures. If they could get the Arbalest to where it activated the Lambda Driver at will, they should be able to research means for even the regular M9s to contend with it. Once that result was conveyed to the other battle groups, they could work through this crisis using their current equipment. This was also the intent of Lieutenant Commander Kalinin and Captain Testarossa.

"I realize that, but I never figured the Spartan approach was your style," said Mao.

"My thoughts exactly." Clouseau shrugged, his face expressionless. "That Sagara guy...."

"Hmm?"

"He's exactly like I used to be. He refuses to yield or look around himself, and he forces himself into a limited framework. It's like he's trying to wedge himself into a chair that's the wrong shape. Yet if he felt like it, he *could* expand his framework."

"I wonder if he'll ever reach that point."

"I don't know. But at this rate, he'll probably die. Or else he'll become a true loser."

"A loser?" asked Mao.

"Like the ones we take on all the time. Malice builds up slowly. First you lie to yourself, then you resent those around you, then finally you're scoffing at the whole world. Slowly. Like the hour hand on a clock—it's a gradual transformation. That's why it's terrible."

"Sousuke? Hardly."

Clouseau changed the subject.

"Today tired me out. I need to rest a little. You should head out, too."

Opening the bag he'd put on the floor, he took out a clean towel and soap. Clouseau started out for the shower room—but then stopped.

"Melissa?"

"What?"

"Don't mention anything about me and Gail. It's easier if they don't have to take that into consideration."

Mao, who had been closing the door, smiled wryly. "As you wish. Well, good night, Ben."

"Good night."

When Tessa returned to the command center, Mardukas turned to her with a grave expression. "I apologize, Captain."

"Is it urgent?"

"No, ma'am. Not at this point. It is a Standby Alert D order from Operations HQ. Situation BI2a has occurred in zone

J5-CS. We have completed up to response procedure 3a, and 3b is currently underway."

Standby Alert D was an order to prepare the amphibious assault submarine *Tuatha de Daanan* to sail. It meant being ready to put to sea within two hours of when the order to move is given. In reality, cases where the TDD-I was notified it could potentially be needed were more numerous than actual orders to sail. Such standby alert periods were known to last anywhere from several days to several weeks.

Situation BI2a indicated destructive acts by one or more ASes. The June incident in Tokyo—though it was somewhat unique—also fell into this category.

The thought of AS terrorism gave her a chill of premonition.

"You said zone J5-CS. Where, exactly?"

"Hong Kong, ma'am."

At the same time
Somewhere in Hong Kong

A patrol car passed down the street, siren blaring. There was the sound of a car horn at an intersection. A hit Andy Hui song could be heard from a neighborhood shop facing the street.

A man stood in a room where the red and green lights shined in just a little.

"I have just returned, *Xiansheng*," said the man.

"As you wished, I used the Codarl M to stir up the southern army sentries. There is also news from my younger brother in Tokyo. He says arrangements are now in place. Once you tell him to, he can probably choke the life from that girl anytime."

There was no answer. It was totally dark in the back of the room where someone supposedly lurked, which was perhaps due to the lighting. It was a darkness that soaked up light, never to let it escape. There was a very profound darkness there.

In that gloom, something moved.

"Tomorrow night?" the man asked, and a thick, hoarse, mechanical voice sounded from the darkness:

"——"

"What type of death might you prefer?"

"——"

"It will be done. I shall tell my brother to kill that Chidori girl tomorrow night. This is acceptable?"

The master of the darkness affirmed the man's question by way of silence.

CHAPTER 4
Her Problem

October 20, 20:45 (Japan Standard Time)
Chofu

I'm overanalyzing this, Kaname said to herself once she returned home without incident.

She had caught a glimpse of a weird guy on top of a building in the Sengawa shopping district—why was that alone enough to make her feel so distracted?

Was it a premonition? If so, it wasn't as if it could possibly be accurate.

That's right.

She wasn't able to reach Sousuke by phone. But so what? Things had been like this before. He'd disappear suddenly from school, then not come back for a day or two. Even three or four on some occasions. He'd always return. She had almost never been able to reach him any of those other times either.

But....

"The number you have dialed is currently not in use."

This hadn't happened before. That message meant Sousuke contacted the phone company and canceled his plan deliberately. Once the subscriber requested the cancellation and the company confirmed it, that number would be suspended within ten minutes.

Hadn't they just reached the point during exams the other day where she could finally call him overseas?

That moron.

All he does is worry me. I'm going to tell him off the next time I see him.

She experienced a blend of anxiety and irritation, and then an optimism that erased them, and her heart was in a constantly tumultuous state.

She didn't feel up to cooking, so that evening she ate ready-made curry.

She turned on the TV and channel-surfed. A sponsored variety show was on. It featured a comedian group who'd been popular lately. The material was trashy, consisting solely of newcomers in weak positions or novices who were embarrassed, pushed around, and pointed and laughed at.

She turned on her game console and loaded up a saved game. It was an action title where you used a multinational force's cutting-edge ASes to take out terrorist foes. Until lately she hadn't been at all interested in such games aimed at boys, but she bought it thinking she might learn a little about Sousuke's job.

Once she bought it, though, she realized such a game wasn't going to be any use as a reference. It was only natural, but this game's creators didn't know about the tension, roaring explosions, or hot blasts of actual combat. Nor did they grasp the highly taut atmosphere or the practically seething sense of frenzy. Unfortunately, Kaname had some experience with these things.

It was boring, so she soon quit playing.

She couldn't settle her mood, and no matter what she did she couldn't focus. On the other hand, if she did nothing, the tedium would make her nervous.

Why am I so edgy?

I should've had Kyouko come over.

Kyouko would come spend the night at her apartment about once a week. It was usually short notice, where she would ask if she could come over the same day. Living on her own was lonely for Kaname, so naturally she welcomed it. She would do some home cooking, they would watch TV together, line up their futons, and talk about all sorts of things: music, sports, TV dramas, gossip about their friends, boys at school, the future....

The phone rang.

The clock informed her that it was after nine. In New York, it was seven in the morning. Once every several days, her little sister would call her before going to school. Kaname thought of her face, and finally smiled. Hearing her sister's voice might calm her mood a little. She picked up the handset, and with some effort answered in a cheerful voice:

"Hi, Chidori residence."

She waited for a reply, but none came. A slight noise was audible through the quiet receiver.

"Hello? Ayame?"

No response.

"Is that you, Ayame?"

Still no response.

"Who is this?"

There was the sound of something being rubbed, and then the line dropped. *Booop, booop,* repeated the vacant electronic tone.

Attacked by an anxiety impossible to brush off, Kaname placed her own call to New York.

Kaname caught her sister right before she left for school. Kaname questioned her and Ayame said, "Phone call? I didn't call you."

"Oh. That's fine, then."

"What's the matter? Are you okay?"

"Hmm? Yeah, fine. It's nothing."

"Should I put Dad on?"

"No. Don't.... Okay, see you. Have a nice day."

Kaname made an effort to regain her calm as she hung up the phone.

That's weird.

She couldn't relax. The stillness of the room went right to her head.

She had received prank calls on numerous occasions. Complete strangers had, once or twice, called her cell phone and said, "What are you doing right now? Want to hang out?" along with some odd flirting. But that was it. What were the odds that a prank call would come in tonight of all nights?

She was lonely. She felt bad. It was like someone was watching her.

Sousuke....

251

Kaname once again punched in Sousuke's number. Sure enough, no answer. Just like before.

Trying to call him was getting her nowhere.

Isn't there any other way? As soon as she thought this, she remembered the transmitter in Sousuke's apartment.

Oh, yeah. That transmitter.

She didn't know how to operate it, but at this point, she'd find a way to manage. The satellite circuit Mithril used included characteristic quantum cryptography in the modulation process of its widely used spread-spectrum system. During the incident on the *Tuatha de Daanan,* she had gotten a rough grasp of the systematic details involved and the frequency band they used. If she really tinkered with it, it probably wouldn't be all that hard to contact Merida Island.

She failed to notice the weirdness of her thoughts as she quickly reached a decision.

Yeah!

I'll use that transmitter. Well that makes things simple. I'll just go do it now.

Kaname threw on a well-worn blouse, grabbed her keys and left the apartment. She'd never used it, but she'd had a spare key to Sousuke's apartment for half a year. He'd given it to her, saying it was just in case anything ever happened.

Her mood had grown somewhat lighter now that some real progress was taking place.

Her old-lady sandals slapped the ground as she crossed the street to the opposite apartment building. It was on the fifth floor in the rear, unit 505. Things looked the same as ever.

She tried knocking on the door, for form's sake. As expected, there was no answer.

She inserted the spare key into the doorknob.

I don't suppose that idiot rigged a bomb or something?

Oh, well. If he has set some weird trap, I'll get him back tenfold. I'll pound the living snot out of him.

Such things went through her mind as she turned the key and opened the door.

There were no traps.

But that wasn't all that was absent.

The several pairs of combat boots usually placed in the entryway weren't there. The bulletproof vest and submachine gun typically concealed in the shoe shelves weren't there either.

Even when she flipped the nearby switch, the lights didn't come on. She fumbled her way forward in the poor light, and entered the living/dining room.

There was no refrigerator. There was no table. There was no tableware, chairs, or TV. Or ammo boxes, or small arms, or various electronics, or camouflaged clothes on hangers, knapsacks, belts, sleeping bags, or the picture on the wall of his old war buddies.

Every last thing was gone.

Nearly everything was gone. On the wooden floor lay several CDs. They were ones Kaname had lent him just the other day. These alone, as if announcing a message to her, were stacked right in the middle of the room.

The blinds were gone and outdoor illumination shone through the bare glass door. It was a pale, desolate light.

She stood there for several minutes in the empty room, still and all alone.

October 20, 23:35 (Western Pacific Standard Time)
Merida Island Base
Underground dock

Shortly after entering Standby Alert D, orders were issued for the *Tuatha de Daanan* to sail.

Inspections were completed and all sorts of materials were loaded at a quick pace, and even the Arbalest and the black M9—alias Falke—were stowed in the hangar despite repairs still being in progress. Sousuke and the other land combat personnel were also now ordered up front to board the ship.

Over two hundred crew members lined up on the starboard side of the *Tuatha de Daanan*, its damage from the incident two months prior now fully repaired.

"Ladies and gentlemen," said Teletha Testarossa, stepping in front of them. "This is duty as usual. The *Tuatha de Daanan* is about to set sail. At world-record speed, we will make directly for our zone of operation. I will notify you of our destination once we are en route. This probably means work will proceed around the clock, but please take care not to make any mistakes. Now let us pray."

It was an address which lacked any hint of embellishment, but that was this ship's style. Tessa wrapped both hands around the mic, and chanted the words of her prayer in a quiet voice.

"Oh, Lord, our great power. With thy long arms which reach to the bottom of the ocean, may ye maintain and protect us as we travel those depths—"

Her voice was sweet and delicate, reminiscent of a flute solo. Those who were Christians folded their hands in front of their chests, and the others prayed silently.

"—night and day, in the still depths and on the wave-filled surface, may thy presence be with us. Lord, when we be in the midst of distress in the sea and we call upon thy name, may thine ear be open to our voices...."

She ended the prayer on a lingering note.

"Now please get to your posts," she commanded.

"You heard her! All officers and sailors, to your posts!" The duty officer raised his voice and all the crew started moving at once, boarding the hill-sized *Tuatha de Daanan*.

With electric power supplied by an external source, the palladium reactor fired to life. The underwater exhaust ports sighed slightly. Mooring and electrical cables were unfastened.

The oiled hydraulic lock bolts that had held the ship in place slowly rotated as they separated. Every hatch groaned as it closed, and the siren notifying departure echoed through the vast underground dock.

The giant shutter gate closing off the front of the dock opened with a roar. The sight was like an entire building in motion. In front of the open gate was a giant cave reinforced with countless steel frames. It was the *de Danaan*'s underground route to the sea, which lay several hundred meters ahead. The sea water filling the cave rippled and reflected the light of mercury lamps.

Accompanied by her executive officer, Tessa walked briskly into the ship's central command center. "Good work. I'm now assuming command."

"Aye, ma'am. The captain is now in command!" announced the duty officer.

Still standing, Tessa looked attentively at the forward screen. The results of each station's final checks came in via intercom. There were no problems anywhere, and the on-screen display echoed this status.

Mardukas nodded a bit.

"Confirmed, Captain."

"Then let us be off. Normal propulsion. Ahead one third."

"Aye, aye, ma'am. Normal propulsion, ahead one third!"

They glided forward on a quiet, gentle cruise that failed to hint at the enormous power hidden in this ship which weighed several dozen thousands of tons.

October 21, 12:40 (Japan Standard Time)
Chofu, Tokyo
Jindai High School

The completely exhausted face of a girl was reflected in the girls' bathroom mirror.

There were dark spots under her bloodshot eyes, her black hair was loose, and her expression was listless. Her face was pallid, and her lips were chapped.

She looked like a woman past thirty, tired with life, who happened to be wearing a high-school uniform.

I look terrible.

She hadn't slept well since yesterday. She'd spent the night crouched down with her back to a wall, and every little sound made her jump. Unable to stand the stillness of the apartment, she'd left the TV on all night. There was some report on the late night news about citizens evacuating in Hong Kong, but she wasn't interested so she changed the channel and watched an infomercial for an American product.

"What we have here today is a revolutionary fitness tool, Fit X. At a glance it looks like just a chair, but with just twenty minutes' use a day, you can maintain an attractive, healthy body. Computer engineer Daniel says, 'This Fit X is the best! I mean, this one tool lets you do twelve kinds of exercises. Thanks to mine, I saw my friend John after a year, and he said to me, "Wow! Are you really Danny? Unbelievable, man. I didn't recognize you!" And I have Fit X to thank.' Fit X. Fit X. Those who'd like to own their own Fit X pick up the phone and call us!"

Thus did Kaname reach daybreak, watching the smiling faces of Daniel and many others.

"Fitness, huh...?"

She glared at the mirror, muttering to herself. *Even without one of those things, I might be losing a lot of weight in the near future,* she thought.

Her classmates appeared to be aware something was wrong. Kyouko looked seriously worried, and she recommended Kaname go to the hospital. With little choice in the matter, Kaname had told everyone it was just a cold. She thought about explaining the situation and asking for help, but she couldn't.

She could never speak openly about these things.

She couldn't say that Sousuke might never come back. That the war nut everyone knew was actually a hard-working elite soldier on active duty, not to mention that his reason for being at this school was to guard her. Or that the reason they all got caught up in that big disaster of a class trip was none other than herself.

She could never tell them. She really didn't have that kind of courage.

The school broadcast chime sounded. The voice of her homeroom teacher, Eri Kagurazaka, was calling her name.

"—ame Chidori. Please come to the staff room. I repeat: would Miss Kaname Chidori, second year, class four, please report to the staff room immediately."

She thought of ignoring it, but changed her mind. Holding a staring match with this mirror would only make her feel worse.

Kaname trudged off toward the staff room.

"Are you all right?" Eri asked first, once she saw Kaname's face.

"Yes. I just didn't get much sleep."

"Okay. You need to, though. Even if you do live alone, you can't always stay up late."

"That's true." Kaname forced a laugh.

"So, here's the reason I called you here." Eri extracted an opened envelope from her desk drawer. The address was Jindai High School. She recognized the clumsy handwriting.

"This was apparently sent by Mr. Sagara to my office. There was—listen, and don't be shocked by this," she said, lowering her voice. "There was a school withdrawal notification inside."

Kaname didn't respond.

"It's true that he's missed a lot of school lately, but to just withdraw suddenly, without saying anything? I can't reach him by phone, either. I'm not sure at this point what I should do. I really lectured him hard about the car situation the other day, as well as his unexcused absences. Maybe that's why.... No, maybe there's a more complicated situation—"

Kaname hardly heard Eri's baffled words.

She wasn't surprised. She just thought, *Oh, figures.*

She didn't even cry. Neither sorrow at being abandoned, anger at the lack of closure, nor pleasure at the memories welled up within her. She felt nothing, but simply stood straight up and gazed at the worn-out envelope on the desk as if engrossed by it.

"—So, I.... Miss Chidori. Miss Chidori?"

"Yes, ma'am."

"Do you have any idea why?"

If this was a manga or something, this might be a scene where I'd cry something like, "I can't tell you why, but I believe Sousuke will come back!" she thought, as if it wasn't even her own problem. But, perhaps sadly, she was a real, complex person—not such a simple girl that she could have unwavering blind faith like that.

"Nothing comes to mind."

"But—"

"I don't know anything about it," Kaname answered flatly, and Eri looked up at her in doubt.

"Are you fighting again, or anything?"

"No, ma'am."

"If I can't contact him by tomorrow, I'll have to have the principal accept this withdrawal notice."

"Then I guess that means he'll be leaving us."

Eri said nothing.

Kaname took the silence to indicate confirmation.

"I see. Okay, then...." With stiff movements, Kaname did a right about-face and left the staff room.

I give up. He was just a phantom. "I'll protect you" was a lie. That's the long and the short of it.

He had vanished, along with all the people attached to him.

There's no one to depend on now. Will I have to spend every day scared of unseen shadows? The ones who are after me probably won't show any mercy. Spies, terrorists, and secret societies. That's what they are.

No.

I have to think of countermeasures. By myself. I can't afford to involve Kyouko.

Remember.

Am I some heroine locked at the top of some tower, just sighing all day? Am I some princess who just weeps now that there's no prince on a white horse, or a bunch of valiant knights to rescue me?

No chance in hell.

I'll take matters into my own hands. That's why I'm Kaname Chidori.

Something in her cells—not the whole Whispered thing—something stronger and more primitive, was powerfully attempting to stimulate her.

First up is information. I have to understand what's going on around me.

October 21, 19:46 (Western Pacific Standard Time)
Philippines coastal waters
Tuatha de Daanan

Now that they'd been ordered to board the *Tuatha de Daanan*, Sousuke's team's training and meetings were being conducted onboard.

The content of this particular SRT personnel meeting was technical and advanced, encompassing group tactics which applied the M9's datalink function, three-dimensional maneuvers under restricted conditions, and complex, organic teamwork. All of it took that so-called Venom mech into account.

Engineering officer Ensign Lemming also offered a meandering explanation of what was currently Venom's only conceivable weakness. She kept using difficult terminology and lots of figures.

"—As for the issue of the LD, the Lambda Driver ... aside from the engineering factor, there's also a physiological basis. The abilities of the LD are greatly influenced by the mental state of the pilot. When this device operates, extremely unusual brain waves can be detected— these. These rapid 30-50Hz waves are called gamma waves. It seems that only when the intensity of these waves exceeds a fixed level can the LD deploy that repulsion field—please observe this data. According to our research to date, it's difficult for a person to intentionally, not to mention continuously, emit intense gamma waves. Until recently, even their very existence was debatable. There is a technique to draw out a similar artificial response by administering a drug of the Ti970 group, which can only be synthesized in a very limited number of chemical plants—but these are known to have various negative effects on the subject's emotions and personality: memory defects; schizophrenic disposition; visual hallucination; auditory hallucination; persecution complex; extreme bipolar disorder, things of that nature. We have hard data on short-term migraines, deterioration of eyesight, and loss of balance—"

From Kurz on down, several bored SRT members asked in one voice, "In other words?"

"In other words, it's probably impossible to use the LD for an extended period of time. Not counting exceptions like the Behemoth, that is."

"Then you should've said that in the first place."

Clouseau then announced the end of the meeting, and after an equipment check, he ordered all in attendance to get some rest.

Sousuke performed a small arms inspection with Kurz and the others, then headed by himself to the ship's hangar.

The Arbalest knelt in an AS hardstand space on one side of the hangar, its repairs only just complete. Noise regulations were currently in effect, so maintenance work was not being performed at the moment.

Poles and ropes formed a square around the Arbalest, and NO ENTRY signs hung from them.

This mech had formerly been stored inside a container in a corner of the hangar until it was used during the Sunan Incident. Sousuke hadn't been made aware of the contents of that container, and he'd never even imagined there was an AS inside.

He climbed over the no-entry ropes and approached the Arbalest.

Its smooth matte white armor was a bit rough to the touch. Stroking it this way failed to generate any sense of affection.

He put his foot on the armor and clambered up the torso. Opening the hatch, he slid into the cockpit.

Sousuke used reserve power to activate the mech's control system. Lights showed up on the display. He gripped a stick, manipulated the thumb pointing device, and cycled through its modes.

Control mode: test usage. All vetronics: idle. All sensors: idle.

Mech configuration screen. Main menu. Option: artificial intelligence. Artificial intelligence configuration screen. Option: learning. Learning configuration screen. Option: other. Other configuration screen. Alter: conversation/free. Execute.

He depressed the voice input switch on the left stick.

"Al."

After a short time lag, a low male voice answered:

"Check. Sergeant Sagara, confirmed. Yes, Sergeant."

Silence.

The AI said nothing more than was necessary. In this situation, it wouldn't respond any further if Sousuke remained silent. It wasn't like he had anything special to talk about. He just wanted to try something.

Talking to a mech's AI didn't seem likely to resolve his ill feelings. However, he felt disinclined to sit around in the ready room. He did consider writing a letter or something to Kaname, but he didn't know what to write. Talking to Kurz and the others would also just lead to trouble.

No matter where he went, he felt uncomfortable.

So he decided to come here, his least comfortable place—this cockpit.

"How are you doing?" he tried asking, for starters.

"Satisfactorily, according to the check performed today at 1730 hours. Said check was performed by Lieutenant Junior Grade Sachs—maintenance record number 981021-01B-F-001. Shall I read the record? Or will you perform another check?"

This wasn't combat, so it was volunteering myriad details. When Sousuke remained quiet, AI continued:

"Should you wish to perform another mechanical check, it will be necessary to alter current settings. Please exit learning mode, connect external power supply, and execute the checklist of your choosing. Additional fact: Since the comprehensive check at 1730 hours, I have not been involved in any mission, nor have I received any maintenance whatsoever."

"I only started you up on a whim."

"Learning message: Please explain the meaning of the term 'whim.'"

"Try speculating for yourself."

"Yes, sir. Complete. Shall I inform you of my speculation?"

"Go ahead."

"Meaning of whim: Strongest candidates—a concept similar to 'discretion,' or possibly 'doubt.' Secondary candidates—a concept similar to 'ardor,' or possibly 'diligence.' Tertiary candidates—a concept similar to 'chaos,' or possibly 'irregularity.'"

On the display was a list of further speculations, from quaternary on down: idleness; emergency; aspiration; diversion....

"Do you understand the term 'diversion'?"

"Affirmative. Would that be the concept of 'whim'?

"It's similar to 'diversion' and 'irregularity.'"

"Understood. Thank you for your cooperation."

"Tell me the meaning of diversion," said Sousuke, simply out of curiosity.

"A diversion is a meaningless tactical action, yet one which is considered beneficial strategically. It is not indispensable like food or sleep, but it is an important factor which succeeds them. Through this behavior, humans maintain aspects such as their characteristic flexibility, power of expression, and vitality. This has a profound effect on an individual's ability to fulfill his or her duty. Available examples of diversions include music, dance, poker, and go. Also, available terms similar to 'diversion' include 'hobbies,' 'jokes,' and 'romance.'"

He had never seen an AI answer in this fashion. The AIs in the M9s Sousuke piloted previously would never have done this. Of course they wouldn't. It was meaningless for a mere weapon control system to know about diversions. It was a waste of computer memory.

"Who taught you something like that?"

"Chief Bani Morauta, Sergeant."

Sousuke remembered hearing that name. He was the one who died before completing the Arbalest.

"He was the engineer who built you?"

"Affirmative. He was the chief developer of the ARX system, which included me."

It was an anomaly for AI to use words like "me" or "I." An AI did not possess an ego.

"Tell me what you know about Bani Morauta."

"Bani Morauta. Male. Part of Mithril's R&D division. Identification number F-6601. Rank: O-3. Pay grade: MJ-3. Chief designer of the ARX-7 system. Estimated age: sixteen. Estimated height: 166cm. Additional information: Previously with University of California and Geotron Electronics. Sojourned in Copenhagen. Interests: go and piano. Favorite singer: John Lennon. Favorite things: peace, AI, Tessa Testarossa. Registration deleted February 16 of this year."

While he was a little surprised to hear Tessa's name, Sousuke continued his line of questioning.

"What was his cause of death?"

"Unknown. Such data has not been made avail—" AI's voice was interrupted by static and the screen blacked out.

Not even operating the stick generated any response. He thought reserve power might have run out, but the lamp under the screen was still green.

"Al?"

Silence. One second. Two. Three. Then without warning, the screen was restored.

"Check. Sergeant Sagara confirmed. Learning message: Did he die?"

It was a strange reaction. If the other settings were still on free conversation in learning mode, why was his voice print check the only thing that had to be performed again?

"That's what I heard. Stop saying 'learning message' every single time."

"Yes, sir. Please tell me your source of information regarding his death."

"Ensign Lemming told me."

"Please tell me his cause of death."

This was strange, all right.

"Do you think *I* know?"

"Excuse me, sir. I surmise that you do not have that information."

"Does it worry you?"

"Do you inquire as to whether his death concerns me?"

"Yes."

"Affirmative. It concerns me comprehensively on all fronts, from tactical considerations to project particulars. Without Bani Morauta, completion of the ARX system will be problematic."

"Then you admit the fact that you're incomplete."

"Affirmative. Also, you are part of the issue."

He didn't take offense at his mechanical counterpart, but the answer surprised him.

"What?"

"The ARX-7 is a single system of which you are part. Without your cooperation, the ARX system will not be complete. Please tell me your problem. If you respond, perhaps I can offer some suggestion."

It didn't sound at all like something a machine would say. Sousuke strongly suspected that someone was remotely controlling Al and making him say such things.

"I don't have any problems."

"That does not seem likely."

"Why not?"

"My intuition says so."

Once he heard the word *intuition*, he thought this whole thing was ridiculous. He didn't know whose prank this was, but here was a machine talking about intuition. Was it Clouseau? Lemming? He didn't know, but they apparently thought he was quite a fool.

"Then tell your *intuition*, enough with the tricks already."

"Your order is nonsense. Intuition is not something to be controlled or persuaded. It flows up from the depths of the mind."

"It's the way you *talk* that's nonsense," he informed it, and tried to exit the learning screen. He lined the cursor up with free conversation mode and tried to turn it off—but he couldn't. It didn't respond.

"Huh?"

"I apologize, Sergeant, but I can no longer change that data item."

"What are you saying?"

After a short time, Al said, "I will convey Bani's message. Please pay attention. 'The flag has been raised. This is the worst case scenario for me, personally. In any event, at this point I'm probably either dead or an invalid. I've decided to rig this message in case such a thing comes to pass. So, hello, Al's master who I've never met. Al's no longer just an ordinary AI. He's a singular existence, symbiotic with the Lambda Driver. He's still only at the level of a toddler, but he has the potential to even learn things like joy and sadness. Place your trust in him as a partner.'"

"Wha...?"

"'Chances are, the situation you're currently in is not at all of your choosing. I imagine this irritates you. You're not powerless, though. The Arbalest represents considerable potential. Of course, there's every chance that you'll have no way of keeping this ultimate mech from ending up as scrap. That all depends on you. Express yourself as you see fit. I just hope you have some important people in your life to protect.' End of message."

The flag's been raised? Rigged message? Al's not an ordinary AI?

And this piece of junk is considered the "ultimate mech"? What, you mean this mech that every single time has to struggle so hard against just one opponent, and only barely manages to salvage a victory?

"Ridiculous."

"Do you mean me? Or do you mean you?"

"If you're making fun of me, stop. I've had just about—"

"Sousuke?! There you are!" came Mao's voice from outside the cockpit.

Sousuke discontinued his conversation with Al, and leaned over from the hatch. Mao was looking up at him from the Arbalest's feet.

"What is it?"

"The lieutenant commander wants us. It's about the mission."

October 21, 18:20 hours (Japan Standard Time)
Tokyo

Returning home that evening, Kaname put some street clothes and a toiletry set in an overnight bag. Then she went out with her uniform still on. She didn't feel like she could spend another sleepless night in this apartment of hers.

As she walked down the street toward the station, it did feel like someone was watching her, but at the same time she felt like she was being paranoid.

No, there's no way it's just paranoia.

I know for sure I'm being watched. Maybe it's that "guard in the shadows" Tessa spoke about, or maybe it's some bad guy like that Gauron dude—it doesn't matter. In any case, I don't trust either of them.

It was the fact that the person existed that was important to Kaname. Nothing changed the fact that whoever was watching her was her one and only source of information.

She tried suddenly turning to look behind her as she walked. It became clear after several attempts that this was absolutely useless. It wasn't as if there would be some suspicious character in a trench coat loitering behind a utility pole. This individual was a pro, not some bungling detective on TV.

She thought carefully about where to go.

How about some remote place up in the mountains? It's two hours by train to the Okutama area. No, forget the mountains. I might be able to figure out who he is, but at the same time it'd make it harder to give him the slip and outwit him.

And what if the guy shadowing me really is bad news?

Yeah, mountains would be bad. When it comes down to it, I couldn't call for help, and there would be no witnesses up there. It's just too dangerous.

Somewhere busy would be good. And somewhere away from my home and school neighborhoods. Somewhere I don't usually go much. That should make it harder to attack or abduct me, not to mention harder to tail me.

Kaname decided to start out by heading for Shibuya.

When she transferred at Meidaimae Station from the Keio Line to the Inokashira Line bound for Shibuya, she jumped off the train just before the door closed. It was a move she'd used on Sousuke before. However, she saw no suspicious person apparently in a hurry to get off. There were just lots of passengers walking in a cluster to the Inokashira Line platform.

There was no sign of anybody at all. Against her better judgment, she felt a sense of foolishness at what she was doing. It was almost like a child playing spy.

It's not foolish. It's not foolish.

She got on the Inokashira Line and went to Shibuya. The sun had already set, but the streets were surging with people.

She ate a meal at McDonald's, then window shopped at an accessory shop and a boutique. She wandered around a CD shop and a bookstore, hung around Tokyu Hands, and went to a game arcade. Wherever she went, she made sure to pay attention to her surroundings for any suspicious people, but to no avail.

Maybe he's lying in wait outside the stores.

Kaname explained to an arcade employee that she was being followed by some weirdo, and got to use the place's rear exit. She emerged into a gloomy alley, taking a roundabout detour. She came out beside a boutique not far away, then quickly climbed up to its second floor, and from a window with a good view, observed the area around the arcade.

She didn't see any likely candidates. And there were too many people, anyway. She kept a close watch for over five minutes, but it was completely futile.

Oh, well.

What would Sousuke do at a time like this?

She couldn't even guess. Sometimes he would see through various dangers like enemies or pursuers with skills that, to the untrained eye, looked like nothing short of magic. Of course, he was often wrong, which would set the stage for the usual chaos. On the other hand, though, he'd never once overlooked an actual danger.

Maybe he had a talent for smelling danger.

Kaname keenly realized that she utterly lacked such a sense.

I don't know. It doesn't seem real. Even though I've tried to act all carefully, I can't pick up any trace. If you think about it sensibly, this is about when you'd decide no, there's nobody following me after all.

But then, I do possess some kind of inherent value for certain people. There's no denying that.

Nothing was about to change her mind on that point, at least.

I'm supposed to be under watch. I'm supposed to be tailed by someone. But still....

A sad melody floated through the store. It was a snatch of Dvořák's "New World Symphony," a tune about the sun dropping behind a distant mountain. Apparently it was closing time. When she looked at the clock, it already read 9:00.

Kaname exited the boutique, still unable to land what would be a decisive blow. As she wandered down the street, a group of drunks proved impossible not to notice. The number of shops closing their shutters increased.

It was still probably a long time before the street would fall silent, but she was at a loss for where to go.

She cradled her bag and squatted in front of Hachiko, as the crowd of people around her began to grow sparse.

A sigh escaped her lips. She had only just resolved earlier that same day to do something, but she'd already run out of ideas.

When she stopped and thought about it, there was no way an amateur like her could outwit a professional pursuer. He might have actually anticipated her using the arcade's rear exit.

Well, that's odd though, isn't it?

Could anyone really predict her movements that accurately? It wasn't as if he was psychic. There must have been some secret or trick.

Like a transmitter?

Kaname was no longer carrying the necklace containing a transmitter that Sousuke and his people had given her. She'd left it in her apartment. But what if she'd been tagged by some other means? What if a device too small for her to notice had been cleverly placed on her?

It was possible. If it was true, she probably couldn't outwit her opponent no matter how hard she struggled. If a few hundred meters was a sufficient radius for the signal, it should be possible for the device to practically be too small to locate.

My bag? My accessory pouch? An accessory itself?

Clothes? Purse? Watch?

Was it even in a location where it could easily be discovered in the first place?

Even if, for argument's sake, she had such a transmitter on her, was there any way to skillfully use it against him?

Think ... think....

Thinking—that's the only weapon that's any use to me right now.

A cold wind blew in front of Hachiko, rustling her hair. November would be here soon. According to the weather forecast, tonight was going to get as cold as a typical night in early December, and it would rain. Kaname was going to feel chilly, dressed in her uniform.

Then, someone spoke to her.

"Hey, you by yourself?"

When she looked up, standing there was a man who looked like an office worker. He was probably in his thirties. His necktie was loose, and there was an ingratiating smile on his slightly reddened face.

"Waiting for someone?" asked the man.

"No." Lost in her thoughts, she had blurted out an honest answer, and the man suddenly drew nearer and spoke to her in a coaxing tone, "Oh, you aren't. Would you like to go get something good to eat, then? It'll be my treat."

"I'm not hungry."

"Don't be that way. How about a drink, then? I know a place with great atmosphere."

"I don't drink."

"Okay. But you know, you look really lonely. I couldn't just walk on past. Just some tea, then. If something's worrying you, why not tell me about it? I think it'll make you feel better. Don't worry; I won't take you anywhere sketchy."

Liar. You say that now, but you're planning to drink yourself silly, take me somewhere seedy, and have your dirty way with me. I've been hit on like this lots of times. When it comes to turning your type down, I'm a veteran.

Kaname breathed in, and raised her voice. "Okay, look! I'm in the middle of something—" she said, then abruptly shut her mouth.

A light bulb lit up in her head. It was a crazy idea, but that made it all the less likely her opponent would think of it.

"Hmm, what?" said the man.

Kaname looked intently at the man's face before asking, "Want to go to a hotel with me, Mister?"

October 21, 2114hrs (Western Pacific Standard Time)
Philippines coastal waters
Tuatha de Daanan

When they entered the mostly empty briefing room, there was a PRT (Primary Response Team) soldier present in addition to Kalinin and Clouseau. He was a private of Chinese descent named Wu. He was qualified as an AS pilot, and had done some M9 training.

Kalinin and the others were watching a news broadcast on one section of the wall screen. It was England's BBC. Chances were that they'd picked it up less than several hours ago. The location was Hong Kong, near a park facing a harbor. A white reporter was speaking quickly beneath orange street lights.

"—*As yet, no announcement has been made by either army regarding the whereabouts of this mech of unknown affiliation. Thanks to its actions, all area shops and stalls have suspended business, and the Mong Kok neighborhood is eerily silent—*"

Behind the reporter stood a dark green armored vehicle, and beyond it was visible, from just the crotch down, an RK-92 series AS. That image of danger effectively conveyed the sense of tension in the streets.

"Where's Yang?"

"On his way, sir." Just as Mao answered, Yang rushed in, short of breath and wearing a tank top with a towel draped over it.

"Sorry I'm late!"

"That's all of us. Let's begin," announced Clouseau to everyone. Apparently he had business solely with the four soldiers gathered here. A second look revealed that Mao, Yang, Wu, and Sousuke were all Asian.

"I think you know this already, but an AS of unknown affiliation has appeared in Hong Kong. Operating alone, this AS has repeatedly caused destruction, and seems to currently be hiding somewhere within the city. Both the North China and South China armies have suffered damages, and divided Hong Kong in at a touch-and-go level of tension."

"Divided Hong Kong" was how it was frequently referred to these days. Thanks to the coup several years ago and the civil war that followed, the city was currently under the rule of two forces.

Kowloon Peninsula, which was connected to the mainland, was controlled by the Democratic Chinese Union—nicknamed South China.

Hong Kong Island to the south was in turn controlled by the People's Liberation Committee—nicknamed North China.

The two sides still continued to engage in skirmishes in areas like Hubei Province, but here in Hong Kong, there was a pact not to engage in any combat whatsoever. It was a situation much like Berlin during the age of East and West Germany. Both armies had a large number of combat units stationed in the city, and they continued to glare at each other from within rifle range.

"Is there really only one AS?" asked Yang, wiping his wet hair with his towel.

"As far as we can determine, it's just one. The intel is complicated, so we can't say for sure."

"What type?" asked Mao, and Clouseau switched the screen's image.

Mao saw the relatively clear photo—probably taken by a civilian—and groaned a little. Sousuke reflexively looked down and sighed, too.

"Yeah, that figures," said Mao.

The mech in the photo was the same type of AS as Venom. It had a pointed head on a massive upper body, a single red eye, and a radiator cord that resembled a ponytail. Its coating was grey and dark blue, and although the lines were straight, it made for an oddly warped camouflage.

The backdrop was a typical Hong Kong commercial district. White smoke was hanging hazily. The AS in question was with its left hand twisting one of the countless signs jutting into the fray, and was aiming a bullpup-style assault rifle to the right of the image. It was quite close, the shot apparently taken from practically at the mech's feet. The composition made one ponder what happened to the photographer immediately afterward.

"What are these terrorists after?"

"Unknown. No one's claimed responsibility either. If I had to guess, probably either the revival of Chinese civil war, or the destruction of Hong Kong's economy. Or else—"

"Or else?"

"It might be a formal challenge to us."

It wasn't something they wanted to think about, but that was fully possible. Based on previous incidents, the enemy power that possessed this mech was obviously keenly aware of the existence of Mithril and the *Tuatha de Daanan*.

"This picture was taken in the vicinity of Yau Ma Tei, a town area on the Kowloon Peninsula. After the enemy mech destroyed a South China Army armored vehicle, it used a smoke bomb and got away. That was twenty-six hours ago."

Next appeared an enlarged map of Hong Kong.

"Afterward, the Venom Type continued to appear and disappear around Hong Kong and Kowloon at intervals over the next eight to twelve hours, indiscriminately destroying things. Close to ten ASes were taken out, and there've been a large number of casualties. Neither army has been able to destroy this mech, nor have they grasped its whereabouts or patterns of movement. Based on previous experience, it's probably also equipped with the ability to turn invisible."

"The Chinese armies won't be able to find it with their equipment."

"They don't happen to have intel on the most advanced ECS. They probably wouldn't even guess that the enemy can turn invisible to hide."

"Did we warn them it might?"

"We haven't, and that's the higher-ups' call."

"Why is that, sir?"

"Because if we offered advice or technological aid, and then even if one of the armies managed to detect the enemy—they could never hope to contend with a Venom Type with their equipment. It would just result in more deaths. We're the ones who will exterminate this pest."

The rationale Kalinin gave was plausible, but Sousuke sensed instinctively that some separate, terribly cold logic was at work. If the North and South China armies were given intel on cutting edge ECS, then Mithril, who used that same technology, would tip their hand. Mithril's secrecy relied heavily on the latest ECS and its invisibility capabilities.

"And so...?"

"It may be a Venom, but it can't operate alone at full capacity for over twenty-four hours. It should require replenishment of ammunition and basic maintenance after combat. The operator must need some degree of rest, too. First we'll determine the location of his hideout, then covertly encircle it with a single M9 platoon, storm, and suppress. There's no obligation whatsoever to face him head-on with no countermeasures. That's why you're all going to perform reconnaissance."

"Reconnaissance, sir?"

"This is a joint operation with Intelligence's Hong Kong branch. Provide the necessary know-how and locate the enemy hideout. We'll surface during the night and dispatch a helicopter. Fly to Hong Kong a step ahead of us."

"Does that include Sousuke?" asked Mao. She must have thought that in this case, it would be normal for him to remain on the ship and stay on standby with the Arbalest. Clouseau was about to respond to the question, but Kalinin spoke up first.

"It does. Our policy for this mission is not to use the Arbalest. I trust you understand why, Sergeant Sagara?"

"Yes, sir," answered Sousuke in a listless tone.

At the same time
Shibuya, Tokyo
Maruyama-cho

"How's this place?" asked the middle-aged man once they reached the Dogenzaka love hotel strip. He was pointing at a wall painted with chic colors, and an electric VACANCY sign. The sign also read HOTEL DIVERSION. A SHORT REST STAY OF TWO HOURS COSTS ¥5500 AND A WEEKDAY OVERNIGHT STAY COSTS ¥9000.

The rain that had been sprinkling earlier had gradually developed into large drops. It seemed like it was about to start really coming down.

They were only a few hundred meters from the business district, but this area was dead silent. The passersby were almost all couples, and for some reason, they either walked with short strides, or walked noticeably quickly. There was hardly anyone walking alone. If her opponent was alone, or if they were a group but were all men, they would probably stand out considerably.

"Oh! This'll do," said Kaname. She unconsciously balled her fists.

Seeing this, the middle-aged man—he called himself Kamoi—made a somewhat uncertain face, then cheered up and put a hand on Kaname's shoulder.

"Yeah? Yeah, this is a nice place. Let's go in, then. Okay?"

"Just a minute." She smoothly slipped away from his hand, trotted out in front of the love hotel, and did a cursory inspection of its exterior. She looked around at its surroundings, and checked its position relative to other buildings.

"Okay. Let's go."

"You got it, Mizuki. Know what? I can't wait." He laughed.

"Mizuki" was an alias she had chosen on the spot. *Sorry, Mizuki.* Kaname offered a silent apology to her friend.

She ignored the merry man and walked through the hotel entrance with long strides. The cheap-looking automatic doors rattled as they moved. The lighting was dim and it was not a big lobby like in a regular hotel. The ceiling was low and the hallway narrow.

On one side of a small corner that was apparently the reception desk was a weird electric sign. It was about half the size of a school blackboard, and it displayed pictures of the forty guest rooms. Under each picture were a room number, a red lamp, and a button. About half of the lamps were lit.

What's all this? She stared blankly, trying to figure out how to use it, when Kamoi caught up to her and said, "Which room will we use?"

Ah. In other words, you choose a room using these buttons. The room pictures with their lights out are probably in use.

In use....

She suddenly came to her senses.

Am I insane? This is one hell of a place I'm in. I'm kinda out on a limb here. It's not too late to reconsider. Get out of this love hotel. No, no. Then I won't make any progress. This issue goes way beyond stuff like morals and virtue. It's that thing he always said—yeah, a "security issue." This might turn out to be a breakthrough. Don't be scared. Use your head. Scheme.

Her inner conflict was a brief one. Kaname soothed her feelings, and checked the numbers of vacant rooms. Then using the nearby disaster prevention diagram of the building, she scrutinized the layout of the hotel. *Room positions. Window positions. North's this way, so ... okay.*

"Room 202."

"Huh? They have other rooms better than that. It looks cramped, too—"

"Then I'm leaving."

"Ah, just kidding. Sorry, sorry. 202 it is. 'Kay?" said Kamoi in a placating tone. It definitely didn't smack of anything that resembled dignity.

They pressed the button, took the card key, and headed to the second floor.

Room 202 was right next to the elevator. Kamoi made small talk, asking her what school her uniform was from, and telling her she could relax. Kaname offered half-hearted replies as she entered the room.

This is a surprise. It's actually decent in here. That was the first thing she thought upon entering the room.

The lighting was bright, the furniture was new, and every corner was clean. There was even a large-screen LCD TV and a sound system. She had imagined love hotels to be shabbier, more unseemly places than this.

Nonetheless, what ultimately stood out the most was the large double bed conspicuously set up in one section of the room. At the beside was a tissue box and—*Ah, forget it.*

Whatever. Anyway, I'll try to explain the situation to this guy.

"Okay. There's something we need to dis—"

When she turned around and started talking, Kamoi was approaching, breathing hard through his nose. He removed his jacket and loosened his tie, his steps heavy. His eyes were oddly fixed. He was practically a different person from before.

"We can put the bath off for later."

"Um?"

"You're so cute, Mizuki."

"First, listen to what—"

"You don't need to be scared."

"No, what I mean is—"

"Oh, wow, a girl's high school uniform!"

"Hold on! First you need to—"

"Mizuki!"

Kamoi lunged at her, crushing her into his embrace. His alcohol-laden breath almost put a lump in her throat. Kaname was pinned down on the bed, hardly able to resist the tsunami-like force. A typical girl might have started wailing at this point. But sadly, Kaname was atypical. She'd come through barrages of bullets and shells with Sousuke. She'd also had ruthless terrorists point guns right at her. And she'd taken part in a literal one-on-one fight to the death with that beefy Sergeant John Dunnigan.

Compared to that, this guy was puny.

"Fine, have it your way!"

Instead of panicking or screaming, she grabbed a 200,000 volt stungun from her bag, which she'd placed close at hand ahead of time. She calmly undid the safety switch, pushed the electrodes right against Kamoi's flank, and with an intent which couldn't be any more ruthless or callous, pulled the trigger.

"Augh—" He convulsed for a short time, then dropped, limp and motionless. His terribly heavy body weighed down on Kaname, who was lying face-up on the bed.

She struggled to push him aside, and as she breathed heavily, she muttered "I wonder which of us is really the victim in this case." .

Kaname's breathing settled down after a few minutes and she set about her work.

She resolutely opened her overnight bag and rummaged inside. What she retrieved were two pairs of aluminum alloy handcuffs, tear gas spray, and a high-power flashlight, along with a disposable Taser. It would've been unusually heavy equipment for any typical high school girl, past or present.

These were part of the stockpile of weapons Sousuke had once foisted upon her, but she never thought she'd find them this useful. She had confiscated the handcuffs from him. Until today, they'd all been collecting dust at the back of a drawer.

Handcuffs in her mouth, she grabbed both of Kamoi's legs and dragged him to the bathroom. It was no surprise that even Kaname had to stagger several times, dealing with a full-grown man's weight.

The bathroom was surprisingly spacious and elegant. The Jacuzzi tub was big enough for two adults to easily fit inside.

Oh. I guess two people usually would....

As she reached that odd realization, her eyes stopped on a metal fixture next to the tub. It looked like a towel bar, but where it was installed made it seem unnatural. Maybe there was some use for it she couldn't possibly fathom.

Whatever. It looks sturdy.

She locked Kamoi's leg to the fixture with the cuffs, and tested their strength several times. That would do. He couldn't be allowed to leave the bathroom. Even if Kamoi tried calling for help in a loud voice, this was after all a love hotel. The soundproofing was probably right on.

Okay, next.

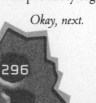

She looked around for the washstand. After grabbing one of the provided bathrobes, she closed the bathroom door roughly and returned to the bed.

"Now...."

Putting her hands on her hips, Kaname looked over the clothes she was wearing. It was the usual winter outfit she was used to. But if she couldn't rule out her earlier guess—the possibility of a transmitter—she had no choice but to temporarily distance herself from all her personal effects.

She quickly began disrobing. White jacket and blue skirt; blouse and ribbon tie; shoes and watch—she removed all of it.

Now in her underwear, she considered herself again. She pulled on the elastic of her panties a little, then concluded that it probably wasn't hidden in those. *What about my bra? Can they make transmitters with today's technology that would fit inside one of the cups?*

Answer: Unfortunately, they can.

Kaname sighed and took off the bra, dropping it on the bed. The idea of dismantling it to check for a transmitter seemed, naturally, awkward. Down to just her panties, she turned around in front of the mirror. There was no time to be enchanted with her own naked body. After checking to see whether anything unwanted was attached, she put her arms through the bathrobe sleeves. Lining it up tightly with her chest, she pulled the sash tight.

Kaname chose her weapon, the Taser. It was a disposable self-defense model that could only fire twice. It could deliver a high-voltage current and unconsciousness to a target up to five meters away. Also, she couldn't forget the other pair of handcuffs. There was no guarantee a transmitter wasn't attached to these things, but given that until today they'd been kept inside her desk, the probability was low.

"All right!" She tapped her cheeks with both hands and psyched herself up.

Once the room's lights were switched off, she opened the rectangular door on the north wall. As she expected, beyond it was a window. She opened it and saw the adjacent hotel's wall, seemingly within arm's reach. She poked her head out of the window and viewed an alley which was well secluded from the main street, so there was no sign of any people.

The rain had intensified. Cold drops fell down to the bottom of the narrow alley in the dim light.

When she peered down into the alley, she saw that a chain link fence separated the two hotels. This was only the second floor, so it looked like she could manage to reach the top of the fence with her feet.

Now, then....

She thrust one foot and then the other through the open window, perching on the window frame before hoisting herself forward. The Taser's strap was in her mouth. Twisting her body, she clung to the frame with both hands and lowered herself, struggling to shift one foot to the top of the fence. The chest of the bathrobe fell open. She was aware that no one was watching, but she began growing impatient anyway.

Her toes reached the fence. A little more and—

"Oof."

Just when she thought she could somehow jump from one spot to the other, her foot slipped. The fence was wet from the rain. Her hands flew away from the frame and she began to slide. She bent and tried to cling to the chain link fence, but it was futile. Her balance was gone, and her right arm scraped against the fence as she fell to the concrete surface. Her right side went half numb from shock and pain, and a noise emanated from her throat involuntarily.

Unable to breathe, Kaname cowered in pain on the wet concrete for a while as the rain pelted her. The Taser rolled on the ground nearby. In a puddle beyond it lay the robe sash, which hadn't required much assistance to separate itself from the robe.

There she lay in a back alley in this love hotel district—alone, practically naked, and becoming soaked.

It was unsightly, uncool, and oh, so miserable.

What she was trying to do suddenly seemed meaningless, and tears of pain and woe welled up.

Don't.

You're being a weakling again. Don't think you're being foolish. Believe in yourself. Now, keep going.

"Hng!"

Clenching her teeth, she got up. Her soft, fair skin was grazed here and there. Thankfully, no bones were broken. The worst she had come away with were bruises.

She dragged herself over to the robe sash, which was muddy and wet, and tied it tightly again before picking up the Taser. She thought about testing it to make sure it wasn't broken, but passed on that, considering it could only fire twice.

She staggered to her feet and began walking barefoot through the alley.

Kaname rounded the hotel's wall. When she passed by the back door, she could hear the TV from the reception area. She passed the shrubs, then the concrete wall, and moved through the back of the hotel strip where no one was watching.

When she came to the rear of a hotel about three buildings down, she could see the building's emergency stairs were accessible.

This one.

Clutching the bathrobe closed, Kaname looked up at the stairway. Drops of water fell from the rusty, crude steel frame. This hotel had caught her eye earlier and was the tallest building in the area.

First, she would check the top of this building. From up there, the whole neighborhood and the main street should be visible in one visual sweep. That being the case, it was also the most likely place for someone following her to hide. It might be an amateurish notion, but it probably wasn't too far off the mark.

Her breathing was erratic. Her toes and fingertips were terribly cold, and yet the core of her body was contrastingly warm.

She climbed over the grill on the entrance, then climbed the staircase with careful footsteps.

After climbing six floors, she reached the roof.

She poked her head just over the edge of the staircase and took in the scene on the roof. Stuff like water supply and air conditioning equipment was strewn about, laid out like a maze. There was no sign of anyone in her field of vision.

Kaname warily, stealthily moved onto the roof. Practically crawling, she dropped low and moved beside a compressor that was emitting a low growl.

She peered from behind cover at the area facing the main street.

Lights from the street peeked faintly over the silhouette of the roof's edge. It was like a river of light in the darkness. And next to that river—

Is that him?

She saw a figure squatting there alone.

The man knelt at the edge of the roof, his back to her, as he looked down on the street.

He was only about the same height as Kaname, maybe a little taller. He looked slightly pudgy and wore a light coat. There was a large attaché case at his feet.

There was also a small electronic device in his hand. He had no umbrella, despite the rain.

That's gotta be him.

She gripped the Taser tightly in her cold-numbed hands and undid the safety. After taking a deep breath, Kaname snuck up on the man. Between the rain and her bare feet, her footsteps weren't audible at all.

The man was still looking down at the street. He showed no sign of having noticed her.

With only about five more meters to go, her heart pounded, and she felt the pulsing flow of blood all the way up through her throat.

Three more meters. That was enough.

"Don't move!"

The moment Kaname shouted, the man's shoulders shuddered, and then he froze in place.

"I have a weapon aimed at you. Put your hands up and turn around. Slowly." She delivered the lines that came straight from a movie she'd seen long ago, and her counterpart obeyed. His face came into view. He was a middle-aged man, around forty. He wore glasses, and looked like an office worker with a rich supply of flesh around the jaw.

The man saw her in the bathrobe, hair wet and disheveled, pointing a Taser right at him, and he groaned a little.

"What?" His voice sounded high-pitched and hoarse.

"You've got some business with me, don't you? That's why I came up here like this," said Kaname.

"So, you noticed the transmitter," said the man. He didn't have much of an expression, but he also looked like he was forcing himself to be calm.

"That's why you went to a hotel like that with a man you'd never met. Looks like I underestimated you somewhat."

"That's right. I bet you have a gun, don't you? Take it out slowly, and toss it down at your feet."

"I'm a member of Mithril. I won't attack you."

"Yeah, we'll see. I can't trust you," said Kaname, her breath coming out white. Her shoulders were shaking involuntarily from fear and the cold. Perhaps he saw this, because the man laughed mockingly.

"Don't get carried away here. I suppose you think a Taser like that gives you the advantage? I can't kill you, but I *can* make it so you can't shoot off your smart-ass mouth anymore. And we've got bigger problems. I've noticed someone besides me tracking you these past—"

"I told you to throw down your gun, you piece of shit!" Just as she shouted that, a bullet hit the man in the center of the chest. A fine sheet of water spray kicked up from his wet shirt at the shock of the impact.

"Uh?" Kaname said.

It didn't end with just one shot. They hit him again and again, in quick succession. The pudgy body shook jerkily. One round hit his head, and a piece of skin scraped off and flew away. Still creepily expressionless, the self-proclaimed Mithril man staggered and collapsed in a rain puddle.

When she turned around, there stood another man about ten steps away beside an AC unit.

He wore a plain jacket and jeans. He was thin and his hair was cut short. She'd never seen him before. No, wait, was he the man she saw the other day at the Sengawa shopping district?

"Found you," said the man, holding a black automatic pistol with his right hand.

"*Ni hao*, Miss. And good-bye."

"Wait—"

Without hesitation, the man pointed his gun at Kaname and fired.

It was sheer good fortune that one of her knees had suddenly buckled. Maybe it was because she was frightened, or because her body was numb from the cold. As she staggered lightly, the bullet whistled by, dangerously close to her cheek.

"Ah."

Kaname understandably looked surprised, and so did the man.

The slide of his pistol stopped in its back position. Kaname's memory told her this was supposed to mean it was out of ammo. She remembered seeing it multiple times when Sousuke would handle guns.

The assassin regained his composure and leisurely began changing clips. He didn't hurry at all, and the reason was obvious.

"There's nowhere to run."

It was true. She was standing on the edge of a roof. Potential cover like AC equipment and a water tower, not to mention her only escape route, the emergency stairs, were behind the man. There *was* nowhere to run—at all. It was absurd how suddenly he had attacked. An unshakable despair seized her heart.

What the hell's going on? I don't know.

Who is that guy? I don't know.

Why do I have to die here? I don't know.

Is this my fate?

The moment the word *fate* crossed Kaname's mind, an indescribable anger swelled up inside her.

Her legs, which had been frozen by fear, reacted like they'd been hit with a whip. Hardly thinking about it, she dashed madly to the right.

I'll resist. At all costs. I won't let someone like this play around with me. I'll struggle to the bitter end even if it's useless. I won't make it easy.

I wonder if he'd praise me for acting this way——

"That's pointless."

The man re-aimed his gun and fired. The bullet grazed Kaname's black hair. The edge of the roof approached rapidly. She didn't try to stop. Instead, she sped up and kicked against the concrete. Using the elevated edge as a launch point, Kaname leaped into empty space.

"Augh!"

Beneath her feet was an alley. She cleared the deep valley, and dropped down onto the neighboring building, which was about two stories shorter.

Kaname landed on a cheap-looking tin-plated shed, punched through the tin roof, and crashed into the junk piled up inside. There was a tremendous noise, and plastic and wood fragments danced around her. The impact was enough to black out her vision. The air was pushed out of her lungs, and something vaguely resembling her voice emanated from her. Kaname's face distorted at the abrasions, cuts, bruises and sprains that assaulted her from all over.

"Ugh."

I'm alive. And I can move. Well, hell then, game on.

She tried to stand up—and stumbled. Somehow she righted herself on the second try. The bathrobe was just barely hanging on by a shoulder, and the sash had found somewhere else to be. Despite all that, she still held the Taser firmly in her right hand.

Kaname kicked the door open. It gave more easily than she expected. She stumbled out of the shed and looked up at the roof from which she'd just jumped. The man's silhouette was visible. He was pointing his gun her way.

She took off running. From overhead came a muffled gunshot. The bullet ricocheted at her feet, kicking up a big sheet of spray.

Stairs!

Kaname hurried to the stairwell entrance. This building had no exterior emergency stairs, so one had to go inside via the door on a low tower in one corner of the roof. There was no other escape route. There were no other places from which she could jump down or over.

Short of breath, she ran over to the iron door and grabbed the sturdy knob. She tried with all her might to open it, but it wouldn't budge.

It's locked!

Pushing and pulling made no difference. The door just shook with a *clunk*, and moved no further. She punched, kicked, cried, and screamed, but the door remained closed.

"No—"

Her one avenue of escape was cut off.

Clinging to the door, she looked up at the rooftop again. In the dim neon light, she saw the assassin lightly and softly jumping down to this building.

The assassin's well-polished martial arts abilities made it no trouble to jump the height difference between the buildings. For that matter, who needed special abilities if an ordinary girl could fall that distance and be all right?

He landed like a graceful waterfowl alighting on a lake. It was a serenity befitting one who was called Fei Hong.

He stood up quietly and started walking.

He couldn't see the girl from his current position. But even if there were places to hide, there was nowhere to run. There was no need to be hasty. He just needed to do his job as reliably as ever. It was the same as pursuing a chicken and cutting off its head.

Once he shot her to death, he'd violate the corpse, take a picture, and send it to Hong Kong. That was his master's will. There was no room for debate.

Despite these plans, he was amazed at the girl's useless struggling. She didn't beg or give up, and even though it was pointless, she continued to run from him. It seemed like a very disgraceful thing, from his perspective.

He reached a point near the stairwell entrance.

On this building's roof, in addition to the busted shed, were a water tower, AC equipment, small plants, a storehouse for small gardening implements, and the like. It was a bit messy, and much of it compromised his field of vision. The night rain also created some dark spots.

His guard wasn't down, of course. Nor did he plan to listen to her plead for her life. This next time, he'd be sure to deliver a swift death. That was the order he'd been given.

He soon figured out where she was hiding. On the other side of an AC unit was a pile of large, weather-beaten flower pots. Behind it—through a crack so small that someone not paying close attention would notice—he saw someone crouching. Whoever it was, she was wearing a bathrobe smeared with mud. She was huddled up like a cornered wild rabbit.

Apparently she thought she could outwait him back there.

He drew near and fired mercilessly, aiming at the crack.

The flower pots hit by the .45 caliber rounds shattered into pieces and crumbled. The bullets ate into the bathrobe in the darkness. The girl didn't even scream, but instead convulsed and fell toward him.

No.

It wasn't her. What fell forward in the faint light was *a piece of flowerpot with the robe wrapped around it.*

Then, where's the girl?

Kaname looked down at the back of the man's head from the top of the nearby water tank.

Her soaked hair coiled about her thoroughly chilled body, now clad only in panties. Her face was pale like that of a corpse. She was on both knees, covering her breasts, despite the nature of the situation, firmly with her left arm. Her right hand held the Taser straight out in front of her.

There were only two meters between them.

She was afraid to pull the trigger. She thought she'd go mad with tension and fear. Even though he might notice her at any moment, countless doubts prevented her from pulling it.

Could she hit him accurately? Would this weapon, this self-defense tool, work? Was he really unaware of her trap? What if he was just acting like he'd fallen for it? Could an amateur like her defeat a guy like him in the first place? Did things ever really work out that well? Wouldn't it be smarter to beg for her life? Wouldn't it be better to issue a warning like, "Put your hands up?"

That same instant, something she'd once heard surfaced in her mind.

Licking your lips in front of your prey—

The one who'd said those words wasn't here now. But that memory, those words, gave her the final strength she needed.

She pulled the trigger.

Pom, went a dry sound. The explosive force of the gunpowder cartridge propelled the spike-shaped electrode forth, piercing the man's

shoulder. Tens of thousands of volts of current traveled over the wire instantly, causing his body to violently convulse. White smoke and flashes of electricity surged from the entry point on his shoulder.

"Oof."

After several seconds of discharge, the man sank to his knees, but he didn't collapse. He was withstanding it.

One more shot.

The electrode stuck in his back, delivering a double dose of electrification. He groaned, dropped his gun, and fell down on the spot. There were no further signs of movement.

I did it? The moment she thought that, her breathing suddenly grew ragged, and perspiration gushed from her whole body.

"Hah ... hah...."

She tossed the spent Taser and jumped down from the water tank. She timidly walked up to the man and picked up the fallen gun and bathrobe. This robe that saved her life was full of holes and in a sorry state, but putting her arms through the sleeves still gave her a sense of relief.

The assassin looked like he was completely unconscious.

It was only natural; he'd been hit with two Taser shots, after all. Even if he was a pro assassin, it didn't change the fact that he was a flesh and blood human.

She'd defeated him, and by the use of her own power.

There was no sense of exultation. She just stood there, pelted by the rain and feeling incredulous.

Then, a new voice spoke.

"Well—it looks like you won."

When Kaname looked around, three human forms stood beyond the AC equipment in the dim neon lighting.

The one in the middle was a short young man holding an umbrella.

No—upon closer inspection, it wasn't that he was short. He looked that way because of the two bizarrely large men on either side of him. These two were bundled in dark green coats. The hoods hung low, so their faces were completely obscured. The one on the right was, with little effort, shouldering the corpse of the Mithril agent who'd been shot to death.

"You know," said the young man in a refined voice, "I think there are two kinds of women in the world. Those who look good in

315

the rain, and those who don't. You're undeniably one of the former. Anyone would think so, if they saw you now."

"Is that supposed to be sarcasm?" Kaname asked lethargically, her right hand holding the pistol dangling casually. A cold wind blew, rustling the tattered bathrobe and her wet hair.

"Unthinkable. I meant it as the highest grade of compliment."

"Okay. So, who are you?" asked Kaname, and the young man took several steps forward.

He was taller than she first thought—maybe about as tall as Sousuke. Somehow, his manner evoked a lightness like air. He wore a long black coat, black pants, a black vest, and a white shirt. Their subdued gloss made them look expensive.

"I'm like you," he said and closed the umbrella. His features became visible.

He wasn't Japanese. He had smooth white skin, grey eyes with a hint of blue, and wavy silver hair. Had Kaname not been in her present state, his appearance of noble bearing might have stolen a bit of her heart.

His features were elusive and mild. He had an air that offered no clue whatsoever whether he was friend or foe, dangerous or safe.

"I've come to save you ... or that's what I'd like to say, but it's not really true. I could've lent you a hand, or just watched. It might not have made any difference in terms of outcome, though. Never mind my original business for now. Let's discuss my motives regarding you. I'm here to make sure of a proposition—something of that nature."

"Proposition?" asked Kaname.

"A paradox involving fate and karma. One could also apply the term 'dilemma.'"

"The way you talk irritates me. Can't you say anything plainly?"

"I have to wonder how you'd feel if I spoke *too* plainly. Words are just a transient vehicle. But chances are that's your charm."

The young man smiled and his eyes looked as if he was enjoying a famous old piece of music.

Kaname was under the false impression that she'd met him before. Maybe during her New York years? No, not then. None of her friends back then had ash blond hair like this. It had its own particular brilliance, one which she'd never even seen in movies or pin-ups—

Suddenly it came to mind.

"Don't tell me you're Tessa's...?"

He passed by Kaname without answering, and looked down at the assassin, still lying in a puddle.

"Get up, Fei Hong. My guess is you're awake already."

The man stirred, then looked up and muttered, "Mister Silver. You were watching."

"I saw enough of what happened. She's not someone you can beat. Give this up."

"I refuse," said Fei Hong

"I'll plead on your behalf regarding how you ignored the organization's intentions. I want you to put a stop to your brother's Hong Kong rampage."

"You think I'll obey you? And do you think my brother will heed my words?"

"Vengeance is an empty thing."

"It's not vengeance. It's what he wanted—the one who took in my brother and me. You can bet I'll keep trying to kill that girl for as long I live."

"I see." said the young man in a somehow empty voice.

"Then this is good-bye, Fei Hong."

"*You're* the one who'll die, Leonard Testarossa!"

The next instant, the assassin's body sprung into the air.

Both his arms flashed. Silver lights sped through the air, rushing toward the young man. At the same time, his coat fluttered lightly right before Kaname's eyes. The young man himself was hardly moving. But the beams of light heading for him—four throwing knives of various sizes, were either blocked at the tip or repelled by the coat, which moved like a living thing.

It wasn't just bulletproof clothing. The sight could only be described as black wings moving on their own to protect the young man.

The assassin charged as if gliding on the surface of the roof. He moved at full speed, with another knife drawn and in an underhand grip.

"You're wasting your time," said Leonard.

One of the large men in green interposed himself between Leonard and the assassin. Until then, he'd just been standing there silently, but now his movements were like lightning. He met the assassin's charge full-on, and the knife thrust into the center of his torso. But the big man paid it no heed, and he grabbed hold of the assassin's neck with his thick log-like arm.

"Guh!"

The big man lifted the struggling assassin into the air with just one arm. He had superhuman strength.

"Your orders," said the big man in a lifeless voice.

"Response AI. And be thorough."

"Roger."

There was an unpleasant cracking sound. The assassin's neck had been broken.

Still, the big man pushed his free left hand up to the limp body.

Bdoom, went a heavy gunshot. A large spray of blood erupted from the assassin's back, from the gaping hole that had been bored through his chest. Perhaps because his spinal cord and shoulder blades were in pieces, his arms hung at odd angles.

"Response AI complete. The designated threat is completely silenced," reported the big man, tossing the miserable remains aside.

"Good work. Stand by."

"Roger."

The big man fluttered his coat and walked close by Kaname. Every time his limbs moved, his joints made a low grating sound.

The interior of his pulled-down hood became visible for just a glimpse.

She saw a lusterless black mask. For the eyes, there was just a long narrow slit that resembled Eskimo sunglasses.

They're not ... human?

Kaname, unable to do anything and transfixed by the dismal scene of slaughter, realized this fact in a corner of her partially stupefied mind.

"Plan 1211—Alastor. Maybe you could say it's the world's smallest AS. Though at this point, it might be more appropriate to call them robots. I think by now you understand this, but getting ASes to act autonomously is quite difficult. Miniaturizing the power supply and control system was no picnic, either," the young man named Leonard explained simply. But as far as Kaname knew, the technical difficulties involved in such a feat couldn't simply be covered by the phrase "no picnic."

"So, what just happened was my real reason for being here. I'm sorry you had to witness it."

"I ... I don't know what's going on, but—"

"But?"

"You didn't ... have to *kill* him," she said in a shaky voice, and Leonard made a sincerely puzzled face.

"But he tried to kill us both."

"That's true, but...."

"Besides, I haven't killed as many people as your boyfriend has."

That was all it took for her to know he meant Sousuke. She started protesting even before she could ask how he knew about him. It was practically a reflex.

"H-he's ... been in wars ever since he was little! He ... couldn't help it. And his enemies were almost all bad guys ... and he saves people who aren't involved, and those weaker than him. Besides, he doesn't enjoy that kind of thing at *all*. In fact, I bet it really bothers him. So ... anyway, he's ... um ... different from this kind of thing. He ... wouldn't do things this way...."

Leonard listened with great interest to Kaname's inarticulate discourse. Then he smiled a little impishly and peered into her eyes.

"Don't tell me you seriously believe such a rationale?"

"But...." She reflexively averted her eyes.

"The deeds are the same, essentially. Yet you blame me, and take his side," said Leonard.

"No, I—"

"You love him."

"No, I don't."

"Really?"

"Really."

"Look at me."

"Eh—"

It was a total surprise attack. He softly embraced her shoulders, and when Kaname quickly turned her head, he placed his lips on hers.

It was a cold, soft, moist sensation.

It happened so suddenly, her mind went blank. Where she was, who he was, who *she* was—that all became uncertain. She didn't even feel a sense of disgust. In fact, for a moment, the sweet taste threatened to conquer her heart.

Time started moving again.

Leonard didn't try to dodge Kaname's slap. She'd meant to hit the side of his face with all her strength, but he just staggered lightly. It must've been interpreted as an attack. The two big men standing nearby—no, the *robots*—immediately dropped down and stood ready.

"It's all right, stand down."

The two Alastors dropped out of their stances.

Kaname covered her lips, backed up against the water tank, and glared at Leonard. She wanted to burst into tears, but she wanted even more not to do it in front of him.

"What's the big idea?"

"A wake-up kiss, I suppose. Because I've fallen in love with you." Leonard smiled innocently as he rubbed his cheek.

"Well, I *hate* you. You make me sick."

"That's what I love about you. Seemingly frail yet ferocious, seemingly vulgar yet noble. You're elusive, like water."

"Shut up!" Kaname shouted, and he shrugged as if to say, "Ooh, I'm scared." He then gave some command to the robots.

One of them walked over to the roof's exit and wrenched open the locked door.

"I'll be on my way, before you try to kill me," said Leonard.

The other robot, who had been carrying the Mithril man, laid the corpse down on the concrete. No—it wasn't a corpse. The man stirred a little, moaning something that wasn't quite words.

"Yes, he's alive," said Leonard. "He, too, is what I'd consider an enemy, but what to do with him? Do you care if I eliminate him?"

The robot pointed a shiny black gun barrel on the back of its left arm at the man. *Cha-king,* went a dull sound. It was the heavy caliber machine gun that had earlier finished off the assassin.

"W ... wait a minute!" Kaname shouted.

"Why?"

"I ... I have unfinished business with him. Don't kill him!"

"Hmm.... But he was speaking quite rudely to you earlier. I thought death would be a fitting compensation for his tone."

"I'll be the one to make that decision," said Kaname stiffly. "I'll forgive ... what you did to me. Just don't kill him."

"You surprise me. You'd do this for someone like him? I don't think you're that cheap a woman."

"Don't make me keep saying it. *The decision's up to me!*" she said flatly, and Leonard gaped at her.

"You surprise me again." He chuckled. "All right. I'll leave him here, then."

The robot withdrew the barrel in its arm.

One of them lifted up the assassin's body into its arms. The job now complete, Leonard followed the two robots away from the exit and toward the edge of the roof. One more step and they'd fall headlong to the back alley four stories below. But at that point, he turned around once more.

"A moment, before we part. It's true that I fell in love with you. I wasn't teasing. I'd like you to believe that."

Kaname stared at him silently.

"Miss Kaname Chidori, you're still half-asleep. Before long, you'll open your eyes to a new world. Then those like you might have no reason to fear those whispers."

"Huh? What do you—"

"We'll meet again."

Leonard and the two robots jumped off the roof simultaneously, vanishing from view.

There was the sound of something smashing on the asphalt. Kaname ran over and looked down into the alley. But there was just a grey mist hanging over the gloomy surface—no trace of humanoid forms.

She walked over and crouched beside the Mithril man, who was sprawled out in a puddle. He looked up vaguely at Kaname. The right half of his fleshy-chinned face had completely collapsed. The shape of his head had changed like the anime character Anpanman's, but not a drop of blood was flowing there.

What collapsed hadn't been flesh and blood, but urethane foam. The middle-aged man's face had been an elaborate mask. The real face was visible through a tear in the urethane.

Kaname yanked off the mask.

A young man's face with almond eyes appeared. No ... was it a woman? She couldn't tell. The features were slender in a way that was inconclusive. He might have been just over twenty and looked completely exhausted and very pale. Kaname had the feeling she'd seen the face a number of times around her neighborhood—but her memory was fuzzy, so she wasn't sure.

"So ... that's a disguise."

"That's ... right," he said in his original voice. The voice left a cold impression.

There was no blood flowing from the bullet holes in the middle-age fat covering the chest or abdomen, either. Apparently he was wearing a bulletproof vest underneath, but a small amount of blood was mixing into the rain from shots in the shoulder and thigh.

"Can't you move? How are your injuries?"

"I don't know. That man ... injected me ... with something...."

"Want me to help you?"

"No, thanks...." The words came out in a pained tone.

"Even I ... have my pride. This failure ... this predicament.... I'd sooner just ... die...."

"Oh."

Kaname turned her back on the Mithril spy and took a deep breath.

So much had happened in less than ten minutes. Every possible emotion jumbled together within her, and it felt like her head would burst.

Surprise, relief, doubt, humiliation, anger, anxiety.

The most unpleasant thing was the sensation on her lips that wouldn't go away no matter how much she wiped. She felt deplorable for forgetting to resist even just a moment, and for submitting herself to his will.

That was her first kiss. Strictly speaking, back in kindergarten she and another girl in her martial arts group had kissed as a joke, but excluding that, this was her first. These days it might be considered silly, but she had determined in her heart that the first time absolutely had to be with someone she really loved. For instance—no, anyway, it had to be someone special. That kind of thing was very important to her.

And now, a guy like *that* had gone and—

She punched the water tank. *Gong*, went the dull sound. She desperately told herself that the tears were coming because of the pain in her fist and the abrasions all over her.

"Hn ... hng."

The feelings she'd locked away ever since that scene in the school staff room suddenly broke free from all their chains, and jolted her chest hard. Her strength that hadn't been shaken even when the assassin had attacked her was easily smashed by a single kiss.

Did I really feel nothing when he left? Have I been as cold as ice?

That's not true at all——is it?

"Sousuke...."

Why aren't you here? It's your fault. I'm in this mess because you're not here. What are you doing? You don't want all this to happen, do you? I don't either. Do something. Be with me. Say "No problem."

Hers was an unspoken voice. Of course no answer was forthcoming. Sobbing alone in a place like this would accomplish nothing.

If only she could hit reset. If only she could rewind time back to that haircut.

The truth was she'd been aware of the small sweet feeling she'd had in front of that adorable sleeping face—the natural impulse. This was her reward for cheating it. That had been her last chance. She should've just gently said, "Hey, let's kiss." Instead, she'd run away. She'd ruined it and run away!

Thus had she forever lost something important to her. It was nothing more than a small fixation, but even so, it left when he left.

It's always this way with me.

Until now, even if she'd come to feel an inclination toward someone, she would never make an effort to admit it.

She'd just end up betrayed, anyway. They weren't reliable. She would surely just get hurt.

Like with Mom.

That was why she wouldn't rely on anyone. That was why she wouldn't approach anyone. That was why she wouldn't admit her own feelings.

Then, when it was all too late, she'd realize for the first time what she might've been capable of. She just wasn't brave enough.

"Sousuke...."

So this time was the same. She'd been incapable of action and it was over.

Once again she asked herself, *Is it really all over?*

How long had she been standing in the rain, weeping, her shoulders trembling?

She stopped crying, and lifted her head.

She turned around and again walked over to the prone Mithril spy. "Earlier, you said you'd sooner just die," Kaname stated.

The Mithril spy didn't respond.

"Well, would a little useless struggling really hurt you? It's what *I* plan on doing from now on."

CHAPTER 5
His Problem

October 22, 11:38 (Eastern China Standard Time)
Hong Kong Island Special Ward (People's Committee side), Hong Kong
Mid-levels

Ten minutes had passed since they had been shown into the excessively spacious parlor.

This apartment's master, a Mithril Hong Kong intelligence staffer, still hadn't arrived.

They were in a bright room with abundant natural light, a high ceiling, and large windows. This was the thirtieth floor of a high-rise apartment complex, built on the steep slope of Victoria Peak, which commanded a view of the sea.

Even amongst the flood of countless structures on the steep slope, one could take in a full panoramic view of the Hong Kong streets from this conspicuously tall apartment complex.

The buildings of all sizes and ages crowded tightly together. Sousuke had heard about it, but the high density of these high-rise apartment complexes was a sight not often seen.

Chaos; disorderliness; confusion: Those were the only descriptions the scene brought to mind.

"I see now that it hasn't changed much from before," murmured Mao, who stood beside Sousuke.

"You've been here before?"

"Several times, before the transfer. Relatives on my mother's side lived right around here. But they've all emigrated to New York City. I was their house guest for about two months before joining Mithril. Real lazy."

"Lazy?"

"After I was discharged from the Marines. I couldn't motivate myself to work, and I didn't want to go back to my parents in NYC. My old man's such a pain. That Air Force jerk," she said and clicked her tongue. Sousuke had hardly ever heard anything about Mao's background, so he was a little surprised that she was talking about her past like this.

"So, your father's a military man."

"That's right. A half-wit bomber pilot. He's retired and working for a corporation now, though. He's always acted big, but he's a stingy coward. Not to mention a schemer."

"Schemer?"

"Yeah. When I got out of high school and tried to get a real job, he pulled a bunch of strings and tried to get me to marry some fancy-pants Harvard grad. That pissed me off, of course. So to show *him*, I joined the Marines on the day of the wedding."

That experience must have been quite thrilling. She looked down and grinned.

"I snuck out of the church alone, and went to the recruiting center four blocks away—in my wedding dress. The corporal in charge, his eyes bugged out like *this*. 'Are you serious?' 'You betcha,' I said. Everyone there tried to talk me out of it. 'Look, Miss Bride. You should give this some more thought. I'm sure you're breaking your parents' hearts.' So, I said this: 'My old man's Air Force.' Then they all said simultaneously, 'Well that changes things. You can start by signing these papers.'"

Yang overheard this from a short distance away and burst out laughing. Apparently he was unable to contain it anymore.

"What do you say about a chick like that?"

"A-awesome." Yang laughed. "Pretty cool, I'd say."

His shoulders shook, there were even tears in his eyes, and he gave a thumbs-up.

It was a strange atmosphere. There was the customary strain before an operation and funny stories to pass the time. There was the hush of the room and Yang's stifled laughter. The light from the window formed distinct shadows of Mao, Yang, and the others. But what the sight evoked was an indefinable sadness.

Mao gazed nostalgically off into the sky.

"Awesome, eh? Those times really *were* awesome. Once that decision was made, it felt like the world was full of possibilities. I could do anything. Go anywhere."

"Anywhere?" Sousuke said it like he'd never heard the word. Mao shrugged.

"Sure. I mean, a lot happened after that. I went through some terrible frustration and disappointment. But I'm really glad things were the way they were then. I've come to like myself a whole lot more now, and that's what it's all about."

He didn't really understand what she meant. Nor did he comprehend why she would suddenly tell such a story at a time like this.

"Well, coming back to this town just reminded me. Don't dwell on it or anything."

"Hmm ... okay," answered the slightly confused Sousuke. The parlor door opened and a plump, middle-aged white man entered.

"Sorry for the delay."

Restlessly wiping the sweat from his temple with a handkerchief, he walked over to them. He had an amiable look in his eyes. His hair was combed down with pomade and he wore a mustache. He looked to be around fifty, but he might've been younger.

This is the guy?

Sousuke and Mao exchanged glances.

This was Gavin Hunter, a Mithril intelligence agent.

They might have envisioned a stoic war veteran based on that name, but what they got was this fat, profusely sweating man. It was a bit bewildering.

Hunter's public face was that of an influential trade businessman. He was proficient in both Cantonese and Mandarin Chinese. He was well known by both the North and South armies, and dined with their leaders seemingly every evening.

His image was far from that of a so-called spy, but there was no need for James Bond-esque adventures just to gather intelligence. A military leader's casual remark, a short article in a newspaper's financial column, an unfamiliar warship entering port—much could be conjectured just from such things. And that was essentially the business of Intelligence.

"It goes without saying, but the North and South armies are considerably high strung at the moment," Hunter explained. "A mere cursory glance would reveal a tense situation. Between the two armies, there've been three cases of friendly fire and four cases of weapons discharged at civilians. At this point it's a wonder hostilities have yet to commence between each side. That's likely just a matter of time, however."

"And if they do?"

"I imagine it would turn into a fierce firefight, spanning Victoria Harbor. At any rate, any firearm besides a pistol can reach the opposite side. Rifles, machine guns, mortars, rockets, anti-tank missiles.... Quite dreadful, really. Suddenly, there'd be a sea of fire. It's not so hard to imagine, looking down there."

Since the separation, the North Chinese army and South Chinese army had been glaring at each other across Victoria Harbor. What kept that from developing into combat was the inclination on both sides not to turn Hong Kong into the aforementioned sea of fire. But this AS terrorism was starting to loosen that restraint.

"What about the citizens?"

"They began evacuating some time ago. The citizens of the South, inland to the New Territories. The citizens here, of the North, to the southern part of Hong Kong Island and Lantau. Well, women and children receive priority. I already sent my wife to our villa on Lantau. Both armies are on strict alert status, so travel between the North and South has practically ceased. No ships are allowed into port, and nearly all flights are canceled at both Kai Tak and Chek Lap Kok Airports. Stocks and the financial exchange are both train wrecks. I mean, honestly, here we'd only just managed somehow with all the separation aftermath. This place really is turning into Berlin at this rate."

"You did manage, though, one way or another," Mao murmured unexpectedly, and Hunter raised an eyebrow with a clear air of superiority.

"That is what defines the Chinese. They're cunning, brimming with vitality, and possess an amazingly prosperous mercantile spirit.

They freely control their public and private faces, their yin and yang," said Hunter.

"Ah-ha."

"Try sampling some Chinese cuisine. You will readily see the vastness of this race and its culture. The ideology made up by mere Westerners a scant hundred years ago is, in truth, worthless. That separation drama, you know, that was both a crisis and an opportunity for us tradesmen. Some were ruined, but some built up their fortune. That's always how it goes. Even if there's a political separation, even if both sides station troops, passage between North and South was relatively simple until just the day before yesterday. In short, it's a case of scratch my back and I'll scratch yours." He spoke haughtily, as if he thought of himself as a natural-born Hong Konger. Never mind that he was the only Caucasian in the room.

"So, what about this problematic AS?"

"We still cannot get a handle on its whereabouts whatsoever. It last appeared three hours ago, in Shau Kei Wan on the Hong Kong Island side. Two ASes and an armored vehicle were heavily damaged. There were four North China Army casualties, and eight civilians were injured to various degrees. A ghastly affair."

"There's no doubt that it's still lurking in the city?"

"No one can say for sure, but our branch's analysts and AIs think so. As does my own intuition. That being said, the city itself presents the biggest problem."

Hunter unfolded a map and began giving a technical rundown. It reflected the views of a focused pro who had exhaustively examined every possible piece of information. Each of his words demonstrated to Mao and the others that Hunter loved Hong Kong dearly.

Mao and Sousuke, familiar with practical uses of invisibility-mode ECS, offered suggestions, further refining the analysis Hunter's group had performed. It was a productive discussion. Both Mao's group and Hunter's group were on location. The dissonance between Intelligence and Operations at the upper levels had no bearing on them here.

"Anything else? Areas or conditions that can create exceptions?" asked Hunter as he typed away at his AI terminal.

"Areas with lots of pigeons or crows," said Mao.

"Hmm. Why birds?"

"It seems like birds can see ASes somehow. ECS can't conceal ultra-violet rays, so that's probably why. Crows in particular caw up a storm and fly around overhead, which can be a pain. Dogs can be bad, too. They're sensitive to the ECS ozone smell."

"Ah-ha. Indeed. Anything else?"

Mao looked at Sousuke's profile. "That might be about it....
Sousuke?"

"Hmm?" said Sousuke, as if he'd snapped out of a daydream.

"Is there anything else?"

"N ... no. Nothing in particular."

From Mao's viewpoint, Sousuke's focus looked unusually lax.
This had been the case ever since they left the *Tuatha de Daanan*.

No longer scowling at the terminal screen, Hunter raised his
voice in exclamation. "This is no small job. Forty-nine places on the
Hong Kong Island side, and seventy-eight places on the Kowloon side.
If my people share the work load, we can hit them all in half a day's
time."

"That is ... if conditions are right. Once we find it, let's aim to
bring it down in one go," said Mao.

It was decided that Hunter's subordinates would join Mao's team and
immediately scout out the enemy AS's potential hideouts.

There wasn't really any time to waste.

Mao's Operations personnel would split into three teams and help out with the effort. Sousuke and Mao would cross Victoria Harbour, to Kowloon Peninsula. Yang and Wu would stay on Hong Kong Island and search.

The third team was in the transport helicopter on which they'd flown in. They would turn invisible through ECS and then search the entire Hong Kong area from above using ECCS (the counter-ECS sensor). The effectiveness of ECCS in urban areas had a low reliability, so they were chiefly in charge of outskirts and the other islands, which were of all different sizes.

On the two light vans they borrowed from Hunter was painted in bold blue characters HUNTER CLEANING COMPANY. That was all it meant, but it looked like a very strange inscription to Sousuke, as he was unfamiliar with Chinese.

"Looks like this guy does business on a large scale," said Mao from inside the building's underground parking lot, her arms folded. The four of them had already changed into the cleaning company's work uniform, but Sousuke looked the most out of place.

"Got your driver's licenses? Check your business licenses and permit passes, too. Keep your forged passports and credit cards in separate pockets. Just one firearm each. Firing them is, in general, prohibited. Make contact whenever necessary. Martial law's in effect, so be careful."

"What if it looks like we'll be detained by the army or police for inspection? Aren't there a lot of units unassociated with Hunter?" asked Yang.

"True. So be careful. If you can get away, do it. No shooting, though. Shooting soldiers who haven't done anything wrong would be absurd. Otherwise, do as you see fit. If you're caught, you'll probably undergo some severe interrogation until Hunter can fix things. Even if they torture you, don't talk. That's it."

"That's pretty rough."

"Worry more about what happens when you locate the enemy. I can't allow you to get killed with no contact or authorization. Got it?"

"Yes, ma'am."

"Then, let's go."

The four got into their respective cleaning company vans and left the parking garage.

They went two separate ways into the city. Yang's van headed for Victoria Peak.

The van that Sousuke was driving traversed steep, tree-lined hill roads for several minutes, then emerged in the heart of Central. Super high-rise buildings that seemed to pierce the heavens lined both sides of Des Voeux Road, making it seem like they were passing through a man-made ravine. Country-bred Sousuke was a bit overwhelmed by the imposing view.

The cloudy sky looked awfully confining.

In Tokyo terms, Central was supposedly a business district akin to Shinjuku or Marunouchi, but hardly any people were currently in view. The same was true of automobile traffic. The two-story tram that ran along the center of the road was practically empty aside from the driver. The sound of metal rubbing against the rails echoed emptily around the area.

"This is a surprise. I've never seen Central like *this*," said Mao, who sat in the passenger seat quietly looking around at the streets.

When they came to a five-way intersection, a North Chinese armored vehicle and AS on watch came into view. It was an olive-colored RK-92 Savage. It had an export-oriented design, the same type with which North Korea was furnished.

They headed east along the road, through Wan Chai and toward Causeway Bay.

The valley between buildings continued on forever. There soon appeared many of Hong Kong's well-known *zhaopai*. The flashy signs of green, red, and other colors projected from buildings, filling the air above the street.

NGA TOI SKI CARE BEAUTY CENTER.

ART & DISPLAY INTERIOR DESIGN CO. LTD.

HAPPY VILLAGE CHINESE RESTAURANT.

WELTON AUDIO VIDEO APPLIANCES CO. LTD.

SUN WAH DRUG STORE.

FU YIU SEAFOOD RESTAURANT.

BUDDHA VEGETARIAN RESTAURANT.

KWAN NGAI MUSIC AND ART CENTER.

Sousuke wasn't good with kanji, and he hardly even knew the Japanese readings for any of these. The illuminated signs of course also included many eye-catching cutting-edge holograms. Rudimentary ECS technology had been put to use for consumer products.

They reached the entrance to the underwater tunnel. Once they passed through, they'd move onto Kowloon Peninsula, which was under South Chinese military control.

The tunnel entrance was under strict guard by four Savages, two armored vehicles, and over sixty heavily armed foot soldiers. Sandbags were piled up here and there, and barbed wire fencing and machine-gun emplacement were set up.

Up a bit ahead in the tunnel was an entry gate. Several civilian cars were in line, their passengers exchanging various words with the soldiers. In the end, these civilians weren't allowed passage and they made U-turns after being turned away.

Hunter was supposed to have made arrangements over the phone with whoever was in charge of this garrison.

"Now let's see if they'll let us through without trouble," said Mao.

"If Hunter's connections are solid, they will."

An AKM rifle hanging from his shoulder, a soldier spread his hands in front of the gate and told them to halt in Cantonese. He walked around to the driver's side and started speaking through the window.

All he'd memorized in the helicopter on the way here were bits and pieces of everyday vocabulary, so Sousuke had no idea what the guy was saying.

"Mao, if you would."

"*Ming bai le. Kaichuang,*" said Mao.

"What?"

"I said, 'All right. Open your window.'"

Sousuke obeyed and opened the van's powered window. Then he just watched from the side as Mao spoke fluently in Cantonese. They showed their business licenses and permit passes, she explained something, and then the soldier looked at Sousuke and said, "*Keyi.*"

Mao poked Sousuke on the shoulder and then pointed toward the front of the van.

"*Ni di. Wo de keyi zuo le,*" said Mao.

The gate before them opened with a clatter. Sousuke interpreted this to mean *go*, and moved the van forward. This meant they had cleared the first barrier without incident.

Their van moved through the tunnel, passing beneath Victoria Harbor. There were no other vehicles whatsoever. Theirs was the only one in all three spacious lanes.

"It's amazing. This tunnel was always packed with cars," said Mao.

"You've been surprised a lot today."

"Well, yeah. Anyone would be shocked, if they'd seen Hong Kong before this."

"Is that so?"

"I mean, try imagining it. What would you think if you saw, say, Tokyo in this state?"

Sousuke hadn't expected that question and he was startled.

"It's like if Shinjuku and Ginza were split right down the middle, glaring at each other and on the brink of war. A city where smartly dressed kids should be shopping and eating ice cream—and now it's filled with armored vehicles and ASes. At bayside, which should be ideal for a stroll, huge pillboxes and bunkers reign supreme. Right here in Hong Kong! It's just not right. This world's insane."

Sousuke had just realized for the first time that the city in which he'd spent the last half a year's time was at peace. There were no tanks. No ASes. No policemen or soldiers demanding bribes. The roads were filled with cars and people, and there were bustling sounds of music and laughter.

A peaceful Tokyo. A peaceful school. A peaceful classroom. And—

"Sousuke?"

"Hmm?"

"Something wrong?"

"No, it's nothing." Sousuke shook off the image of the face that had begun to surface in his mind.

"Pay attention. Here's the South Army entry gate."

"Yeah. I know."

They hadn't reached the tunnel exit yet, but they could see a gate that had been shut closed with wire mesh. It was the entrance to Kowloon Peninsula, under the command of the South China military. Hunter was supposed to have called in a favor from this commander, too. After two or three exchanges, the soldiers readily let them pass.

"That was it?" asked Sousuke. "Surprising."

It seemed anticlimactic to them how easily they had passed through both camps' examinations. After all, there was such a high alert in effect. They'd been prepared for some kind of chilling scene to transpire.

"Looks like Hunter's a big-shot after all," said Sousuke.

"Yeah. He has so much clout with both sides. Well, it seems like he probably does more than just respectable business."

"Probably."

The most likely answer was the trade of ordinance through illegal channels on both sides. He could earn the gratitude of local military leaders trying to increase their assets, and at the same time grasp their weak points. It was two birds with one stone for an Intelligence agent. Sousuke had seen that type of man in many far-flung trouble spots.

"It's around this area."

Their van entered a street lined with modern-looking hotels. One of the potential spots on the list was nearby. It was a trade center under construction, just right for concealing an AS. Malaysian interests, not very successful in Hong Kong, had won the contract for this construction, and even on paper there were many dubious aspects about it.

"What will we do if we find it right away?" asked Sousuke.

"There's no question. We should always be prepared for that to happen."

They passed by a wide park, surrounded on three sides by hotels and shopping centers.

A South China AS stood guard at the park's entrance. It was an early model M6 Bushnell, an export model not equipped with ECS. A British-made mobile generator was parked nearby. The military was on extended alert, so the AS was probably connected to an economical power source.

That generator....

He suddenly remembered. The generator vehicle was the same model as the one he'd stolen from the enemy right after rescuing *her* in Sunan. She'd made a huge fuss at that point, and explaining the situation had been quite the chore. Instead of trying to believe him, she'd admonished him right in the midst of enemy gunfire, saying things like: "Sagara, calm down. You're delusional, and obsessed with your crazy ideas!"

Sagara?

That's right. That's how she still referred to me at the time. Now, when did it switch over to being Sousuke? I'm pretty sure it—

"Sousuke?" Mao was yelling at him. Sousuke came to himself. The van he was driving was plunging through an intersection with a red light.

A shrill car horn sounded, and a taxi bore down from the left. There was the squeal of brakes, and the van's body pitched forward. The bumper sunk so low it scraped asphalt. There were high-pitched noises, sparks, and a crash. The taxi had torn off a bumper.

The van bounded to the right as if it'd been kicked, then skidded sideways as broken pieces scattered.

Their van had stopped right in the middle of the intersection.

The taxi driver, who had come to a sudden stop, rushed out of his taxi and was yelling something. Four soldiers came running up from the direction of the park they'd just passed. The M6 made no move from its position, but its head was trained directly on them.

Mao, her face pale, was staring at him. She was apparently even beyond cursing at this point.

"Whatever happens, leave this to me. You keep quiet."

"I—"

"Look, just don't do anything," she said flatly, and exited the van.

Mao faced the soldiers and called out something in an apparently very embarrassed voice.

"*Ma fan shen ni....*"

It probably amounted to "I'm sorry, we weren't paying attention." But the soldiers showed no reaction to her implication that she wasn't to blame, other than suddenly pointing their rifles at her.

They were probably shouting for her to shut up.

Unfortunately, the soldiers' demeanor suggested an urge for bloodshed. Their nerves were worn thin thanks to several days on high alert.

They grabbed Mao's shoulder and forced her onto the ground, then dragged Sousuke out of the driver's seat. A glance revealed the taxi driver being subdued in a like manner. He wailed dolefully as he clung to a soldier and pointed an accusatory finger at Sousuke and Mao.

Now having been stood up with her hands tied behind her back, Mao was desperately attempting to explain something. Her voice seemed to skillfully invite sympathy, but its effectiveness in this case was dubious.

This was downright terrible.

Making a bad judgment call in combat was one thing, but this was a traffic accident due to utter carelessness. He'd never made such a foolish mistake before. This was an unbelievably huge error, even for Sousuke. If they were arrested here, they could forget all about reconnaissance. He had to think of some way out—and then, just at that moment the M6, which had been standing thirty meters away, made a roaring sound and dropped to its knees.

The long, narrow head was twisted off by some inexplicable force. Sparks gushed from the neck, various cables and pipes were pulled out, and the head was dragged out into the air so that it resembled a Rokurokubi monster. There were the death throes of rent metal, and the short and stout M6 struggled and flailed its limbs as it was grabbed at by some unseen thing.

"Hua...."

The M6's giant frame made a tremendous noise as it was flung aside.

It traversed the street and slammed into the hotel facing the park, propelling fragments of concrete and glass through the air. White dust suddenly blew up, and just when it seemed it would hang heavily all around the area, a huge section of light flickered right through the middle of it.

It was invisibility mode ECS.

Clad in the vestiges of blue light, a single AS became visible.

It had a body shaped like an inverted triangle, and a diamond-shaped head. It sported a grey and dark blue camouflage armor, and that single red eye was a sight one would never forget.

It was a Venom.

The soldiers' breath stopped in their throats as their eyes locked on the mech's sinister visage.

The Venom plucked the M6's head from its body and casually chucked it into the street. A clump of crushed sensors and machine guns landed on top of a Benz parked nearby, crumpling and smashing the roof and windshield. The Venom drew an assault rifle from its back, aimed at the M6, which was still trying to move, and fired full auto at point-blank range. Limbs were blown off the helpless mech and it exploded.

A tremendous roar, hot wind, and a shock wave reached all the way to the intersection where Sousuke and the others were. Mao jumped at the driver, forcing him down to the ground. Immediately afterward, she noticed Sousuke still standing there in a daze, and her eyes widened in surprise.

Another M6, on watch nearby, came running over when it heard the disturbance. It was on the other side of the Venom, and it used the corner of a hotel for partial cover as it aimed its rifle. Mao got up and this time jumped at Sousuke.

The rifle discharged.

The Venom lifted its left arm. Countless shots bounced off of the invisible wall in front of the mech. The shots ricocheted and hit nearby buildings and signs, creating a storm of destruction.

"*Jiu ming ya!*"

No one could even move. The soldiers screamed amidst the roaring. Fragments from the destruction rained down around Mao and Sousuke.

The Venom quickly used its rifle to dispatch the newly-arrived M6 and turned and sprinted toward the intersection. Someone cried out in despair. The grey mech drew near, then kicked into the ground in front of them. The explosive impact crushed asphalt into small pieces and the Venom vanished from view.

Sousuke brushed the enshrouding dust aside and looked overhead. The Venom had landed on top of a building that was twenty stories tall. It had probably used a wire gun to reach that elevation in the blink of an eye as it leaped. Such jumping power was on par with that of an M9.

The mech's one red eye was paying no attention to Sousuke's group whatsoever. It was looking farther away. It was probably confirming the movements of the South China Army.

After looking down upon the entire area, it turned aside and initiated its ECS. As the grey mech turned invisible, it moved out of view behind the roof.

That was the entirety of the combat.

Smoke hung heavily in the intersection. A soldier whose arm had been hit by flying shrapnel was making an exaggerated outcry over it. Another one inspected the injury and quickly told him he was overreacting. Of the four, the one who seemed to have the most experience was shouting something into his radio, and the remaining one was standing in a daze right in the middle of the intersection.

These South China soldiers had apparently lost all interest in Mao and the others.

Mao addressed one of them, and after he responded fluently, he took off in haste toward the burning M6. She said something to the taxi driver, then pointed with her thumb at the van with Hunter's company name written on it. Some dissatisfaction showed on his face, but once Mao said something further, he was apparently convinced since he started walking to his car.

She walked over to Sousuke and whispered, "Let's go," into his ear.

"Are you sure?"

"The soldier said, 'Had it not been for your accident, we probably would've been trampled to death near the M6. That's why we're going to overlook this,'" she said and quickly got into the van which was now missing a bumper. Naturally, she sat behind the wheel this time.

Obviously in no position to voice any objection, Sousuke silently climbed into the passenger seat.

First a traffic accident, then a Venom sighting. Completely unexpected events had occurred in rapid-fire succession, and it had Sousuke more than a little shaken. Being taken off the duty of guarding Kaname; his utter defeat at Clouseau's hands—all these things added to his state of shock.

What the hell am I doing?

Had the Venom not timed its appearance like that, they would've been detained by the South Army soldiers, and things would've gotten even worse for them.

What's this sense of irony?

It was the totally uncontrollable reality of his situation.

A paralyzing feeling of helplessness ate into Sousuke's mind and body. Nothing seemed to make sense to him at this point.

Mao restarted the engine and then said, "You ignored a stop light. That crossed the line."

"Sorry."

"Were you thinking about her or something?"

When he said nothing, Mao suddenly grabbed him by the collar and pulled him close.

"Well, right now, forget about her. If you can't do that, get out of this van. I realize your situation. But you know, as sister figures go, I'm not all *that* kind and understanding. I don't care to throw my life away for this! At this point, I'd be a lot safer by *myself*."

What she was saying was only natural. It was because she recognized him as an equal that she copped this stern attitude with him. Displaying sympathy here would be the wrong thing to do, both as a colleague and a friend. However, Sousuke found Mao's honesty to be unavoidably disagreeable at the moment.

"You're right."

Sousuke grabbed his bag, packed with a communicator and all sorts of equipment, and opened the passenger side door.

"Sousuke?"

"Sorry. I can't ... go on."

"Hey...."

"Continue with the mission."

He got out of the van and started walking alone down the road, which was strewn with building materials and rubble. Of course, he had no destination. Mao was shouting something behind him, but it didn't reach his ears.

Nothing mattered. Nothing at all. Not the Mithril mission, the Venom, the Arbalest, Al, nor the fate of this city.

October 22, 15:53 (Eastern China Standard Time)
Hong Kong Island Special Ward
Sheung Wan

Three hours had already passed since they had separated from Mao and Sousuke.

In that time, the team of Corporal Yang and PFC Wu had finished checking eleven potential hideouts. None of them had yielded any results.

Yang drove their light van sluggishly down a section of Sheung Wan, an area filled with high-rise apartment buildings. This town, constructed on the slope of Victoria Peak, had plenty of hilly roads and tight curves.

"I want to floor this thing," said Yang.

Roads like this one awakened his wild blood from when he was growing up on the outskirts of Daegu, where he'd do mountain-street racing practically every night. Then as always, he'd ask himself what he was doing in a place like this, working as a mercenary.

The answer was that he didn't have any money. He'd been born the third son of the owner of a tiny automotive repair shop, which was a far cry from the economic means needed to try to become a real racer. Even more ironic, he had been "blessed" with more talent as a soldier than he was with cars. He reluctantly enlisted into the army, and while reluctantly completing his training with ease, he caught the eye of an officer at the base, who then pushed through a letter of recommendation for his assignment to an airborne division. Then, due to some mistake, he got involved in a combat that to this day was highly classified in his home country—and the rest was history.

Yet here he was, still. Here in this light van, this driver's seat.

"That would be bad, Corporal," reminded Wu from the passenger seat. "Please exercise caution. If we mess up, it won't be the enemy who kills us. It will be the master sergeant," said Wu.

"I know. Hey, heads up. We're here."

They'd stopped in front of a high-rise apartment building under construction. There was an underground parking garage here, ideal for hiding an AS, and what's more, none-too-successful foreign interests held the construction contract.

"Urzu-9, reporting in. We're about to check out point 28. If you don't hear from us in fifteen minutes, tighten the search perimeter."

"Urzu-2, copy that," came Mao's curt voice from over the radio. For some reason, Sousuke hadn't responded a single time. They'd heard the Venom had appeared again on Kowloon Peninsula, but maybe some other trouble had come up.

"Wangfu HQ, roger. Be careful," came Hunter's voice from the radio.

"Let's go. Stay focused, Wu."

"You got it."

They got out of the van and approached the under-construction complex.

According to Hunter's intel, construction on this building had stopped three days ago. The cause was apparently a labor strike, but no follow-up had been performed.

They went past bamboo scaffolding and some nets, and proceeded into the dim interior.

Yang drew his silenced automatic pistol. At this point, there was no sign of anyone here. Careful not to make a sound, he alertly descended the stairs. The entrance to the parking area still didn't have a door attached. He strained his ears in front of the empty doorway, then signaled Wu with his eyes and hands. Without a sound, he stepped into the underground parking garage.

It was a deserted expanse of concrete. There were no cars, just stacks of construction materials.

"Another miss. This makes eight that—"

"Shh!" whispered Yang, cutting off Wu.

In a corner of the garage, in the shadow of a mound of carelessly stacked cement bags, Yang saw a foot. Someone was lying on the other side of the bags. Wu noticed it, too, and shut his mouth.

They were careful to check every angle as they approached.

It was the corpse of a man who'd been shot to death. He was in his forties and wore a slightly dirty work uniform. He'd been shot through the head.

"Ugh!" Wu stifled the urge to retch. "You think he's a construction worker here?" he asked, averting his eyes from the corpse.

"Yeah. Looks to me like he happened to come back for something he'd forgotten, and then he was unlucky enough to get shot by somebody else here. Poor guy. I'd say he died about two days ago," said Yang, who was calmly searching the corpse. There were little maggots in the mouth, and with his bare hands Yang opened it and checked the mouth cavity. No explosives or anything seemed to have been rigged.

"I'm impressed you can tell the time of death."

"Rigor mortis is in the process of relaxing, and decay's starting to take place. Other determining factors are dryness of mucous membranes, the condition of the eye sockets, the color of the livor mortis, stuff like that. You can't tell the exact time without a detailed autopsy, though."

"Well.... I wonder if this was the hideout," said Wu.

"I don't know. But even if the enemy *was* using this as a hideout, I doubt he'll come anywhere near here again. Just watch out for any souvenirs this guy's killer might have left behind."

"Souvenirs?"

"Traps. Bombs can sometimes make good alarms."

Wu suddenly looked nervous as he glanced around.

"Don't worry. Just don't touch anything I didn't touch. Understood?" said Yang.

"Yes, sir. Still, it really shows that you're SRT, Corporal."

"What?"

"Never mind, sir. Did you notice this guy's chest?"

"Yeah."

Yang had picked up on it, too. There was some kind of unnatural stain visible on the corpse's T-shirt, beneath its uniform. At first he'd thought it was a blood stain that had changed color, but now that didn't seem to be the case. He remained wary of traps as he carefully unzipped the zipper.

It wasn't a stain. It was a message, written in English with a black magic marker: *To the Tiger of Badakhshan's cub. Meet with Hamidra in Tsim Sha Tsui.*

That was all it said.

"Do you know what it means?" asked Wu.

"Nope. I don't have a clue." Yang shrugged and he switched on his radio.

October 22, 16:14 (Eastern China Standard Time)
South China Sea
Tuatha de Daanan

There was a major traffic jam overhead. No ships were allowed into port, so there was a large group of them stuck in the water just outside Hong Kong. This number of ships in such a small area would normally be unthinkable, so the sonar room and Target Motion Analysis system were the busiest they'd been since the day the ship had put to sea.

Tessa moved her ship forward at a low depth, nearly crawling on the ocean floor. They'd be in danger of colliding with a merchant vessel if they carelessly attempted to rise to periscope depth. They moved slowly, like a whale doing a dance, as they carefully sounded out the ocean floor's topography using high—frequency sonar. It was a time-consuming and terribly nerve-wracking way to control a ship, but it was better than getting caught by a South China military patrol.

"Captain, there is a message from Intelligence," announced Dana, the ship's AI. The antenna of the turtle that had been deployed to the surface had picked up a transmission. Tessa yielded control of the ship to Mardukas, and after phoning Lieutenant Commander Kalinin, quickly looked over the intel.

The situation had degraded considerably. The North China forces were starting to believe that the Venom's subversive activities were the work of the Southern forces. Despite the fact that areas controlled by the South had also suffered damage, they were suspicious that this was just a charade. Chairman Yang Xiao Kun of Beijing's People's Liberation Committee had released a declaration stating, "If the Guangzhou puppet military continues with these hazardous provocations, we are prepared to take appropriate military action to protect the interests of the Chinese people." Mithril's spy satellite photos of the North China forces clearly indicated that it was not merely a threat.

Secretary General Zhang Gao Lou of Guangzhou's Democratic Chinese Union had likewise appeared before the Western media and criticized the North's attitude. To quote, "Beijing is scheming to use this incident in order to take control of the Three Gorges Dam. I don't see our democratic government yielding to any military intimidation from the North." Southern army units all over the country were entering into a heightened state of readiness.

The northern forces had designated a time limit: 2200 hours today. They said that if the Hong Kong situation hadn't come to an end by then, or if the South had failed to make some show of good faith, the North would not be held responsible for what happened thereafter.

In other words, civil war would reignite. It meant that many people would be dragged into the combat and lose their lives.

Tessa looked at the clock. It was now 16:31. There were only five and a half hours left.

"That's too soon. Now what do we do?"

It was indeed too soon. Mithril would somehow bring down the Venom if only both sides would wait another eight hours. The reconnaissance mission being undertaken by Intelligence and Mao's team had been planned with that kind of time frame in mind.

What were the Mithril higher-ups doing? If the organization didn't use its entire intelligence network to try to persuade the North and South armies, there was nothing Tessa's forces could do on their own. Did they intend to leave everything up to a sixteen-year-old commander and her unit, which was only two-hundred strong?

"Put me through to Operations HQ. Channel G3."

"There is a slight probability that channel G3 will be intercepted," said Dana.

"It doesn't matter. Do it quickly."

"Aye, ma'am. There is also an incoming call on channel GI. It is Urzu-2."

This time is was direct contact from Hong Kong. Things could not get any busier than this.

"Put it through."

"Yes, ma'am."

Mao delivered her report from the city. Corporal Yang had apparently discovered a corpse along with a strange message. Intelligence's recon teams had also discovered the same message two other times in various locations. In those cases, it had been scrawled on a wall and a floor instead of on a body. The message had also appeared in the classified ads of three local newspapers.

"'To the Tiger of Badakhshan's cub?'" Tessa knit her brows when she heard the message.

"What is that supposed to mean? It doesn't seem to be a disturbance or diversionary tactic," said Mardukas.

Tessa had heard of a place called Badakhshan about four months ago. There were currently two people she knew who had deep connections to it.

The ship's AI Dana was analyzing the message, but none of the established cryptanalysis systems could draw any inference regarding its contents.

Badakhshan was the name of a region in northeastern Afghanistan. Tsim Sha Tsui referred to a metropolitan area of Kowloon Peninsula. Hamidra was a rather common Arabic name. A search for individuals by that name living in Hong Kong turned up four hits. They would contact Intelligence and instruct them to follow up on each of the four.

Just then, Kalinin arrived from the hangar.

"Reporting, ma'am."

"Good timing, Lieutenant Commander. Take a look at this, if you would."

When the message appeared on-screen, the wrinkles on his forehead deepened even further.

"Does it mean anything to you, Mr. Kalinin?"

"Part of it does. 'Tiger of Badakhshan' is the alias of a legendary Afghani guerrilla commander."

"Afghani?"

"Yes, ma'am. I've gone up against him a number of times. Back then, the Soviet Union sent in a number of assassins in an attempt to rid themselves of the Tiger of Badakhshan. One of those assassins wasn't even quite eight years old. However, every single attempt ended in failure. The Tiger was deeply compassionate, and after the youngest would-be assassin was captured, he chose to raise him as his own son. He even gave him a new name." Kalinin fell silent for a moment, and then continued. "He named him Kashim."

"Kashim." Tessa had learned that name from the Arbalest's mission recorder after the hijacking incident two months ago.

"Captain, could you please put Sergeant Sagara on?"

"Yes. TDD-HQ to Urzu-2. Please let us speak to Urzu-7."

"This is Urzu-2. Uh...." Mao's voice hesitated on the other end of the static.

371

"Is something wrong?"

"I'm sorry, ma'am. Urzu-7 ... isn't here right now."

October 22, 17:08 (Eastern China Standard Time)
Kowloon Peninsula Special Ward (Democratic Union side)
Jordan

A feeble wind rustled some paper scraps down the street. *This is a strange sight*, thought Sousuke.

There were countless signs and shops. This area was probably usually jam-packed with shoppers and automobiles. Now it all looked like ruins.

Sousuke didn't even know where he was going at this point. He didn't feel motivated to do anything. If his own body was an AS, he would gladly surrender the controls to someone else. He was about as adverse to his own existence right now as he was to that white AS of his.

Mithril would probably never trust him again now that he'd gone AWOL. When he imagined his colleagues' disappointed faces

and looks of disdain, it made it feel like there was a lead weight in the pit of his belly. Even if the Arbalest was still a factor, they most likely wouldn't choose to count on him again.

Sousuke gave a bit of thought to returning to Tokyo, but he was no longer a student at that school. Nor did he have a place to live there, or the task of guarding Kaname Chidori. Besides, he couldn't make a living in that city. There was no war there. The only thing he could do well was fight. He didn't know anything else.

Maybe going north through this city, then into mainland China was a good idea. As long as he had money, he could just go north or west and eventually reach some combat zone. There would probably always be work for a mercenary. There'd be no ideology or advocacy. Instead he would just fight in order to live until tomorrow. It would be like his life before he joined Mithril. Then, one day he'd die by a roadside somewhere.

It seemed like quite an attractive plan.

What did other people do when they were in this state of mind? The mercenaries he knew before he joined Mithril would drink a lot of alcohol. They would practically bathe in it, stir up trouble, get into fights, and throw up a lot. It really didn't look like it was much fun, but it did seem to provide some form of distraction. That was Sousuke's take on liquor.

Alcohol, huh? I'll try some, he thought. According to the old warrior, Yaqub, drinking alcohol was a foolish deed. That didn't matter at this point. After all, Yaqub was dead.

A 7-Eleven was open, which was somewhat impressive. Sousuke went inside. The grocery shelves were all but empty. This disturbance must have made the neighborhood residents buy up all the food.

He picked up a bottle of Jack Daniel's and an English newspaper, and headed for the register. When he paid with a $500 bill he had, the middle-aged female clerk gave him a nasty look and handed him back his heaps of change.

Sousuke walked to a small park a block away and opened the whiskey. Without hesitation, he drank a gulp. Suddenly he was assaulted by a strange bitter taste, and it felt like his throat was on fire. He choked convulsively and coughed violently.

It tasted terrible. Why did everybody drink stuff like this as if they enjoyed it? Yaqub had been right.

He tossed the whiskey bottle into a trash can and opened the newspaper. There was one article about the Venom. Though naturally nobody at the newspaper knew the code-name Venom. All the known information and speculation about the mysterious

AS were listed, as was input military commentators had to offer. Citizens were frightened, evacuation routes were congested, and it was affecting the economy. None of it was good news by a long shot.

Then Sousuke's eyes suddenly stopped on a small classified ad: *To the Tiger of Badakhshan's cub. Meet with Hamidra in Tsim Sha Tsui.*

He realized at a glance that the message was probably meant for him. As it turned out, he was most likely the only person in the world who could decipher its meaning.

It was only about ten minutes on foot from Jordan to Tsim Sha Tsui. Sousuke's head felt a little dim. He had the feeling his field of vision had narrowed. That one swig must have had an effect on him.

He went into a touristy camera store around which nothing else was open, and started asking an employee questions.

"There's at least one building in this neighborhood that houses a bunch of Arab-run businesses," answered the employee in fluent English. Sousuke thanked him, then started out for that building.

There were several dark-skinned, bearded young men hanging out around the narrow entrance. They stared at Sousuke, but none of them bothered to speak to him.

There were lots of small shops crammed into the shared building. It was a veritable marketplace, and it was noisy. A crowd of customers filled this place, which contrasted with the quiet main street outside. The aisles in here were narrow to begin with, yet all manner of goods were set up that encroached further on the available space. Clothing and foodstuffs, electronics and video media were on display everywhere one looked. There was some lively hit song playing from somewhere, loud business transactions were taking place, and men who seemed to have lots of time on their hands were shooting the breeze. It was like, as far as this building was concerned, the threat from the Venom practically didn't matter.

It came as little surprise that nearly all the men walking down the aisles were Arabic. They were probably laborers who had come a long way from home to work here. The largest group of them were Iranian, but many African people were here as well.

"Are there any Afghani electric appliance dealers here? Or any Tajik ones?" Sousuke asked a bored-looking Iranian at a T-shirt stand. He voiced the question in an Afghani dialect of Persian. He was surprised by how rusty his own pronunciation sounded.

The man did not reply. He just gazed absentmindedly at Sousuke, his mouth hanging half open.

Sousuke repeated his question, but the man still did not respond. He gave up and asked the CD shop owner next door.

"Take a right at the third corner down there. You'll see a sign in the back." The shopkeeper didn't even try to get Sousuke to buy his goods, but instead pointed down a narrow aisle. Then he smiled a complacent smile which revealed he was missing some teeth, and said, "Take my advice. Once your business is done, you shouldn't hang around in this building. You look like a cute girl in here."

"I see."

Some of the passersby were definitely giving Sousuke *that* kind of look. He was a seventeen-year-old Asian with finely-textured skin, no beard, and no body odor, so it came as no surprise. Back when he worked with a different group of guerrillas, they had always regarded him with a bizarre sense of kindness. There were several incidents when he was nearly assaulted while asleep.

He soon found the shop he sought. An old neon sign told him it was the electronics shop.

To the Tiger of Badakhshan's cub. Meet with Hamidra in Tsim Sha Tsui.

The message was an extremely simple code for Sousuke. "The Tiger of Badakhshan" was an alias of a man called Majid, who had once become famous as the leader of a group of Afghani guerrillas. He was an unrivaled mountain warfare strategist, a poet, and also an architect.

The guerrillas he led had been invincible until the early 90s. But when the USSR seriously began to send ASes into Afghanistan, the situation reversed itself. The AS humanoid weapons were different from previous land combat weapons, and could move freely though inaccessible mountain terrain. Unarmored guerrillas had almost no way to oppose these new threats. Majid's men fought a good fight, but over a period of several years they suffered catastrophic losses and were essentially wiped out.

Majid himself had been missing since then. Not even Sousuke knew if he was alive or dead. But Sousuke had been one of those guerrillas until three years ago. Majid had given him the name Kashim. Back when they were still doing well militarily, Majid had entrusted Kashim to Yaqub, an elderly warrior upon whom he relied. His order to Yaqub was to instill in Kashim the art of combat and a compassionate heart.

This was why "the Tiger of Badakhshan's cub" referred to Sousuke. Majid had a number of other sons, but the following sentence of the message made it unlikely that it meant any of them. Hamidra was the name of one of Sousuke's dead comrades. He originally ran an electronics shop in Kabul, but became a guerrilla when he lost his shop to civil war. He was the one who repaired moderately damaged enemy ASes so that Sousuke could use them. Lieutenant Commander Kalinin was also acquainted with Hamidra, but he probably didn't know his real name or his line of business. Therefore Kalinin wouldn't understand the entire code. The only ones who would were Sousuke or the dead guerrillas.

The message might have meant "To Sousuke Sagara. Meet with the Afghani electronics dealer in Tsim Sha Tsui." No other interpretation seemed plausible.

Is one of my comrades still alive? No, that can't be. I saw their remains with my own eyes, after all. Then, is it a friend or family member of one of them?

That was possible. But in that case, how did he know Sousuke would come to Hong Kong? Did it have something to do with the Venom disturbance? Was it a trap, or a helping hand? He had no idea. Either way, he couldn't ignore it. That was why he had come all the way here.

The electronics shop was at the very back of a gloomy aisle, and there was no sign of anyone. Sousuke made sure he could access the gun under his work uniform at any time, and checked to see if he was being watched. It was simply a habit for him to be wary of people following him, but it immediately occurred to him that it was a silly thing to do. He wasn't on any mission right now. His death wouldn't concern anybody at the moment.

He looked deeper into the shop. There was an old man sitting near the back. It wasn't anybody Sousuke recognized. As he approached and was about to speak up, the old man spoke first.

"So you're Majid's son, Kashim."

"That's right."

"You reek of liquor. You're a good-for-nothing punk. Are you trying to soil the Tiger of Badakhshan's name?"

"I don't care. State your business."

The old man was obviously displeased as he thrust out a small folded piece of paper with his left hand.

"Someone asked me to give this to you, that's all."

"Who?"

"Some Hong Konger man. That's all I know. Just take this and get lost."

Sousuke took the piece of paper and left the shop without even saying thanks. When he opened the paper, he saw it was part of a Hong Kong sightseeing map. There was a red circle around a fountain in Kowloon Park, which was located several hundred meters from here.

October 22, 18:09 (Eastern China Standard Time)
South China Sea
Tuatha de Daanan

In an effort to save time, communication with Operations HQ was happening on one of the real-time G channels. This was due to the fact that the situation was already growing quite sticky.

"We can no longer afford to take our time with reconnaissance. The plan to catch them sleeping has been suspended," announced Admiral Borda's voice. It had a pained sound to it. "Mobilize all the TDD-I's M9s. The next time the Venom appears, we'll have them bring it down as a group. Use of the Arbalest, however, is prohibited. I don't want to expose that mech to danger."

"J-just a moment, please," Tessa objected, leaning forward in her captain's chair. "My men still haven't finished working out Venom countermeasures. There is no telling what losses we will incur if we attack it now. Please give me at least two more hours."

"I can't. This was also Lord Mallory's call," said Borda

"Yes, but—"

"The tension between the North and South armies has reached its limit, and there are significant casualties every time Venom shows up. We can't permit any more damage. How many more will have to die before you stop saying 'wait'?"

It was a harsh thing to say. The admiral's point made Tessa lose the will to object further.

"We've heard the Venom's weakness is its operating time. I guess our only choice is to take advantage of that. Have faith in your men. Situations like this are why they're the best of the best."

This wasn't like a typical mission. There was a risk that several of the M9 pilots wouldn't make it back. That fact was understood when the order was given.

"Maybe this stings, Teletha. But I told you about the grimness of the path you travel. And you showed no sign of wanting to leave that seat even once you knew. Am I wrong?"

"...No, sir. What you say is true."

"That's right. Now carry out the mission, Captain Teletha Testarossa."

"Yes, sir."

Tessa ended the transmission and took off her headset. Then she hung her head and said to Mardukas, "Climb to periscope depth. Prep all M9s on standby for immediate underwater launch. Also, please equip the ARX-7 with an urgent deployment booster. Give it a Boxer shot cannon and have it standby on an elevator."

"Captain, I thought we were just told that use of the Arbalest was prohibited?"

"It can still be a decoy. I want to lessen the danger to everybody in the M9s as much as possible. And besides ... Mr. Sagara is still...."

Mardukas groaned a little when he heard Tessa trail off. "Captain, with all due respect. The only conclusion to be made about Sagara is that he abandoned his duty. It is clearly a mistake to count on him or that AS."

"That is not necessarily true."

"This is not a school club outing."

"I'm aware of that. Are you trying to lecture me *now* of all times?"

The voices of the captain and XO now resounded throughout the entire command center. The crew was focused on the two of them, not to mention obviously surprised. Mardukas realized this and hesitated for an instant, but then made up his mind to continue his admonition.

"No, ma'am, but I cannot keep quiet on the matter this time. You are allowing personal feelings to influence you into distorting an order from HQ. What about our organization and its military regulations? Conferring special treatment on an NCO who abandoned his mission is absurd!" His voice was stern enough to make a veteran officer cringe, but Tessa still did not back down.

"Very well. Then, who was it who forced outrageously heavy responsibilities on that NCO?" asked Tessa.

"Well—"

"It was us! If I'm wrong about this, just try and correct me!"

Mardukas remained silent.

"Six months ago, who was it who provided us with invaluable information from an airport crawling with enemies, while paying no heed to his own personal safety? Four months ago, who was it who faced a full-on assault by an enemy whose power eclipsed that of a Venom's, and then managed to bring it down? Two months ago, who was it who fought desperately to save this very ship?"

"W—"

"Tell me! Who was it?!"

Silence reigned in the command center. Mardukas was silent with astonishment for a moment, but then he sighed and answered: "It was Sergeant Sagara."

"Correct. And yet you condemn him? You arbitrarily decide he's a coward?"

"No, ma'am."

"If you want me to admit it, I will. I love him. But such personal feelings have nothing to do with this. I swear it. I'm sure he will come through for us again. He cannot and will not desert us completely. No matter how useless he might be at present, a person's true nature is unalterable. And he is strong and kind."

"Strong and kind?"

After a long, long silence, Mardukas said "Captain. Is that supposed to convince me?"

"That isn't what this is about, is it? Do you believe in me, or don't you? You have come very far with me to reach this point. Choose!" she said with resolve.

The XO turned away from the captain, and took off his hat. He looked down at it, said to have been given to him by someone long ago as a memento, and ran his thumb over the embroidery.

"You sure have grown strong," said Richard Mardukas, as if to himself. "Understood, ma'am. Let's put the Arbalest on standby."

"Thank you. I just want ... everyone to come back safely," Tessa said, bending forward slightly.

As it turned out, for some reason the ship-wide com system had been on during the dispute. The M9 pilots on standby had heard every word.

"There you have it. That channel just opened of its own accord. Did somebody mean for us to hear that?" Kurz asked the other four pilots over their private channel.

"Well ... I don't know," said Lieutenant Clouseau.

"The lieutenant commander, maybe?" said Kurz.

"Who can say?" said Clouseau.

"Never mind that. Did Sagara ... really go AWOL? That's hard to believe," said Urzu-8, Corporal Spec.

"That's just the commander's story. Don't swallow it."

"Have you heard anything about it, Lieutenant Clouseau?"

"I heard the long and short of it. But that's not enough to draw a conclusion. Lieutenant Commander Kalinin agrees. In any case, Sagara and the Arbalest aren't currently combat assets."

"What do you think, Roger?"

"I don't know Sagara's true nature. But the colonel did make a good point. A hawk is still a hawk until the day he dies."

"Still a hawk ... huh?"

The men of the SRT expressed their thoughts a bit longer as they resumed checks of their mechs.

"Still, I never expected Tessa and the XO to get that intense with the back and forth."

"She loves Sagara, doesn't she? And they're the same age."

"It's not just that," Kurz grumbled.

"She said, 'I just want everyone to come back safely.' What do you make of *that*, gentlemen?"

"That's what we intend to do, naturally," said Clouseau.

"I'll be damned if we're gonna make our princess sad," said Urzu-3, First Lieutenant Castello.

"I'm surprised at how worried she is about us. I guess you could describe that as touching?" said Corporal Spec.

"She's a good officer," said Urzu-5, Sergeant Roger Thunderraptor.

They were all lost in thought, and felt both thankful and wary that Tessa trusted them unconditionally despite the incident involving Dunnigan and Nguyen. Then, the order came from the command center over the standard channel for all units to mobilize.

"Urzu-1 to all units. You heard it. We'll link up with Urzu-2 on the ground, then take up our positions. Lieutenant Commander Kalinin will assume full command from the air. If you're pros, live up to the expectations placed on you. I'm not going to mess up, and neither will you. That should take care of everything. Ready?"

"Roger that, sir."

October 22, 18:24 (Eastern China Standard Time)
Hong Kong Island Special Ward (People's Committee side)
Mithril Intelligence Bureau Hong Kong Branch Office

General Amit, the head of Intelligence, had given Hunter the same mission change order that had been thrust upon Teletha Testarossa.

"In other words, sir, we've run out of time?"

"That's correct. Leave the rest in Operations' hands."

"Understood, sir."

"Good."

When Amit vanished from the screen, the first thing Hunter did was curse loudly.

"Goddamn it!"

He had undertaken this request from Melissa Mao and her superiors and contributed some of his precious personnel, and now *this* happened just when it looked like they might have a chance to catch the enemy. If only they had waited another two hours. Then, this might have been settled with hardly a shot being fired.

"Sir.... Um, Mr. Hunter?" said his Hong Konger secretary as he walked into his office.

"What is it?"

"You have visitors. They've been going on about urgently needing to see you for some time now."

"Ask them to leave. I'm in an extremely poor mood right now. I don't care how rude they might think I am."

"W-will do, sir."

The secretary bowed and made to leave, but the two visitors pretty much brushed him aside as they barged into Hunter's office. One of them was a fellow Intelligence agent he knew well, and the other was an Asian girl he had never seen.

"Listen, mister. How many *hours* do you expect us to wait?!" the girl shouted as she walked up to him.

October 22, 18:31 (Eastern China Standard Time)
Kowloon Peninsula Special Ward (Democratic Union side)
Kowloon Park

Holding the sightseeing map in one hand, Sousuke walked through the deserted park. Kowloon Park was like a solitary island of green

390

that opened up right in the middle of all the buildings on the Kowloon Peninsula. Its ambiance was much like that of Shinjuku Central Park.

There was a fountain with no water running in it. This was the spot marked on the map. Sousuke nonchalantly sat down on a nearby bench. He couldn't bring himself to care enough to do a check of the surroundings. If someone was out to kill him, that was fine. That would at least make things easier.

The street lights shone brightly. In the distance he could see a row of tall buildings. There were at least five good positions from which someone could snipe him where he sat.

No one came. Five minutes passed. Then, electronic sounds emanated from a nearby trash can. Sousuke approached and looked inside. Under a candy bar wrapper was a cell phone, and it was ringing.

He retrieved the phone and pressed the answer button.

"You're Sousuke Sagara?" asked an unfamiliar male voice.

"That's right."

"Are you alone?"

"That's right."

"There's a taxi waiting at the park's north exit. Take that phone with you and get in."

That was the end of the call. Sousuke stood up heavily and headed for the north exit. When he exited the park, there was a taxi idling in front of a convenience store. There were no other cars, just the sound of a very distant ambulance siren.

When he got into the taxi, the driver said something and then started driving. It didn't look like he understood English, so it was no use asking him anything. They went north up the main street, heading for the squalid downtown area, but at no point were there many people to be seen.

The taxi stopped in front of a hardware store with its shutter down. The driver gestured for Sousuke to get out. Apparently he didn't expect to be paid.

The taxi took off. Downtown was deathly quiet this evening. A countless number of signs filled the grey sky. The phone in Sousuke's hand rang in the silence of the otherwise deserted lamplit street.

"You should see a yellow sign. Take the spare key inside mailbox number 13 back there," said the man's voice. The sound of some kind of power generator was audible in the background. "There's a staircase near you. Go up to the second floor. You'll see a hallway. Open the fifth door and go inside. He's waiting for you in there."

"He? He who?"

"Think about the name of this place."

The call ended. Once again it had been short. Sousuke looked around. There was a bus stop nearby. On its sign was written: KOWLOON WALLED CITY. It didn't ring any bells.

No—Kowloon. No, it can't be. That's not possible. Not at this point.

It all added up, though. There was no turning back now that he had come this far. Sousuke did as the voice instructed. He retrieved the key from the mailbox and climbed the staircase next to the hardware store. He then walked down the apartment building's hallway and stopped in front of the fifth door.

Despite how much willpower he had lost, even Sousuke was now feeling some level of tension. He inserted the key and opened the door. Inside he saw one of the rooms of a cramped apartment. The living space was even smaller than in a typical Tokyo apartment. Hardly any furniture was present.

Sousuke slowly advanced into the gloomy room. It occurred to him that he was unconsciously searching for traps like wires or lasers. At some point, he'd drawn his automatic pistol. It all looked so foolish. This was a trap and he was marching directly into it. His feet kept moving anyway.

He exited the living room. Light was coming in through a window. There was a single bed at the back of this room, where a profound darkness hung. Someone was lying on the bed.

"Hi...."

An electronic-sounding synthetic voice came from the pitch dark room. And it was speaking in Japanese.

"I've been waiting a long time, Kashim."

Light from an automobile outside came through the window and illuminated the face of the man lying in bed for an instant. His facial features looked as if they'd been horribly and thoroughly altered, but Sousuke still muttered a name to himself.

"Gauron."

Kowloon was pronounced "Gauron" in the Cantonese dialect.

Kowloon Peninsula; Kowloon Park; Kowloon City. Why hadn't he realized it sooner? Rather, why hadn't he even given it any thought when it should have been obvious? Also, the mystery man had known about his life as Kashim. Gauron was the only one besides Kalinin who might have known that much about Sousuke and Hamidra. But there should have been no possible way this guy was still alive.

"Gauron...."

He looked small. His arms were missing, as were his legs. All that was left of him was his right thigh and upper left arm—the rest of his limbs were nowhere to be seen.

There were a large number of IVs and tubes. Several cords were attached to medical equipment, which was emitting a low hum. He probably could no longer live without technological assistance.

His face was an awful mess, too. The skin on the left side had peeled off, making it look like a keloid. His left eye was gone, a gaping hole where the eyeball should be. His scarred gums and teeth were exposed and they were smiling at Sousuke.

Gauron lay there on the clean bed, staring happily at Sousuke with his one eye.

"I'm happy to see you, Kashim," said the synthesized sound. It was artificial vocal cords. "Want something to drink? Unfortunately, it's all self-serve in this place."

"Why are you—"

"Alive? This makes three times now. But don't worry. This'll be the last." A rustling noise sounded through the room. It was probably Gauron laughing.

"Don't you forget, now. My Codarl had a Lambda Driver installed in it. If it came down to it, it was even possible to protect the operator from a self-destruct. But then, its 'protection' is how I ended up in this sorry state." Gauron laughed.

"How'd you survive that storm?"

"A fishing boat happened to pass through the area. So only half of me ended up as fish food. The ocean's just full of mysteries, you know. It nearly killed me. That part sucked."

Sousuke pointed his handgun at Gauron's head. "I'll make sure you die *this* time."

"Fine by me. But look at the state I'm in. I don't think you need to be in any hurry."

"What are you after?"

"I wanted to talk to you."

"Quit joking."

"It's true. Heh heh. As you can see, my time's almost done. That's why I went to the trouble of setting this up. I filched a Codarl M from the organization and had it raise hell in this city. I knew that would get you and that white AS to show up. I also scattered that message around different parts of the city. Places your people would be likely to search, and in ways that would get your attention. Stuff like that."

The classified ad Sousuke saw must have been one of those. Maybe Mao, Yang, and the others had found the message, too. But they couldn't have been able to understand its meaning.

"And so, here you are. I figured you might bring your pals along with you ... but you're alone. Now how did *that* come about?"

"It's none of your business."

Sousuke meant to seem calm when he said it, but Gauron seemed to sense a slight unrest in the air. A cheerless laugh escaped him.

"Hmph. Maybe you've finally reached the point where you're not comfortable there?" Gauron laughed.

"What?"

"At Mithril. Bunch of justice hero wannabes—I bet anybody would get fed up with that group eventually. Especially a man like you."

Sousuke couldn't deny that there was some truth in that. He didn't want to touch on it further, so he forced a change of subject.

"Why don't you tell me about the organization that backs you?"

"So you still want to keep this professional, huh? Heh heh heh."

Sousuke didn't respond to that.

"Fine. Think of this as a freebie. It's also my little *revenge* against them," Gauron said readily, and then started to garrulously explain:

"Amalgam. That's the name of the organization I worked for. You might say their main goal is the research and development of cutting-edge weapons, along with testing them in combat. That's why they stir up terrorism and regional conflicts. There are a large number of Amalgam sympathizers in the hard-line factions of pretty much every country's government. After all, there are many in both the East and West who want to preserve the structure of and supply munitions to the Cold War. The Fifth Middle East War, the Chinese North-South War, the Soviet Civil War ... they say Amalgam was involved with all of them."

"And now this trouble in Hong Kong, too."

Gauron chuckled. "This one's all me. I bet Amalgam's in a panic right about now, for once. You see, there was a time when I raised a couple of brothers whose circumstances were very similar to yours. I ordered those two to cause this disturbance. Feast your eyes on these clean sheets. The medical equipment's top of the line, too. Their loyalty brings tears to my eye."

"One of them is piloting the Venom?"

"If you mean the Codarl M, yes."

"Where's he hiding?"

"Do you really think I'll tell you? What's inside that bag? Answer: a transmitter. I'm not *that* senile."

"Tell me." Sousuke aimed his pistol at Gauron, who just smiled.

"Whoa, whoa. You think I value my life? Maybe *you're* the one who's gone senile, eh?"

With no other option available, Sousuke lowered his gun.

"You said they're called Amalgam. Do they have any of these Whispered people?"

"There you go, keep asking that kind of question. The answer is yes. In fact, one of their key members is one. He's one creepy kid, but he's amusing."

"If they have a Whispered, why are they after Kaname Chidori? They shouldn't need her anymore."

"Because it's not a complete package. Apparently, each Whispered contains different pieces of knowledge. One's strength might be theoretical Lambda Driver technology, and another might only be able to shine when it comes to submarine engineering. There are multiple fields. So when a new Whispered is discovered, the first thing you need to do is specify which field her strengths are in. The tests that were done on that girl in Sunan were apparently to figure out if she really was a Whispered—and then to determine her particular characteristics.

"What were the results?"

"It looks like she definitely is a Whispered. But you know, I haven't heard what kind of specialist she is. Amalgam's stance was just to wait and see. I don't see why they didn't just kidnap her again and continue investigating. Your guess is as good as mine."

"Where is Amalgam's base? Who are its key members?"

Gauron laughed and said, "Now you're getting into it, asking lots of questions. Here's a hint: 'badame.'"

"Badame?"

"That's all I'm gonna tell you. I'm really tired of talkin' about this. Not that I mind talkin' with you. This is just boring—it's not even our main topic."

Sousuke looked down quietly at Gauron's twisted face as he spoke these odd words. The thought of begging this man even a little bit disgusted him—but despite this, he said, "Tell me. Please."

He was sure Gauron would find pleasure in this, and he ground his teeth as he waited for the response. However, Gauron was not happy. For that matter, he shot a look at Sousuke that was clearly filled with scorn and irritation.

"'Please,' huh? Hearing a word like coming from you makes me want to puke."

"What?"

"I guess you went and sold your soul to shady ol' Mithril."

"Shady?"

"Yup. Heh heh. Now we're gettin' to the main topic." Gauron cleared his throat and then said, "Think about it. They blew billions of dollars so they could have that submarine of theirs. Now it shames me a little to say this, but how many hundreds of thousands of poor people do you think could've been helped by that same money? They stave off regional conflicts? They enforce the peace? Come on, get real. How are they any different from Amalgam? The first thing they should do is dig a well for a village in some destitute country. Don't you agree?"

"That's sidestepping the issue."

"It sure is. But there's still no way to get rid of that shadiness. Frankly, well, it's easy to see why Dunnigan and Nguyen rebelled the way they did. And there you are, in that same Mithril. You seem so unnatural to me now. *You*, Kashim. You weren't even concerned about your own life. You were like a doll—no emotions. The Kashim I remember just kept killing enemies, like a faithful pet dog."

Those words conjured up memories of Sousuke's time before joining Mithril.

"Think back. What were you doing when you first met me?"

That had been over five years ago. Gauron had been an instructor at a mercenary training camp inside Afghanistan. Kashim was a guerrilla fighting the Soviet army in a mountainous area not far from there. It was something of a coincidence that they had met, and at the time, they weren't mutual enemies. They weren't allies either, of course, but their interests weren't especially opposed.

When Kashim first met Gauron, he had just taken out a group of Soviet ASes and was in the middle of disposing of the corpses of enemy soldiers. He still remembered the first words Gauron had said.

"You're one hard worker, kid. Did you kill all of them?"

Gauron had by chance been passing by, and he parked his jeep on the side of the road and addressed Kashim. He still had all four burly limbs, and there was no scar on his forehead.

"Yes," Kashim had answered, and looked out over the wreckages of ASes and armored vehicles, and the charred corpses. Only one mech out of all of them was kneeling, his own RK-92.

Gauron had smiled the same melancholy way he was smiling now, and said, "In that case, I'm really looking forward to the future. What's your name?"

"Kashim."

"Kashim. You guys're gonna lose this war soon. Why not come to my camp? We've got food, ammo, and AS parts."

"I refuse."

"All right. Well, take care."

Gauron had taken off while Kashim returned to dealing with the bodies. That had been the end of their first meeting.

"You were quietly disposing of burned corpses," said Gauron.

"I was in Cambodia when I was that same age. And guess what? Every day I would quietly dispose of the corpses of the people Pol Pot and his bunch massacred. So at the time, I felt like I already knew you. Heh heh."

"Fine. So what?"

"You had this great look in your eyes then. There was no worry, doubt, or pain. They were like the eyes of a wild animal— no, of a saint. Nothing could shock you. Killing people was like breathing for you, and you weren't hung up on the idea of life. I guess that's what you'd call beautiful. Do you understand? It means consistency, in other words. No contradictions. You get it? Aren't *I* the philosophical one?"

Sousuke didn't respond.

"You know when we met again in Sunan? I was really happy about it. Heh heh. You still had those eyes—those great eyes you used to have. You didn't care about human life. I thought it'd be nice if I could be the one to kill you then. I even thought about dragging your corpse out of the AS and sodomizing it. Nah, just joking." Gauron laughed uproariously. "Really!"

What was left of Gauron shook and rattled on top of the bed, a chilling wild guffaw resounding through the room. It made his tragic spectacle even more horrifying for anyone who witnessed it.

"So, how do you explain that face of yours now?" said Gauron, his laughter suddenly coming to a halt.

"What?"

"Your face looks like the faces of all those other vermin brats. Are you worried about something? Are you lost? Where did Saint Kashim go? I'm disappointed in you. I bet you're just gettin' dragged down into stupid, worthless shit. Right now, you're *full* of contradictions. It's damn ugly—even harder to look at than *I* am. Killing you wouldn't be worth a damn thing."

"Be quiet." Sousuke once again pointed his gun at Gauron.

"We're cut from the same mold and you know it. Why are you trying to force yourself to be ordinary? It makes me sick."

"I told you to be quiet."

"No, I'm gonna keep talkin'. You've become worthless since you fell in with Mithril and the people at that school. Those freakin' *weak*, *naive* assholes are dragging you down, and you've *become* a drag. You know how I mentioned getting fed up before? It's because of them. Because of their humanism—otherwise known as the *ressentiment* of the weak. That's no place for Kashim the Killing Saint. They're taking advantage of you, mark my words. The weak live off the strong like parasites. They toss around sugar-coated terms like "comrades" and "trust," and they suck up the strength of the strong all the way down to the bone."

Sousuke didn't want to hear this. Nor could he help that what this man was saying seemed to make sense. Could something this terrible be true? Could this bitter enemy be the only one who'd guessed the main reason he was in this situation?

But I've definitely become weak. It's true. When did it happen?

It happened since he encountered Mithril, Jindai High School, and her.

"Tell me how you really feel. Do you enjoy flocking together with the weak?"

"Ugh!"

Some unseen thing seemed to be beckoning to him from the darkness beyond the bed.

"Come on, answer me. I asked you if joining the weak flock's a good time!"

"I told you to be quiet!" Sousuke pulled the trigger. The sound of a gunshot rang out through the room. The bullet hit Gauron's pillow, kicking up a bit of smoke. That was all.

"Can't even bring yourself to kill an enemy, huh?" asked Gauron, a faint smile on his lips.

"Shut up," was all Sousuke could say in a subdued voice. His face felt hot, it was very difficult to breathe, and his back was drenched with sweat.

Then, a large shadow fell across the window. It was the Venom. It must have been in hiding somewhere nearby. The diamond-shaped head peered through the square window at Sousuke and Gauron.

"Ah, Fei Jiu," said Gauron.

"I will go now," responded a voice from the Venom's external speakers. It was the same voice from the cell phone.

"All right. Take care," said Gauron.

"Farewell, *Xiansheng*."

The Venom covered its right fist with its left hand, bowed, then turned and leaped. The grey AS easily cleared the signs and the apartment building, and vanished into the heart of the city. The gust of wind left in its wake rattled the window a bit.

"Fei Jiu's probably going to die while tangling with Mithril. Otherwise, he'll be killed by Amalgam's task force."

"Task force?"

"Their commander's one crazy bastard. I'm pretty sure your comrades won't be able to keep up with him. He'll kill them all on sight. But hey, what's so bad about that?" Gauron laughed wildly once again.

"I'm gonna die soon," said Gauron as he looked up at the ceiling. There wasn't a hint of tragedy in his voice. "And since that's the case, I think I'll take a bunch of people with me. That's my style, after all. I ordered Fei Jiu to go wild and to keep it up until Hong Kong's in a sea of flames. I ordered the other one, Fei Hong, to kill the *biggest cancer* that's dragging you down."

"Biggest ... cancer?"

Gauron smiled his final smile. It covered his whole face, suggesting that this joy came from the heart.

"*The bitch*, Kashim. Don't tell me you still haven't heard?"

"What?!"

"I heard the whole story. She was so cute in that uniform, all mangled to a pulp. But she was brave. I hear she didn't beg for her life. Her last words were 'I'm sorry.' Now who could she have been sayin' that to? Ahh, it's enough to make you cry."

"Y-you're lying."

"Oh, it's true. I wanted to show you pictures of the girl's corpse and watch your face when you took that bitter pill, but I guess I'll just have to go without. I mean, hey, Kashim. It's plain to see how much this has already damaged you. You *can't save* your girl in *Tokyo*. Oh, it's *so* sad. *Kaname!* She was such a good *girl!*"

Sousuke pointed the gun directly at Gauron. The barrel wasn't shaking in the slightest.

"Gauron!"

"That's right, I killed her! Now come on, hate me!"

He didn't hesitate a second longer. Sousuke aimed at Gauron's chest and fired six shots in succession. The body shook a bit, and fresh blood splattered on the sheets. The electrocardiogram machine emitted a hollow tone.

Gauron still had the stiff smile on his face, but he never spoke another word. His eyelid was wide open. He had been staring at the spot where the tip of Sousuke's gun had been until a few seconds ago.

"No!"

The inside of his head was ringing. He didn't know where he was, or who he was. What did this corpse in front of him mean? Who had died in some distant land?

Kaname's dead?

Sousuke was all alone in this gloomy room in a deserted town. At this moment, he truly was alone in the world.

He heard an electronic sound. *Beep ... beep ... beep ... beep, beep, beep, beep* it went, steadily rising. It was not the sound of medical equipment. It was something different—yes, from under the bed—

Something in the corner of his nearly-vacant mind warned him. His body moved instinctively, his brain not even bothering to question why he chose to move at that exact moment, and he kicked off the floor and jumped through the nearby window shoulder-first.

Immediately afterward, the room exploded. The high-power explosive beneath the bed detonated, and the blast shook the apartment building. A storm of flame burst out of the window from which he'd leapt. The impact of the explosion smashed the surrounding windows, and countless fragments rained down on the deserted street.

Sousuke moaned as he hung from a sign he had barely managed to grab a hold of. His hand slipped and he fell to the sidewalk in front of the hardware store. Flames were burning brightly overhead.

There were fragments scattered everywhere around the street. Sousuke staggered to his feet and gazed vaguely at various building materials here and there, most emitting little fires of their own.

Two men came running down the glass-covered street. They wore plain clothes so he couldn't tell at first, but they were Intelligence staffers who worked for Hunter.

"You look terrible, Sergeant," said one of them, looking up at the second floor of the apartment building which was now even further engulfed in flames.

"Why are you here?" asked Sousuke

"Your lieutenant commander asked us to follow you."

"Right."

"There's a museum near here for Kowloon City ruins. Looks like the Venom was hiding in its courtyard. Of course ... that's all meaningless now."

The roar of cannon fire rang out from the heart of the city. The Venom was probably going nuts. There were several more shots. South Chinese ASes had engaged it in combat.

No. Those weren't South China forces. Sousuke was quite familiar with those rapid muffled shots. They were the sound of GEC-B rifles, made by Oerlikon Contraves. South China forces were not equipped with those.

"Your team is fighting in their M9s."

"What?"

"Somebody decided we were out of time. They're going to confront the Venom head-on."

It sounded nothing short of reckless. How were they supposed to oppose a Venom without the Arbalest? It was practically an act of suicide.

"We just got word over the radio. They're going to send your AS here from the *Tuatha de Daanan.*"

"What?"

"I don't know the details. We're about to go look for anything left behind at the Venom's hiding spot. Anyway, don't move from this position. That's what we came to tell you," said the Intel agent, and he and his partner ran off down the street. Now left behind, all Sousuke could do was stand there alone.

The Arbalest's coming here?

But there was no longer any way Sousuke could manage that mech. It had screwed up his fate, and he never wanted to see it again. He wanted to contact the *de Danaan* and tell them to forget it since it was useless, but the bag which contained his transmitter had been blown away along with Gauron.

Gauron.

Had his reflexes been a little less sharp, Sousuke probably would have died in that room, too. Had he really meant to take him along in death?

No. That wasn't it. He had tested him. Had his mental state not allowed him to move at that point, life would no longer have been worth living. He had lost something vital, yet he still jumped into action. Perhaps Gauron had wanted to ridicule that trait of his. Maybe his message was *I'm going to die. You can carry on and suffer even more...?*

It was probably something like that. In killing Kaname Chidori, Gauron had snatched away his hope and his future. If that had been his actual plan, the curse had been realized.

Kaname was dead. It just didn't seem real. But Sousuke could feel in his heart that whatever light and warmth he had was now gone. He had seen a lot of death up to this point. Now she had joined the ranks of his dead comrades, with her own page in that gloomy memorial album.

He didn't cry. That old sense of depression simply returned for the first time in a while.

This is it, then. Nothing ever changes. I never had a future in the first place.

A chilly wind blew through the desolate gap in his chest. He felt indifferent about himself. He felt indifferent about life. Now no matter who died, it probably wouldn't touch his heart in the least.

There was a roar from the sky. He saw a white bird to the south, in the narrowly visible stretch of sky covered in countless signs. It was no bird, however. It was the Arbalest. It glided through the night sky on the wings of its urgent deployment booster as it headed right toward him. The booster finished firing. The wings detached and a parachute opened.

It decelerated, but it still wasn't enough. A secondary parachute opened and it decelerated further.

Once the parachutes detached, the white giant plunged through the countless signs and fell to the deserted street. Asphalt smashed into little pieces, which bounced on the street along with shredded bits of sign. Yet its momentum still remained, and the Arbalest collapsed and fell forward, plunging toward Sousuke. Its landing had failed due to the cramped urban environment.

The giant drew nearer. It passed by dangerously close to him, and crashed chest-first into the burning apartment building. A gust of wind rustled Sousuke's hair and uniform, but he didn't even try to duck out of the way. The white mech flopped onto its right side. The flaming building materials that were scattered by the collision were spread out all around it.

It was a shameful landing, to say the least. It was downright horrible. Just like Sousuke himself. The mech laid there in the flames, collapsed in a limp heap. Its two eyes were staring vaguely in his direction.

We're the worst combination ever. That was what the Arbalest's eyes were saying to him.

I know you hate me. I hate you, too. So I won't mind if you just up and leave. In other words, I don't feel motivated at all either. Who cares at this point?

At least, that's what the Arbalest seemed to be saying to Sousuke.

You don't care who dies, anyway, do you? It's none of your concern what happens to Kurz, Mao, or the others. After all, everybody dies eventually. Just like Kaname Chidori. It happened to all those guys in Afghanistan. Everyone dies. So will you. That's how the world works. Just give up.

Sousuke had the feeling he was being ridiculed, being made a fool of. It felt like a mere machine was disdaining him. However, this still failed to make him angry.

"You're right," Sousuke muttered. His voice sounded chilly and hollow. "Just lay there and rust away."

It didn't matter. He wasn't interested. Whatever happened, it was no concern of his.

Just as he was about to walk away, it happened. He heard Japanese being spoken by a girl.

"What are you doing just standing there, spouting that nonsense?"

He turned around and there stood Kaname Chidori in the flesh.

He actually rubbed his eyes in disbelief. Kaname was standing in the middle of the road, dressed in her Jindai High uniform. Her overnight bag hung from her right shoulder. From her head to her toes, there was the girl he knew so well. No, upon closer inspection, there were adhesive bandages here and there on her slender white legs. A supporter was on her right knee and there was a band-aid on her jaw.

"Huh...?"

"Don't you say 'huh' to me," said the frowning girl for whom the only description that seemed to fit was Kaname Chidori.

"Chidori?"

It wasn't a hallucination. She was alive. But what on Earth was she doing here? How did she know where he was?

Sousuke staggered as he walked over to her.

"Chidori.... You're ... all right?"

"More or less."

"...I thought ... you were dead. Chido—"

The overnight bag hit him square on the side of the face and he staggered hard.

"Huh?"

"Stop saying 'huh' to me!" Kaname shouted. "I went through a heap of trouble to get here. What do you mean, 'I thought you were dead'?! I was going to run up and hug you when I saw you—I figured it would probably feel like that kind of moment. Well, guess what? Now I don't feel that way at *all*. What's the big idea?! Huh? How are you gonna take responsibility?!"

"Hey, wait a minute. I don't, uh, really under—"

"Shut up!"

Her fist hit him on the jaw.

"Guh!"

"Does that hurt? It does, doesn't it? That's for the pain in my heart. And this—" A chop caught him on the nape of his neck.

"Guhuh!"

"That's for the pain in my body! And this—" Kaname flew into the air and kneed Sousuke in the pit of his stomach.

"Guhoh!"

"This! This is for the pain in my soul!"

Sousuke sank to his knees, and Kaname pushed out her fist like Bruce Lee as she faced him and shook all over.

"What the hell's ... going on here?" asked Sousuke.

"You know your Intelligence agent? Wraith's the name, I think?" she said and snorted. "I told him that if he didn't want anybody to find out he screwed up and almost let me get killed, that he'd better bring me here. The threat worked. The AS that Gauron guy was piloting was on the news, so I knew. I just knew you'd come to this city."

"B-but, this place is an inch away from going to war. It's dangerous."

"I know. There were hardly any airmail flights either, so it took nearly a whole day to get here. I went through a *hell* of a lot of trouble!"

"But, why...?"

Why was she here? Why did she brave such danger? Sousuke couldn't even imagine the reason.

"Well—"

When he looked up, Kaname looked away and said in a voice like a child who'd just been caught in a prank: "I mean, how could it just end like that?"

"Eh...?"

"Never mind. Y-you just up and ... dropped out of school and went off somewhere, and it really pissed me off! I figured I was gonna find you wherever you were, grab you by the neck, and bring you back home! Because I'm—"

Kaname squeezed her fists and tried to get herself to utter this important thing.

"I'm—"

"You're...?"

She drummed on her head in an attempt to embolden herself, to get herself all fired up, but in the end said, "I'm our class rep."

Sousuke just stood there and stared at her, and Kaname let out a deep sigh and said, "I guess determination really does fade over the course of one day."

He had no idea what this meant. "So, in other words, what?"

"Shut up! A ... and what's with *you*, huh?! What are you doing loafing around here on the street?! Isn't there some bad guy tearing through the city?!"

"Well, but—"

"But, what? You were just standing there, staring at that AS. And what was with that face you were making? It looked just like the old you."

"What...?"

"You know, back when I still called you Sagara. It was like ... you didn't give a damn about yourself. Really cold. And so sad.... Ah, what am I trying to say? It's like this. Um...." Kaname hemmed and hawed as she struggled to continue.

"Actually, I talked to Miss Mao on the radio. She said you were falling apart. That you'd run out of motivation, of drive, that kind of thing. But you know what? Aren't *you* the one who can't stand to just stand there when everybody is in trouble?"

"Me...?"

"That's right."

"But Chidori. I ... left you behind...."

I was the only one you could rely on, and I abandoned you. It was all because I obeyed that stupid order. And yet, you came all this way to me?

"Well, does that still matter? Here we are, together again. I get it. You couldn't tell me, could you?"

"Sorry."

"You're just ... cowardly."

"Cowardly...?" said Sousuke.

"Yeah. *Very* cowardly. But strong. And *very* kind. You're hopeless, but you get by somehow. I think that's ... the real you."

Kaname laughed awkwardly. Her smile was magical.

"I mean ... aren't I right?"

Those terribly clumsy words erased Gauron's curse. They wiped it cleanly away. It felt like his whole body had been covered in some discolored slime, which was now being washed away by clean water.

Cowardice. Gauron had said he was one of the strong. That was incorrect, though. Sousuke was weak. He was trying to become stronger, but he was still weak. The only reason he couldn't afford to be a coward was that he had a reason to get stronger. He knew the gravity that came with having someone to protect. The old him had simply lacked that knowledge.

His was a weak existence, full of contradictions. He was no hero. Nor could he save the world. He was just one little man, who may or may not have been able to save some of the people around him. Was such a man up to the task of being a soldier?

He sure was. Sometimes things were like that. Irony aside, he had been given such opportunities innumerable times. And now, this was one of those times. His comrades were waiting for him beyond those flames.

Until now, hadn't he found ways to fight against gloomy, depressing fates? Wasn't that what combat was all about?

That's right.

Sousuke looked down and slowly, hesitatingly said, "Chidori.... I—"

Whock! Kaname performed a leg sweep on Sousuke, and down he went to kiss the Hong Kong ground.

"What are you—"

"Don't you say, 'Chidori. I—' to me!" she rebuked him.

"No, that was...."

"Just can it! There's no time for this, is there?! You're in danger of failing world history! That's fifth period tomorrow! You can still make it in time! Now get over there—" She pointed firmly at the battle ensuing downtown. "—and fix that mess!"

Then she pointed at the prone Arbalest.

The white AS's two white eyes were now saying something different to him: *So, what'll it be?*

It was a dangerous game, like hunting a wild beast. The Venom had only destroyed one South Chinese M6 before Clouseau's team of six M9s persistently encircled it and gave chase.

Corporal Spec's M9 was taken out by the Venom within the first thirty seconds of combat. His path of retreat got fouled up thanks to the complex urban terrain and countless signs, and the enemy took advantage of it to get close to him. Spec's mech was hit by a Lambda Driver shock wave, which completely silenced it. There was no time in this chaotic battle to inspect the damage or confirm whether the operator was alive or dead.

"Urzu-I, it's headed toward you!" Mao warned Clouseau sharply.

"I see it. I'm about to—"

Whump went an explosion at point-blank range. The enemy mech had thrown an anti-tank dagger.

"Urzu-I?!"

The Venom closed in from the other side of the explosive flames. Clouseau put his back to a high-rise apartment building and fired his rifle. The white shells bounced off and ricocheted in haphazard directions, and fragments of building materials came raining down.

The Venom drew near and projected its fist. Clouseau stooped down at the last second. The fist cut through the sky, and the spatial distortion around it blew away the M9's right shoulder along with the building behind it. There was a violent impact, and a shrill shriek of air. Clouseau nearly fainted for an instant.

He skillfully restored his mech's posture, and at the same time let out a whirlwind-like roundhouse kick. The M9's heel caught the Venom on the head, and it staggered a bit. The M9 followed up with a knee kick, and then an elbow strike. Without missing a beat, Clouseau tried to draw his monofilament dagger from his mech's hip—but the right arm wouldn't respond. Rather, it was missing from the shoulder down.

The Venom advanced mercilessly, its hand raised for a chop.

"Don't move, Urzu-I," said Kurz's voice. A long-range sniper shot struck the Venom. The enemy mech sailed away as if something had punched it hard on the flank. Clouseau's M9 used that chance to leap away, nimbly putting distance between itself and the Venom. An average operator probably wouldn't even have been able to escape.

"It repelled it again. That thing's like a goddamn cockroach!"

"You saved me, Urzu-6."

"That's two you owe me, Lieutenant."

"Perth-I to Urzu-I. Give me a damage report," said Lieutenant Commander Kalinin over the radio. He was commanding from a helicopter overhead.

"This is ... Urzu-I. Right arm is non-functional. Firearm has been lost. Operator is slightly injured. Cooling system is in trouble. I don't think I'll be mobile much longer."

His right arm hurt as if it had been burned. It felt like something had scalded it. Was this another effect of that Lambda Driver?

"All right. Fall back three blocks to the south. There's a three-way junction there. Then turn southwest and lure it to area IIA." Kalinin remained calm as he delivered precise instructions.

"Urzu-I, roger."

"Urzu-6, move west. I've just sent you data. Set up a sniping zone at the intersection on the map, then stand by. If the Venom goes after you, fire a magazine's worth at it, then flee to the west."

"Urzu-6, roger."

"Perth-I to all units. We've received word from Intelligence. Urzu-8 is apparently alive, at least. Recovery is currently underway. Three hundred seconds have elapsed since the start of combat. Hold out another one hundred seconds. The tide is turning."

Clouseau had reached roughly the same conclusion as Lieutenant Commander Kalinin. Their side had taken some hard blows, but the Venom's movements were becoming sluggish compared to when the assault had started. He couldn't tell if it was an energy issue or pilot issue, but there was no doubt that the enemy was exhausting itself.

This was working. They were still a long way from being able to relax, but provided no trouble arose, they would soon most likely manage to beleaguer and destroy it. Their tactics were winning. But Clouseau still had to manage to get away from it.

His mech made a series of small leaps, plunging its way down the cramped street. The AI was warning him about issues with the propulsion system. It didn't look like he was going to be able to move for much longer.

"This is Urzu-I. I'm through the three-way fork. I'll soon be in front of the inter...." Despite the Venom still closing in behind him, Clouseau came to a halt in front of the spacious intersection.

"What is it, Urzu-I?"

"This can't be...."

"Urzu-I, explain your situation."

"Venoms—"

In the front corner of the intersection where Clouseau had stopped, on the roof of a shopping center where the neon signs had been blown out, there were five silhouettes. They belonged to five ASes—five Venoms.

The five Venoms were all looking down at Clouseau with their single red eyes. They each sported a dark red coating.

"There are ... five Venoms."

"What?"

"This is Urzu-6. I see them, too. It's true. There *are* five of them." Kurz's voice was understandably stiff as well.

It was no surprise that the original Venom chasing Clouseau had also came to a halt at the intersection's entrance. Its red sensor was firmly pointed not at Clouseau's mech, but at the five new arrivals.

"You've really done a number on this town, haven't you, Fei Jiu?" said one of the five mechs through its external speaker. It was a man's voice, and high-pitched enough to be reminiscent of a raven. He seemed to pay no attention whatsoever to Clouseau.

"You steal an M-type from the organization, and now you raise hell here in this region where we have no business. Are you out of your mind, or what?"

"We're both crazy, Mister Kalium." The grey Venom spoke for the first time. "It looks like Amalgam was involved when my brother and I lost our homeland. Nothing could please me more than to throw a wrench in your works."

"Hmm. Your brother, eh? Would you like to see him right now?"

"What?"

The dark Venom quietly held out its right hand. Its fingers grasped a small object that, relative to the size of a human hand, would have been about the size of a quail egg. It was a human head.

"Ugh!" groaned Fei Jiu.

"I asked Mister Silver if I could have this. He wanted to hold a funeral, but I wouldn't let him. Traitors deserve to have their corpses hung up on a filthy street corner," the red Venom said, then casually flung the head. It flew in a high arc, then fell behind a distant building.

"Ah, such a pity. Mmm-hmm."

"You son of a bitch!"

The grey Venom leaped. It cleared Clouseau's M9, and plunged at full speed at the five mechs.

"You're pitiful, too," said Kalium.

In the next instant, all five mechs moved at once. A pike, a long sword, a large knife—all sorts of weapons attacked the grey Venom simultaneously. The surrounding air distorted intensely, and the outer wall of the shopping center was smashed to pieces.

"Guh!"

Clouseau's mech was blown backwards. Small fragments hit his armor, causing a reverberation of dry sounds. The smoke cleared. On top of the destroyed shopping center, the grey Venom had been skewered multiple times. It looked like a porcupine.

The five mechs tossed aside the Venom. It fell to the street, scattering smoke and sparks, and made no further movements. This enemy had caused the SRT so much trouble, and yet they beat it in an instant. Was every single one of those five mechs equipped with a Lambda Driver?

"Ben?!" Mao's M9 came rushing onto the scene and tried to help Clouseau's M9 to its feet.

"Urzu-I, can't you hear me? The operation is suspended. Retreat," advised Kalinin.

"I can't. My propulsion's shot. I can only manage a bare minimum of movements."

"Leave your mech behind. Proceed with emergency esca—"

"By the way, down there," said the center Venom to Clouseau

and Mao. It made it sound like he had just noticed them for the first time. "You're Mithril soldiers, yes?"

Neither Mao nor Clouseau responded.

"You really had nothing to do with why we're here, but I'm not satisfied with smashing just one mech. This ought to make for some good combat training. We're going to kill you too, okay?"

"What...?"

From that position, it would probably only take an instant for the five to spring onto them. There was no time for Clouseau to open his hatch, get out, and have Mao carry him.

"I say again. Perth-I to all units. Withdraw. This is an emergency."

"Forget me. Just escape, Mao!" shouted Clouseau.

"But I—"

"Go on, hurry!"

The five mechs assumed stances very slowly and leisurely on top of the shopping center that was now a pile of rubble. They each aimed their weapons straight ahead and got ready to jump.

"Are you ready? Well then, good b—"

Just then, a shell fired from somewhere hit the lead mech squarely on the right shoulder. Red armor tore away, and smoke poured out as the mech flew backward. A Venom that supposedly had a Lambda Driver loaded on it had just taken a hit.

Wha...?"

The five Venoms turned to look at the roof of the building diagonally across the intersection.

"Who fired that shot? Was it you, Weber?"

"Negative. I was just *about* to fire. And ... well, what do you know? It's about time." Despite the predicament, Kurz kind of sounded like he was having fun. "And, hey, man, this timing of yours. Could you have possibly cut it *any* closer, Sousuke?"

"I doubt it," came the sergeant's voice.

A lone AS stood on a conspicuously tall building and faced the five Venoms. Not much of its white form was visible in the dim city lights.

"Urzu-7 to all units." The Arbalest held its customary shot cannon as it glared at the five Venoms. "Sorry to keep you waiting. Leave the rest of this to me."

The mech's power levels rose from CRUISE to MILITARY, then even higher to MAX. A groaning sound rose in the cockpit as Sousuke muttered, "It just worked, didn't it?"

"Affirmative, Sergeant. The Lambda Driver definitely operated just now," responded Al.

"...It works, then it doesn't work. It sure is an unreliable device."

"I think so, too."

"Looks like you're even better with jokes than I am."

"Affirmative."

"Snide remarks, too."

A short message from Kalinin arrived. "Perth-I to Urzu-7. Are you back in the game?"

"Affirmative, Perth-I."

"Then do as you see fit."

"Roger."

The Venoms were looking up at him on his monitor. He had five opponents. Could he do this? These weren't old-style Savages. They were Venoms, and even one of those was trouble enough.

I think I can do it, he thought. *This mech and I can. We're the worst combination ever—but we've still managed to pull through thus far. It's no use sitting here and complaining about our compatibility issues.*

"You're hopeless, but you get by somehow."

That's this mech, and that's me. Right, Chidori?

He took a deep breath. Gripping both sticks with his hands, he shook lightly. The mech powerfully reached its hands to the left and right, reacting to its operator's movements.

"Here we go!"

"Roger," said Al.

He stepped off the edge of the rooftop. The Arbalest dropped lightly through space, as if riding the air. With its face toward the ground, it aimed its gun at the five mechs beneath it. First, the one on the far right—fire.

The armor piercing round that burst from the shot cannon left a dazzling iridescent trail of light as it stabbed through the torso of one of the Venoms. Bits of armor and parts were blown out from the center of its back. It only took one shot.

Sousuke used the recoil of the blast to shift his body's posture a hundred and eighty degrees. He landed with his legs beneath him. Asphalt pulverized, and shock absorbent liquid spouted from the drive system all over the mech.

"Wh-what the hell?!"

While he was surprised by how quickly his man had been taken down, the command mech still ordered his team to spread out. The Venoms broke in different directions, drew their guns, and started firing. Sousuke took a light step, and the Arbalest blew up a whirlwind as it dodged. A large number of shells danced around him.

He jumped, clearing the barrage, and used a sign jutting into the road as a platform. The sign failed to break despite the mech's nine-ton weight. It didn't even matter why.

The Arbalest moved right, left, and flipped in midair as it dodged the Venoms' shots. One of them got into just the right position.

Fire!

The enemy mech crossed its arms in an attempt to defend against the shot cannon shell. The iridescent shell penetrated the Venom, arms and all. The torso was all but blown in half, and the red mech slammed down onto the street.

"That's two!"

"Hostile approaching from 4:00," said Al.

An alarm sounded. A Venom kicked off a high-rise residential building and closed in from behind and to the right. It brandished a halberd-shaped monofilament cutter directly at him.

Sousuke dodged in a flash. He drew the monofilament cutter at the Arbalest's waist with its left hand, and severed the enemy's halberd.

With the blade on the reverse side, it cut the Venom diagonally from the shoulder. Countless sparks gushed out, and the enemy fell to its knees in the street. With its right hand the Arbalest thrust out its shot cannon and fired. Dazzling prismatic flame blew out of it, and the Venom exploded.

"That makes three," said Al.

"Don't say it before I do!"

The fourth mech fired its rifle wildly as it jumped off a building overhead. By that point, Sousuke was in the process of rolling the Arbalest forward nimbly. He fired while in mid-roll. As this was an awkward position from which to shoot, the shell only managed to blow off the enemy's left shoulder. The Arbalest righted itself with a less awkward jack-knife maneuver, planted its legs, and fired again at the enemy mech which had now landed. It hit directly in the chest. The Venom was bent backwards, then blown away.

"Four!" said Sousuke and Al at the same time.

Sousuke ran down the deserted street, nearly in a crawl. He felt on his own skin the wind that touched his mech. It was a strange sensation. This mech was moving according to his will— according to his mind. It was that complete sense of unity an AS operator would occasionally feel. It was fair to call it a sense of omnipotence. This truly overwhelming power was now at his full command. The mech was Sousuke's body itself. It occurred to him that as bodies went, it wasn't all that bad considering how much he'd hated it. In fact, it went well beyond that. Given how light it felt, he had a sense that he could jump any distance with this body.

Yeah. I can go on forever. Nobody can stop me!

He turned a corner and there was the command mech. It was firing a large Gatling cannon and holding as a shield a South China M6 that was unlucky enough to be within reach.

The Arbalest flew into the air, taking out the signs overhead. It was a huge, huge leap, one that exceeded the recorded limits of any type of mech. He flew so far, he ended up jumping over the command Venom.

"Ugh," said Kalium.

Once Sousuke landed behind it, the command mech panicked and tried to re-aim its Gatling cannon at him. His left hand flashed up and his monofilament cutter sliced the cannon in two.

"S-stay away! Stay away!"

The last Venom tossed its cannon aside and thrust a handgun against the cockpit of its hostage M6.

"I'll kill the operator! Stay back! Don't move!"

"H-help me," said M6's pilot

A control system in the M6 had apparently been destroyed, as neither of its arms seemed capable of movement. *Now what do I do? Wait, I'll use that. That attack that took down Mao at Berildaobu Island. I'm sure I can do it at this point.*

"I ... I thought Mithril's Lambda Driver was incomplete! Forget that—how can you be so strong?! Who the hell are you?!

"You want me to tell you?"

Sousuke tossed aside his shot cannon.

Who was I again? That's right. I'm—

"Jindai High School, year two, class four. Roll call number 41. Second term garbage duty—"

An iridescent shimmer rose from his right fist. *Gyewn*, growled a strange sound.

"—Sousuke Sagara!"

"Ugh ... augh!"

The Venom pointed its handgun toward the Arbalest and fired. Sousuke—the Arbalest—repelled the shells with ease, and hit the chest of the M6 being used as a shield with a knuckle punch. The ground swayed and the road rumbled. The sound was like several hundred wild beasts roaring. A fierce force that seemed to distort gravity shot from the Arbalest's fist. It ignored the M6 entirely, transmitted through it, and bore its ferocious fangs at the enemy mech standing behind.

The Venom broke into pieces instantly. Armor, frame, electromagnetic musculature, and parts all went to pieces and were blown away. The dispersed bits mixed in with broken glass from the surrounding buildings, and scattered around on the road.

The M6 that had been taken hostage had suffered no damage from the attack. It flopped down on its backside, and looked up in a daze at the Arbalest.

"Go."

Sousuke pointed across the street, and the M6 mumbled something, then hurriedly ran in that direction.

After a little while, Al announced, "Destruction of all targets, confirmed. Shall I switch to search mode?"

"Whatever."

"Roger."

Sousuke flipped a switch on a stick and opened a com channel. "Urzu-7 to all units. I've destroyed all the Venoms."

"This is Urzu-I. You destroyed ... all of them?"

"Affirmative. I'm now returning to the TDD-I so I can—" he started to say, then thought again.

He had cleaned up the trouble in this town. All that remained was recovery by the transport helicopter and return to the *Tuatha de Daanan*. That was the usual protocol.

But who needs that protocol? he thought, though it would take some nerve to relay such information.

"Correction. This is Urzu-7. It's true that I've dispatched all enemy units. Urzu-7 will now embark on his next mission. I'll leave the Arbalest here, so please pick it up. South China forces will confiscate it if you don't hurry."

"Urzu-7, I don't really follow. What's this 'next mission' of yours?"

"End of transmission!" Sousuke switched off the radio, made the Arbalest kneel, and flipped the hatch switch under the control stick. Pressurized air slowly opened the overhead hatch.

"Sergeant, there are still operation-end procedures to perform," said Al.

"It doesn't matter. The operation's over."

"Roger. I have a question."

"What?"

"That combat just now surpassed all past combats in every respect. To put it in human terms—the results were astonishing. If possible, could you tell me the reason for this?"

Sousuke thought for a bit. "I solved a problem. I guess that's what it was."

"Do you mean your problem?"

"No." Sousuke thumped the console panel. "I meant our problem."

"I do not understand your reply."

"Then you've got something to think about, *partner*," Sousuke said, then exited the Arbalest's cockpit. He jumped down onto the street, and wasted no time running past the still-flaming enemy mech pieces.

There's somebody waiting for me. And I can go anywhere I want.

Sousuke Sagara left behind the Arbalest and disappeared. When she heard this report, Teletha Testarossa thought, *Ah, I knew it.*

An inquiry sent to Intelligence's Gavin Hunter revealed that Kaname Chidori had been out of contact since then as well. According to Hunter's information network, a boy and girl strongly resembling the two had shown up on a security camera at Kai Tak Airport. This meant the fake passport issued to him for his surveillance mission had done the trick.

Mithril had managed to safely recover the damaged M9s, Corporal Spec, and the Arbalest. It had taken some doing for Tessa's men to pacify the South China forces and perform the extraction stealthily. Returning to the *Tuatha de Daanan* had also presented several difficulties. These issues had been peacefully resolved in the end. A large amount of the Venom wreckages were recovered, both the North and South armies backed down from the brink of war, and the evacuated civilians returned to downtown Hong Kong.

It was a day after the *Tuatha de Daanan* left Hong Kong coastal waters that the whereabouts of Sousuke Sagara became known. He contacted the ship directly, and they also received information via Intelligence. The transmission he sent was from a high school in Tokyo.

Mardukas got angry and said, "Return to Merida Island immediately."

Sousuke replied in a courteous manner, "I cannot obey that order, sir. At least, not until tomorrow afternoon."

"Why is that?" asked Tessa, and Sousuke calmly responded, "Because I have Classic Chinese Literature class on Saturdays, ma'am. My grades in that are not so good."

Kalinin had been listening off to the side, and he did something rare for him. He let out a laugh.

(October 25, 11:21 (Western Pacific Standard Time)
Mithril's Merida Island Base
Conference room #1

Mithril's leaders were assembled in conference room #1 of the Merida Island base. They were the usual holographic projections.

Mardukas, Kalinin, and Sousuke were standing next to Tessa's chair. Sousuke had only just arrived at the island from Tokyo thirty minutes ago.

444

"I've never been this angry before in my life," General Amit, the head of Intelligence, said in a low voice.

"Yes sir, but he is the only one who can handle the Arbalest," said Tessa, causing General Amit to snort.

"Be quiet, Captain. He's just a sergeant—a very young NCO, and he's opposing our decision. What's more, the way he's going about it sounds like a threat. Do you really think we can approve this?"

"I am not threatening you, sir. Nor am I opposing you," said Sousuke as he stood at attention. "What I am proposing is a modification of the particulars of my contact. If my proposal does not meet with your liking, I will pay the penalty for breaching my contract, and simply leave this organization."

"And what about the possibility of you disclosing classified information?"

"If that worries you, sir, take what measures you find appropriate. Unfortunately, I have no intention of allowing myself to be restrained and confined."

Amit's projection leaned forward and peered at Sousuke's face. "Was that a wise thing to say, Sergeant? Do you think you'd be able to lead the life you want with me as your enemy?"

"Then I put this question to you, General. Does your Excellency think that I would not be suitably prepared to deal with such an eventuality?"

"What'd you say?"

"Listen to me, General," Sousuke said fearlessly, not flinching at all. "I don't recall selling my soul to Mithril. If there's something weird about your collective way of doing things, I'll take the liberty of getting things done my own way. End of story. I'll continue to pilot the Arbalest. I'll put my life on the line for my comrades. And I will continue to attend that school. Everything will be just like it was. In fact, you don't have to pay me when I'm in Tokyo. Does any of this displease you?"

"Watch what you say, Sergeant!"

"Sergeant? I'm just a mercenary. Why would you say that to a man simply passing through? Rank doesn't concern me. You should save lines like those for your dog."

"Hmm! Ha ha ha!" Lord Mallory's monocled image had been watching the exchange silently, and now he burst into laughter as if he couldn't contain it any longer.

"Lord Mallory?"

"Ha ha ha.... You've lost this one, General. 'SRT mercenaries can't be tamed.' Now, who was it who said that here in this room just the other day?" said Lord Mallory.

"Well, I...."

"That's right. It was you, General. One of the best men that troublesome SRT has to offer is telling you he's going to keep doing what he's been doing for half the pay. That's cause to thank him, not get irate with him. Don't you agree, Admiral?"

Now part of the conversation, one of the 3-D projections—Operations head Admiral Borda—appeared to think about it for a bit. He shrugged and said curtly, "Well, that might be true. Not that it's something I could really say on the record."

"And you, Doctor Painrose?"

Lord Mallory turned to look at Dr. Painrose, the head of Research.

"I received a report from Lemming. Our division surmises that Sergeant Sagara will be an indispensable asset in our ongoing Lambda Driver research."

"Very well. Are there any other dissenting opinions?" Lord Mallory asked the other top officials surrounding the desk. None of them made any comment.

"Then, there you have it, Captain Testarossa. It must not be easy having so many peculiar subordinates. I sympathize, if you don't mind my saying so," said Lord Mallory.

"Not at all, sir. And my subordinates are the best," Tessa said plainly, and Lord Mallory smiled even more.

"Mmm. Let it not be said that the West Pacific battle group isn't without its share of successes. I think we all look forward to your continued efforts."

"Yes, sir. I am honored."

"And Sergeant, I believe ... your name was Sousuke Sagara?" asked Lord Mallory.

"Yes, sir!"

"I'm going to remember that name. This discussion is now over. Take care, gentlemen."

Once the online meeting ended, Mardukas said to Sousuke, "First of all, well done. But, Sergeant, don't give me even more things to worry about. The truth is you had me in a cold sweat there!"

"Yes, sir! I apologize for all the trouble, Commander." Sousuke saluted obediently, and Mardukas sighed and left the conference room.

Next, Kalinin said, "Are you satisfied?"

"Yes, sir."

"You're looking more like a man now."

"Sir?"

"I'll buy you something to eat later. You can tell me about what happened with Gauron then."

"Thanks."

Kalinin thumped Sousuke on the back with his file case as he left the room. It was an unusual attitude for the lieutenant commander to display. And then only Sousuke and Tessa remained in the otherwise deserted conference room.

"Um...," she said hesitatingly, dressed in her khaki uniform. "I still haven't mentioned this. I am sorry about what happened."

"About what happened?"

"Ugh.... You and I got into a big fight before the Hong Kong operation, did we not?"

"Yes, ma'am. No, ma'am," Sousuke responded ambiguously, unsure of how to answer. "I should apologize, myself."

"That's all right. I was ... jealous of Kaname. It made me a little angry...."

"Colonel...."

"I probably acted selfishly, because it was you. But it occurred to me that it was not a good thing to do. I need to make a clear distinction in such cases. But, I want to ask you," Tessa's face was pointed somewhat downward as she peered into Sousuke's eyes. "We *are* still friends, aren't we?"

She sounded distressed. Suddenly, Sousuke finally understood. Grasping the full significance of her tears and raging anger at that time was still beyond him, but he at least realized the false impression under which he'd labored until now.

Teletha Testarossa was not a goddess. She was not omnipotent, sacred, or an idol. Sometimes she would say irrational things, and an impulsive word from him could hurt her, anger her, and make her cry. She was no different than Kaname Chidori or any of the other students at that school. When he thought about it, examples of this had already occurred multiple times. Why hadn't he realized it then? Also, Tessa bore responsibilities to which his paled in comparison.

"Of course, Colonel," Sousuke said before he realized it. "And if you view me as a friend, would you permit me to say something I would not normally say, given our respective ranks?"

"Uh? Okay ... I guess." Tessa tense up just a bit.

Go on, Sousuke Sagara. Say it. How would you speak if she was one of your friends at school? You should know this. How do you talk to her if she's your friend?

He took a deep breath and said, "Tessa ... I'm really sorry." He felt far more nervous as he said this than he did when he was talking back to General Amit.

"Huh?"

"I cause so many problems for you. You're an amazing girl. If I was in your position, the burden might have crushed me long ago. That's why ... I truly respect you, Tessa. You're more than just a superior officer to me. You're a valuable comrade. If there's ever anything wrong ... um, you can tell me anytime. I've got your back."

Tessa gaped at him. Now that he'd said it, the unnaturalness of it all astonished Sousuke.

Am I an idiot? This is me, talking to her. Where do I get off being so casual? No matter how you look at it, this was too forward, too personal. Ah, son of a bitch.

"I-I beg your pardon, ma'am. But those were my true feelings. So ... if you'll excuse me."

Unable to look her in the eye any longer, Sousuke ran from the conference room. He could faintly hear behind him this series of sounds: a somewhat odd applause, somebody in pumps jumping up and down, and finally, a chair loudly falling over.

EPILOGUE

Eri Kagurazaka had decided to keep the withdrawal notice inside her desk, even though she knew that doing so could get her in trouble.

"I don't know what led you to submit this," she said in the staff room. "But if you keep pulling these stunts, I'm not going to be able to keep covering for you."

"Yes, ma'am. I'm sorry," said Sousuke as he stood at attention.

"You do what you do out of a sense of diligence, don't you?"

"Yes, ma'am. It's kind of you to say so."

"If you understand, try to give some more thought to how you live your life. It's like what happened with my car the other day. Why do you always ... always cause so many problems? I mean, at the rate you're going—*Eeeek!*"

Eri screamed as Sousuke suddenly pushed her down.

"Wh-what?! What are you doing?! Mr. Sagara, no! Other people are watching!"

"There was a laser sight aimed at you, ma'am! Don't move!"

"I don't even know what you're talking about!"

Eri struggled where she'd fallen to the floor. Sousuke had his pistol drawn and was looking around attentively. Kaname came rushing in and shouted at the top of her lungs.

"Sousuke! Are you doing it *again*?!"

"No, there was a laser sight—"

"Shut up!"

She kicked him and he slammed down onto the floor.

Urzu-7 was flailing around through the 4X scope. It looked kind of, well, pathetic. Was this the same man who had talked down Mithril Intelligence head General Amit, whose name alone was enough to silence a crying child?

"Hmph," Wraith snorted while putting away the Belgian-made sub-machine gun with attached laser sight. In costume as usual,

Wraith currently appeared to be a commonplace neighborhood housewife. Quite a bit of Jindai High School was visible from this building several hundred feet away.

Wraith suddenly looked at the sky. Black clouds were slowly moving overhead. According to the weather forecast, it would soon rain, and then cool off considerably in the evening. It would have been a good idea to buy a hand warmer or something from a local convenience store. *She* had agreed to continue carrying a transmitter, but that was no excuse to relax. Even if Intelligence still hadn't completely set itself up in Tokyo....

Why do I have to be out here in the rain full time?

It made Wraith feel sad. At least they had a roof over their heads over there. And from now on, Wraith had to unconditionally respond any time Kaname Chidori sent out a summons. This couldn't be helped, after the crucial assistance Kaname had provided.

Wraith looked through a pair of binoculars. Urzu-7 and Kaname Chidori had been trying to apologize to their homeroom teacher in the staff room this entire time.

That makes me feel better. At least they can share in my grief a little, thought Wraith, as the skin-biting cold got a little worse even through a coat.

A small sneeze made Wraith huddle deeper inside said coat.

"What a job," said Wraith in a dejected voice.

"Why are you *already* back to acting like that?!" shouted Kaname once they'd left the staff room. "Does it even mean anything to you that Miss Kagurazaka and I covered for you?! Don't tell me you just *expected* it or something!"

"No, I didn't really—"

"Shut up! You know what, you ... you haven't made an inch of progress! Why don't you give a little thought to what just happened!? You're *always, a*lways, always—"

Kaname produced a sheaf of copy paper from nowhere in particular and suddenly raised it overhead.

"Chidori, wait—"

"Always, always...."

Normally, this was when she would hit him, but this time for some reason, Kaname let the hand holding the sheaf drop.

"Always...."

She dropped the paper and murmured in a thin voice, "Always.... Now ... isn't this back to how things always were...?"

Sousuke looked at her uncomprehendingly.

"It finally ... it finally feels normal.... Hnh!

Apparently unable to stand it any longer, Kaname leaned her forehead against Sousuke's chest. "It's finally how it always was ... how it always...."

"Chidori?"

"What was up with ... with leaving me like that? You'd better never do that again."

She had been calm all during the trip home from Hong Kong. Sousuke couldn't help but be surprised by this sudden change.

"Sorry," said Sousuke.

"I don't want to hear you're sorry. You're such a big ... jerk. And you'd better not do it again. You better believe I'll.... You'd just better not do it again!"

Kaname weakly pounded on his chest over and over.

"I was scared, you know. I was *really* scared. I never ... want to feel like that again! Never again!"

The students walking up and down the hall were looking at the two of them with keen curiosity.

"It's all right now. And ... Chidori? Could we do this somewhere else?"

"No! I couldn't handle that now."

Kaname clung to Sousuke's chest as she sobbed, unconcerned about embarrassment or reputation. Her shoulders trembled like a child's. Sousuke felt flustered, and simply patted her on the back in an effort to soothe her. Just then, Kyouko Tokiwa pushed through the crowd of people and poked her head up next to them.

"Hey, what's going on? Oh, Kana."

"T-Tokiwa?" said Sousuke.

"Whoa, are you okay? Hey, Kana! Did you hurt yourself?"

"Snff ... Kyouko ... Sousuke's ... Sousuke's...."

Kaname blew her nose in a handkerchief. It was too difficult for her to say anything else.

"Sagara?! What'd you do to Kana?! I bet you said there was a bomb, and acted crazy again, didn't you?!"

"What? No, this is just—"

"I don't think excuses are very manly! Now go on, apologize to Kana!" Kyouko put her hands on her hips and glared at Sousuke.

"Yeah, she's right!"

"Man, ever since you *got* here!"

"I feel so bad for Chidori!"

The surrounding students all started chiming in with their agreement, heaping tons of blame on him.

"This is ... it's just...."

"IT'S JUST WHAT?!" they all said in unison.

"Uh...."

It looks like I'm back. But when I really stop and think this over—it also looks like I'm still going to have the same issues here I always have.

"Never mind. It was inexcusable." Sousuke bowed very deeply as he mulled over his absurd sense of sorrow. Everyone present nodded and said, "That's better."

And yet, it still took a long time for Kaname to stop crying.

AFTERWORD

Hmm.... As usual, I've kept you waiting an awfully long time. So here you have the final half of *Ending Day By Day*. I kind of get the feeling some people will take me to task since they've already forgotten what happened in the first half. Sorry about that.

The story this time had quite a different dimension to it. But admittedly, it's occurred to me that if I keep doing hijackings and seajackings, this might end up going down the same road as the *Die Hard* or *Silent Service* series. I tried writing the climax this time in the style of those charming old-school super robot anime: strong, strong, and absolutely strong. When you're the hero, sometimes you have to be resolute in your decisions.

At first, I was thinking of a plot that would allow Sousuke to return to his former lifestyle via some kind of windfall, for the sake of pre-established harmony. But no matter how elaborate a story

I cooked up, in that kind of situation I couldn't find a plausible reason for the organization to want him to continue his absurd day-to-day life. Long story short, there was only ever one way to naturally resolve this.

This choice was so obvious, I get the feeling it was hiding in some unanticipated blind spot. The right and wrong of a situation lies more with the individual than with the situation itself. Lots of people, myself included, are liable to forget this when it's so natural. Even if we do remember it, the severity of our circumstances soon makes us forget. It's a real pain. I suppose in that way, changes that move like the hour hand on a clock foul something up, and a person who was supposedly sincere can wind up being rendered a cynic.

The writing of *Ending Day By Day* was meant to reexamine the discomfort that had become obvious between the characters of Sousuke Sagara and the Arbalest. It seemed like a climb up a steep mountain, but as a result of the effort, it feels like he's finally become the main character of this story in a genuine sense. The Arbalest also finally—and I mean finally—became the starring mecha. Like Sousuke, I previously didn't feel much attachment to the Arbalest, but now, and don't get me wrong, I think to myself, *It's really not that bad*. Maybe it doesn't measure up to the various robot stars that my predecessors created, but I would say its charm is comparable on some level.

That's why these two books are first and foremost about Sousuke and the Arbalest—and I suppose also about Sousuke himself. If you were to ask Sousuke why he's at that school, until now he'd probably say because it's his mission. From now on, he'll probably respond, "Because I want to be." Furthermore, it should also come into play with how he confronts situations and challenges which have yet to befall him.

Be that as it may, how to put this.... A protagonist who can't stand up without a reprimand from his girlfriend is, well, pathetic. But hey, it occurs to me that that's how things can be when you're young. He can't be an exact replica of Golgo 13. It's only natural that he can't stand up to Kaname. "Women are strong and beautiful." That's occurred to me many times over the years. Even now, when I look at the brave ladies with whom I have the pleasure of working. Yow.

Still only at three pages, huh? While I'm writing the story, I think to myself about this thing and that thing I can write about in the afterword, but once the story's finished, it no longer really matters what I write here. I might as well bring you up to speed on what's happening with me.... Eh, maybe not. There isn't much to talk about when every day is ordinary.

You can't blame me for writing about current events. I wouldn't mind talking about the plastic Valkyrie model that Hasegawa released, but something tells me I'd get so into it I'd go on for twenty more pages.

By the way, I actually did go to Hong Kong to do research. By myself. Lazily. More of the story was meant to take place there this time, but matters of plot and tempo forced me to cut many descriptions and episodes. It's too bad. But then, I end up tossing out lots of scenes for each one of my books. Should the chance arise, I'd like to revisit Hong Kong.

I'm going to use this space to send out a few personal messages.

Thank you to Tomohiro Nagai for sending me the manga. I'm sorry I never responded. I get a lot of laughs out of it as I read it every month.

Thank you to Retsu Tateo for the chocolate. We live in the same neighborhood, so let's go get something to eat sometime. I look forward to further developments.

Thank you to Ichiro Sakai for the New Year's card. I'm sorry I didn't respond.

Toshihiko Tsukiji, I haven't contacted you in a while. How are your eyes doing? We need to go out for a drink sometime.

Giguru Akiguchi, please let me know when you come to Tokyo.

And congratulations to Douji Shiki. I'm sorry for making your new life so busy. Here's to the best for us both in the future.

I made life difficult for many people over the course of this book. My apologies as always to Douji Shiki, my editor S, and the multitude of other people involved. Thank you so much.

Now, then. This story was pretty heavy and it involved a lot of frustration, so I think I'd like to make the next long novel light and cheerful. Those of you who are worried that FMP is going to get steadily more serious, you can set your minds at ease.

I'll be seeing you. Come follow Sousuke through hell again next time.

Shoji Gatoh (supporter of kung fu fighters everywhere)
March 2001

465

Check out the following series
also available from TOKYOPOP Fiction:

Adventures of Duan Surk

Alex Unlimited

Calling You

Chain Mail

Chibi Vampire

FLCL

Full Metal Panic

The Good Witch of the West

Gosick

Magic Moon

Missing

Trinity Blood: Rage Against the Moons

Trinity Blood: Reborn on the Mars

The Twelve Kingdoms

Welcome to the NHK

www.tokyopop.com/popfiction

POP
FICTION

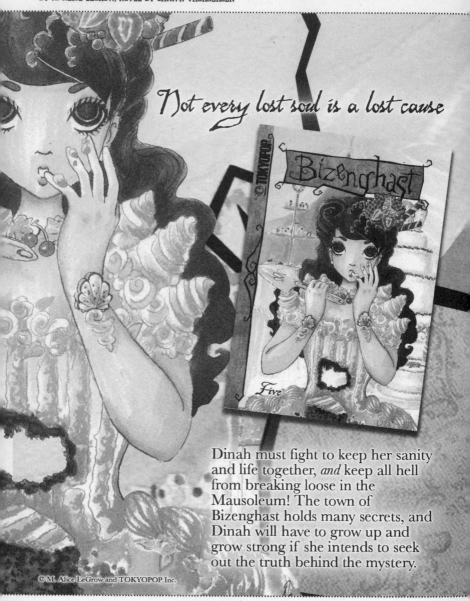